THE CHINESE CULTURAL REVOLUTION

The Chinese Cultural Revolution

by Adrian Hsia

Translated by Gerald Onn

McGraw-Hill Book Company

New York   St. Louis   San Francisco

Library of Congress Catalog Card Number: 72–3940

ISBN: 07-073780-0

Original edition: *Die Chinesische Kulturrevolution,* © 1971 Hermann Luchterhand Verlag, Neuwied and Berlin.

First American Edition

Printed in Great Britain by
Western Printing Services Ltd, Bristol

CONTENTS

INTRODUCTION

PART I. CONTRADICTIONS IN CHINESE SOCIETY BEFORE THE CULTURAL REVOLUTION

CHAPTER I

THE YOUTH OF CHINA

PART II. CONTRADICTIONS IN CHINESE
SOCIETY DURING THE CULTURAL
REVOLUTION

CHAPTER V

THE YOUNG REBELS

CHAPTER VI

WORKER AND PEASANT REBELS

CHAPTER VII

THE PARTY AND THE ARMY

CHAPTER VIII

MAOISM

Ruth

INTRODUCTION

The Ideological and Historical Background
to the Chinese Cultural Revolution

Conceptual Problems

In the middle of 1966 the Chinese cultural revolution suddenly
became front page news. The international press printed countless articles, eyewitness reports and travellers' tales, which
merely succeeded in blurring the real issues. Today scarcely
anybody knows what the cultural revolution was, or was supposed to be. To write competently and objectively about
China now is far more difficult than it was years ago. Amongst
other things, the modern sinologist needs to speak Chinese, he
needs a thorough knowledge of both the old and the new China,
and he needs to be familiar with Marxism-Leninism. Such
qualifications demand long years of intensive study, and it is
hardly surprising that many of our so-called authorities on
China are not proficient in even one of these branches of study.
As a result, a great deal of bogus knowledge has been circulated. For example, it is widely believed that Europeans are
referred to by the Chinese as 'white devils'. But any Chinese
will tell you that he has never heard this expression in his native
tongue; and if it were translated into Chinese, the only people
who might conceivably understand it would be those who had
already heard it in a European language. In fact, most Chinese
would be at a loss to understand what is meant by a devil. They
know what a 'ghost' is, and they know what a 'demon' is. But
a 'demonic ghost' or 'demon-ghost' – which is how 'devil' is
expressed in Chinese – means very little to them, and a 'white
demonic ghost' means even less. The only people the Chinese
think of as 'white' are Albinos. As a rule, Europeans visiting
China are distinguished by their long noses, their deepset eyes,
the colour of their hair (if they are fair- or red-headed types),
and possibly by their coarse, hairy skin and their powerful
physique. True, if the southern Chinese wish to refer to a
European in pejorative terms, they will call him a 'barbarian
ghost' – i.e. a barbarian who looks like a ghost – whilst their
compatriots in the north will speak of a 'little ghost that has
crossed the western ocean'. But in both cases the idea of the

'ghost' will be purely incidental. What matters in these expressions is the concept of the stranger, the barbarian (in the Greek sense of *barbaros*). 'Ghosts' are unimportant in this context whilst 'white devils' are quite unknown. We can only assume, therefore, that those 'authorities' on China who see themselves as 'white devils' are projecting their own ideas on to the Chinese. The process is reminiscent of the kind of racist projections which originated in colonial days. Then there is the fantasy that Liu Shao-chi, the Chinese President who was deposed during the cultural revolution, comes from a Chinese Jewish family. We know that some seventeen Jewish families emigrated to China in the tenth century, and that they erected their first synagogue there in 1163. By 1702 the Jewish community in China numbered some 3,000, and by 1919 all but about 120 of these had been absorbed into the Chinese national community. But there is no evidence that Liu comes of Jewish stock.

With the advent of the cultural revolution – or, rather, with the appearance of the Red Guards – many observers who had been trying to follow the course of events in China were at a loss to explain the new interpretation that was placed on the concept of 'culture'. Normally, culture is understood as the sum total of intellectual and artistic accomplishments. However, the word culture can have a wider meaning than this. The dialectical – objective and subjective – nature of culture was pointed out, first by Hegel, and then by Marx. As a creative process culture is subjective; but once this process is completed and cultural objects have been created, it operates as an independent system which establishes fixed norms for human behaviour. Cultural objects and values are objective; the act whereby they are created is subjective. In these terms, the cultural revolution is a subjective attempt to bring about a fundamental transformation of traditional Chinese culture. However, culture does not develop in a vacuum; it is not a private monologue, but communication, and is conceivable only within a community framework. It usually reflects the prevailing power in the community without which it would not be widely disseminated. Conversely, however, such power depends on culture, because it is in culture that it finds its theoretical justification, and because it is, ultimately, one aspect of culture. The reciprocal relationship between 'power' and 'culture' is well illustrated by the French revolution: it was the political ideology and institutions of the *ancien régime* which prompted the French Enlightenment, and so triggered a 'revolution in men's minds'. Without its intellectual base the French revolutionary government could never have survived. Seen in this light, the proletarian cultural revolution in China appears as a subjective attempt to dispose of established cultural values by the use of political power. It consciously set out to destroy the existing bourgeois culture – to destroy it so utterly that it could never again be revived – thus paving the way for an 'entirely new proletarian culture' that would serve as a guiding light for the entire population.

The Cultural Revolution as a Stage in the Permanent Revolution

Under a dictatorship of the proletariat the cultural revolution is a necessary stage in the establishment of a Communist society. When the political and economic revolution has been accomplished, when collective farming has been introduced and industry is reorganized on socialist lines, a cultural revolution eradicates the traditional culture of the old bourgeois society. Soviet ideologists speak in this connexion of the *'remnants* of capitalism in the minds of the people, the *remnants* of bourgeois morality and religion', and of 'old social ideas and theories, conceptions and feelings' which are tenacious and likely to survive for a long time to come. Consciousness is determined by social activity, which is to say that material factors – above all, the relationship between the forces of production and the conditions of production – are reflected in people's attitudes, for 'in the fight against the remnants of the old basis' the new socialist superstructure 'helps to remove those remnants'. Although both the Party and the State in China have launched countless political and ideological campaigns in an attempt to eradicate traditional patterns of behaviour, and to re-educate the people in accordance with proletarian criteria, and although the industrial and agricultural economy of the country was placed on a socialist footing as far back as 1957, Maoist ideologists hold a completely different view from their Russian counterparts. In China the old bourgeois culture is not regarded simply as a compendium of *remnants* which are 'tenacious of life' and are 'likely to survive for a long time to come', but as a vital, dynamic force which is still deeply entrenched at all levels of society. The representatives of the Chinese bourgeoisie have been accused of using the ideological superstructure – literature, the theatre, films, music, the fine arts, the press, magazines, radio, publications, and scientific research both in schools and elsewhere – to propagate 'bourgeois, revisionist poison in order to corrupt men's minds and establish the system of "peaceful evolution" as a first stage in the restoration of capitalism, both in the ideological sphere and in the sphere of public opinion'. Unless this tendency is constantly opposed, the political superstructure – i.e. the State – will be threatened and capitalism might be restored. Hence the cultural revolution. Provided the understanding and political consciousness of the people was sound, the proletarian State and the Marxist-Leninist principles on which it was based would be secure, and the threat of a relapse into capitalism removed. The emphasis in the Chinese theory is on social activity being determined by consciousness – and not *vice versa*.

The Soviet Union is paraded as a bogeyman:
'After establishing socialist conditions of production the Soviet Union failed to carry out a genuine proletarian cultural revolution. Bourgeois ideology gained the upper hand and corrupted men's minds. It quietly undermined the new socialist conditions of production. After Stalin's death public opinion was subjected more openly to counter-revolutionary influences by the Krushchev revisionists. Subsequently, this group gained control of the party, the armed forces and the government by a "palace revolution" and overthrew the dictatorship of the proletariat.'[1]

By now the Chinese thesis is quite clear: After entering upon its socialist phase a genuinely socialist government has to ensure that a cultural revolution is carried out, carefully and thoroughly, so that the correct proletarian ideology is maintained and disseminated, thus safeguarding the dictatorship of the proletariat and paving the way for the transition to Communism. Unless this is done, revisionism is bound to set in and lead inevitably to a relapse into capitalism. The risk of such a development taking place is all the greater in so far as petit-bourgeois ideas, which are naturally conducive to capitalist tendencies, are liable to appear quite spontaneously, even in a socialist society. That is why the cultural revolution has to be instituted – to purge the socialist superstructure, preventing it from undermining the conditions of production, and enabling it to counter any attempt to restore a capitalist system. Once it has been purged, the socialist superstructure is also supposed to enable the infrastructure to increase production. In other words once the people have become truly revolutionary and proletarian, they will produce 'faster, better and more economically' in order to achieve their distant objective. This idea is synonymous with the 'great leap forwards' and was formulated by Mao Tse-tung himself.

If we take a closer look at the political campaigns conducted in China since the establishment of the People's Republic in 1949, it soon becomes apparent that political and economic factors have never been treated separately, although on occasions one may have been emphasized more than the other. From the collectivization of agriculture and the socialization of private industrial concerns to the 'Hundred Flowers Campaign' or the 'Great Leap Forwards', and from the 'Socialist Education Movement' to the 'Cultural Revolution', the interpenetration of the political and economic spheres has been clearly demonstrated. Moreover, the end object of these campaigns has always been the same: to ensure the establishment of a Communist State at the earliest possible moment, a task which, in the final analysis, can only be achieved by the people. We see, therefore, that the cultural revolution is not just an isolated phenomenon, but a specific phase in the socialist revolution, and the one which happens to be dominant at the present time.[2] It must not be forgotten, however, that in underdeveloped countries such as China the socialist revolution – which is defined in the *Fundamentals of Marxism–Leninism* as 'the sum total of the political and economic changes leading to the complete abolition of capitalism and the building of socialism'[3] – presupposes an initial bourgeois-democratic revolution which, according to Lenin, will be conducted by the proletariat and will lead to the emergence of a socialist and, eventually, a Communist society. From this it follows that the Chinese cultural revolution is a phase, not only of the socialist revolution, but also of the 'permanent revolution'; and for the Maoists it is doubtless the most important phase of all. Lenin commented on the continuing revolution as follows:

> From the democratic revolution we shall at once, according to the degree of our strength, the strength of the class conscious and organized proletariat, begin to pass over to the socialist revolution. We stand for continuous revolution. We shall not stop half way. [4]

The concept of the permanent revolution was more clearly defined by Karl Marx:

> ... the *proletariat* rallies more and more round *revolutionary socialism*, round *communism* ... This socialism is the *declaration of the permanence of the revolution*, the *class dictatorship* of the proletariat as the necessary transit point to the *abolition of class distinctions generally*, to the abolition of all the relations of production on which they rest, to the abolition of all the social relations that correspond to these relations of production, to the revolutionizing of all the ideas that result from these social relations. [5]

Both Marx and Lenin held that if the revolution was to achieve its ultimate objective – the abolition of all class differences – it must proceed from one stage to the next without interruption, albeit in an appropriate manner, ('according to the degree of our strength'). Nowhere do they mention the possibility of taking a 'great leap forwards', avoiding one of the transitional stages, nor do they consider the possibility of dissension in the Party's own ranks, which was of course one of the principal features of the cultural revolution in China. But the Maoists have evolved their own version of the continuing revolution. At one time they gave their unreserved assent to the ideas advanced by Marx and Lenin. This happened after the failure of the 'Great Leap Forwards', the campaign designed to carry China straight into the Communist era by the introduction of people's communes. 'We advocate the Marxist–Leninist theory of the continuing revolution. We hold the view that no 'great wall' can, or may, be erected between the democratic and the social revolution, or between Socialism and Communism. But we also give our approval to a second Marxist-Leninist theory, which states that the revolution will proceed by stages, and we are of the opinion that these different stages of development will reflect qualitative changes, and that these qualitatively different stages should not be confused with one another.[6]

But this resolution of the Party Central Committee on 10 December 1958 was quite exceptional. In general, the Maoist conception of the permanent revolution is more in line with Trotsky's view, a situation that is not without its irony since in China, as in Russia, Trotsky is regarded as the arch-traitor. None the less, the similarity between the Maoist and Trotskyist position is quite manifest. In 1930 Trostky wrote:

'All social relationships will be transformed over an indefinite period as a result of constant *internal* struggles. Society will change for the better. This process will necessarily retain a political character, it will develop as a result of *clashes between different groups* in the society that is being transformed. *Outbreaks of civil war* and external wars will alternate with periods of "peaceful" reform. *Revolutions* affecting the *economy, technology* and *science*, the *family*, and all traditional *customs* and *practices will interact in a complex pattern of development and prevent society from settling down into a fixed routine*. Such is the permanent character of the socialist revolution.[7]

And in 1966 a Maoist propagandist, writing in the *Renmin Ribao*, defended the Chinese cultural revolution in almost identical words:

'A thousand, ten thousand or even a hundred million years from now there will still be contradictions. There will be contradictions in the universe, even if the earth is destroyed and the sun is blotted out. All things are caught up in the flux of contradictions, conflict, and change ... And that is the only thing that can promote our socialist cause.[8]

Where Trotsky spoke of an indefinite period, the Chinese author was more explicit. But, this apart, their statements are virtually interchangeable.

Permanent Revolution and Continuing Opposition

The cultural revolution is to be seen as a phase in the continuing revolution, which apparently goes on for ever. And since this revolutionary process is continuous, we must assume that the roots of the cultural revolution – which is to sweep away 'all dark elements', re-form the 'ideology of the people' and move 'its soul' – are to be found in the period of the bourgeois-democratic revolution. Consequently, if the revolution is to have any chance of success at all, the Party must take steps, during the initial bourgeois-democratic phase, to win over new Party members or allies from that section of the community which is not natallyur predisposed towards it and which, as we shall come to see on a later page, makes up the major part of the population in China. But in taking such steps the Party must inevitably sow the seeds of future opposition; many of these will germinate during the period of the bourgeois revolution whilst the others will undoubtedly appear at a later stage and grow into luxuriant plants, which will then have to be unmasked as 'poisonous plants' in every season of every year. This, certainly, would seem to be the implication of the socialist cultural revolution in China.

Already in 1945 Mao Tse-tung stated: 'The people are our most valuable asset. Under the leadership of the Communist Party, all we need are people, for with them we can perform any miracle.' But he failed to mention another diametrically opposed trend in the Chinese revolution. Events have shown that as the continuing revolution progresses, more and more people can be alienated from it, especially those who pledged their allegiance during the initial period. This means, in effect, that the growing dynamism of the continuing revolution is matched by the growing dynamism of the 'continuing opposition'. The radical policies which are adopted as the revolution progresses can drive more and more people into active or passive dissent, so that opposition to the revolution increases both quantitatively and qualitatively. The conflict between these two trends becomes progressively more pronounced until, in the end, it precipitates the 'proletarian cultural revolution'. Today – for the first time since 1949 – it is no longer possible to distinguish between friends and enemies in China. Previously, this had been quite simple. Enemies of the people were either former members of the alliance or deviationists of one kind or another. These former members were clearly recognizable by virtue of their class, and the deviationists were relatively few in number, which meant that the Party was able to proceed against them as a more or less united body. But now the situation has been completely transformed. Instead of misguided elements being disciplined by the Party, the Party itself becomes suspect, for it has been infiltrated by the 'continuing opposition' and many of its functionaries have been exposed as opponents of the Party.

The proletarian cultural revolution in China constitutes a further attempt to purge popular attitudes, both inside and outside the Chinese Communist Party, so as to preclude the restoration of capitalism, and ensure increased production and the unimpeded progress of the continuing socialist revolution. But the realization of these objectives is hampered both by the former members of the alliance – who were recruited for a specific purpose – and by traditional Chinese culture and its advocates. Consequently, this culture has to be destroyed and its influence on the people eliminated. In addition, the members of the alliance have to be re-educated, and conform to the Party line, which has been changed approximately every three years to date. As a result, many friends become enemies. This process whereby friends and allies – many of them Party members – are progressively alienated has its origins in the magnanimous and conciliatory policies adopted prior to 1949. These policies, which were initiated by Mao Tse-tung, enabled the Chinese Communist Party to overthrow the corrupt Kuomintang government, but they also sowed the seeds of the conflict which has broken out time and again both inside and outside the Party and government. The most recent example of this conflict is the cultural revolution. And if we wish to understand this revolution we must analyse its origins.

From 1935, the year in which Mao Tse-tung became chairman of the Politburo, to the middle of 1955, when the socialization and collectivization of the Chinese economy was suddenly stepped up, the Party had pursued a 'national front' policy. During the Sino-Japanese War of 1937 to 1945 the Party had to gain the support of all anti-Japanese sections of the community. Consequently, class conflict was not vigorously pursued during this period. Patriotism was the order of the day. The estate owners and kulaks were treated with consideration; they were given assurances that their land would not be confiscated and redistributed amongst the peasants as had been the case prior to 1935. Even Chiang Kai-shek was found to be honourable. The advocates of 'English and American imperialism' were also allowed to join the national front, as were the capitalists and warlords (local military commanders of private armies). Once Japan was defeated, however, these groups were declared 'enemies of the people', and the Party allied itself with those opposed to the Kuomintang government and 'US-imperialism'.

Meanwhile, when he announced his tactical measures for the prosecution of the war, Mao Tse-tung made his position quite clear on three major points of policy: 1. The national front had to be conducted in such a way as to undermine the Nationalist Chinese as a political party; 2. The national front, on which the outcome of the war against Japan depended, had to be led by the Chinese Communist Party, which was the only group capable of conducting effective military resistance; 3. The national front was a necessary stage in the political development leading up to the socialist revolution, which remained the ultimate and unalterable aim of the Chinese Communist Party. These policy statements were intended for Party members. The Chinese people were called to resist the invaders by patriotic slogans such as 'Save the Land of our Ancestors', designed to promote a sense of national unity. The Communist Party claimed that it was the true representative of all the Chinese people, and in order to maintain this position was even prepared to concede that it had no objection if the Chinese bourgeoisie continued to 'make lots of money'. It should have been quite apparent from the outset that the national front policy was a tactical measure taken on a temporary basis. Mao Tse-tung stated on December 27, 1935, that although, in its present form, the revolution was bourgeois-democratic and not socialist, in the future it would undoubtedly enter upon its socialist phase. But in the atmosphere of patriotic fervour induced by the new sense of national unity, little attention was paid to this statement. The national front – or 'anti-Japanese united front', as it was called by the Chinese Communist Party, which was at pains to stress the urgent need for the Chinese people to stop fighting amongst themselves and unite against the common enemy – gained immediate support amongst the common people, especially those whose homelands had been overrun by the Japanese army, and subsequently also received the backing of the upper classes. Moreover, it was due to this strategy that the Chinese Communist Party was able to conclude an official alliance with the Kuomintang. In 1936 Chiang Kai-shek was seized by his own troops, who saw the need for national unity, and was not released until he promised to make common cause with the Communist Party against the Japanese.

Mao Tse-tung once stated that the Chinese Communist Party differs from all other communist parties in two essential respects: 1. it collaborates with the bourgeoisie; 2. it is carrying out a peasant revolution. In fact, these characteristics are a natural consequence of the special conditions obtaining in China where, as Mao Tse-tung has also observed, the revolutionaries and the reactionaries between them accounted for only a minority of the population. The majority, which is made up of peasants and farmers on the one hand and petits-bourgeois on the other, occupied the middle ground between these two radical factions. Consequently, it was imperative for the Communists to gain the support of this majority group. At the same time, they had to contrive ways and means of dividing the enemy camp and so prevent it from competing effectively in this respect. In other words, if the revolution was to have any chance of success, the Chinese Communist Party had to adapt to reality, and by taking due account of these twin characteristics it was able to do so. Thus, during the war with the Japanese, the great alliance between the four classes was concluded. This provided for: 1. an alliance between the historical leadership of the revolution – i.e. the proletariat or its vanguard, the Chinese Communist Party – and the peasants and farmers; 2. an alliance between the workers and the peasants and farmers on the one hand and the petits-bourgeois on the other; 3. an alliance between the workers, peasants and farmers, and petits-bourgeois on the one hand and the national capitalists on the other. (These national capitalists came into being when the Communists divided the traditional capitalist class into two groups: the left wing national capitalists – or national bourgeoisie – and the reactionary right wing comprador – or monopoly – capitalists); 4. an alliance between the workers, peasants and farmers, petits-bourgeois and national capitalists on the one hand and the comprador capitalists on the other. Thus, the members of all these different groups became members of the alliance. Their rank within the alliance was also determined at this time. Although the workers – for whom, according to Mao

Tse-tung's own testimony, the Communist Party was directly responsible – were in a minority and had to accept the peasants and farmers as 'close allies', they or their representatives were none the less regarded as the leaders of the alliance. As for the members of the alliance, here the most important group were the peasants and farmers, and the second most important the petits-bourgeois. We have already seen that these two groups, which between them accounted for the overwhelming majority of the population, occupied the middle ground between the left and the right wings, and that whichever of these two radical factions was able to gain their support would gain control of the country. In the tripartite alliance between the workers, the peasants and farmers, and the petits-bourgeois, the workers and the peasants and farmers were the leaders. But in the great alliance all three combined to provide the major part of the membership. The third most important group amongst the members of the great alliance were the national capitalists, i.e. the left wing of the traditional capitalist class. Between them these national capitalists and the three classes mentioned above – the workers, peasants and farmers, and petits-bourgeois – formed the left wing line-up in the nation as a whole. The right wing of the nation was, of course, formed by the comprador capitalists, who were represented in the great alliance by the Kuomintang, the most unreliable faction within the anti-Japanese national front. The alliance with the comprador capitalists was entered into by the Communists only because the country was threatened by an external enemy. Before the Sino-Japanese war the compradors had been branded as 'enemies of the people', and when the war was over they reverted to this category.

The Shedding of the 'Members of the Alliance'

Long before the end of the Sino-Japanese war it was readily apparent that the alliance between the Chinese Communist Party and the Kuomintang was only a temporary arrangement. It came as no surprise, therefore, when Chiang Kai-shek was once again vilified after the war by the Communist as a 'cruel *intriguant*', 'the political representative of the Chinese estate owners and capitalists', an 'agent of the American imperialists' (who began to replace the Japanese imperialists from 1945 onwards), a 'fascist leader' and an 'enemy of the people'. When the civil war broke out, the anti-Japanese united front was dissolved and a new united front was formed in its place. This was composed of workers, peasants and farmers, the petits-bourgeois and the national capitalists, and was directed against the comprador capitalists. In the new united front the national capitalists came to hold the same marginal position as that occupied by the comprador capitalists in the anti-Japanese front. Like them, they were regarded as unreliable allies, and were eventually branded as 'enemies of the people'. Initially, however, they were assured that the Chinese Communist Party had no intention of destroying the capitalist economy, with which it had common interests, since it wished to protect and promote Chinese industry and trade; consequently, although the Party was determined to extirpate the comprador capitalists it proposed to permit the national capitalist economy to operate in the new society for a long time to come. The same assurance was given to the petits-bourgeois, especially the small independent business men. Mao Tse-tung issued a personal directive which stated that the 'leadership' must provide 'those who are led' with material advantages or, at the very least, protect their existing interests so as to ensure that they remained willing members of the alliance. If this directive had come from anyone but Mao, it would have been denounced in the cultural revolution as a blatant example of economism.

Like the members of the bourgeoisie and the upper levels of the petite-bourgeoisie, the peasants and farmers were treated with special consideration at first. In China this class was divided into three groups: big farmers, small farmers and peasants. The small farmers were on a par with the petite-bourgeoisie, and the peasants with the semi-proletariat. Mao Tse-tung has estimated that the peasants made up approximately 20 per cent of the rural population, whilst the big farmers and estate owners accounted for approximately 8 per cent of all agricultural holdings. During the Sino-Japanese war the kulaks also belonged to the united front, and the Chinese Communist Party did its best to ensure that they were not alienated any more than could be helped at that time. It studied their interests wherever possible, and amongst other things refused to permit the redistribution of their land. But on May 4,

1946 this policy was dropped and the Party reintroduced its former line: 'the land belongs to the man who ploughs it.' The kulaks' lands were then confiscated and redistributed. In the prosecution of its new agrarian policy the Party could rely on the backing of the peasants, and by coming to terms with the small farmers, it was able to proceed against the big farmers and estate owners with the support of 90 per cent of the rural population. The terms granted to the small farmers – who were all self-employed – were quite exceptional. Although their support for the new agrarian reforms was less energetic and less reliable than that afforded by the peasants, they were none the less accorded preferential treatment. A directive was issued by the Party leadership stating that the interests of the small farmers were not to be prejudiced and that where disputes occurred between them and the peasants over the redistribution of land, they were to be granted special concessions. In fact, sympathetic consideration was to be given to all their needs. The Party also recommended that politically active members of this group should be invited to serve as functionaries in the 'Farmers' Association', one third of whose delegates were to be drawn from its ranks. The Party was so eager to conciliate the small farmers that it even promised to apologize to them if their interests should be prejudiced in any way. One thing the members of this group were not allowed to do, however, was join the 'Peasants' Association'. Essentially, the position of the small farmers was the same as that of the national capitalists. Initially, they were treated with consideration and respect. But when no longer useful, they became enemies, unless they were prepared to abandon their old class ideas and embrace the new egalitarian ethos. Identical tactics were used in the cultural revolution.

One interesting aspect of the agrarian reform is the fact that, after they had been dispossessed, the kulaks and estate owners were regarded as potential workers, and arrangements were made to 'educate' them accordingly. Thus, although the class to which these people had belonged was to be extirpated, the people themselves were not. After successfully completing five years' manual work a former estate owner could be reclassified on the basis of his new occupation. In the case of the big farmers this probationary period was reduced to three years. One would have thought, therefore, that the number of people considered to be unreliable on account of their class associations would have gradually declined. But this did not happen, primarily because, even after the collectivization of agriculture, the Party still retained the old class categories which were used not only for former members of these classes but also for their children. It was assumed that, since children were reared by their parents, they must also be influenced by them. And so, far from declining, the number of people classified as estate owners or kulaks actually increased. But the number of big farmers and estate owners also increased in real terms. Many new estates have been created since the agrarian reform, and from a remarkable statement made by Mao Tse-tung we learn that most of the poor peasants in the old 'liberated districts' have now become small farmers, and some even big farmers. Consequently the number of unreliable elements in the countryside has constantly increased.

The poor peasants, of course, were also members of the alliance; like the less reliable and unreliable elements in the national front, they too had to be educated, i.e. they had to acquire a 'proletarian outlook' appropriate to the new society. Moreover, although the agrarian reform had been introduced on their account, the way in which it was implemented was determined by the needs of Party policy and the assessments of local functionaries. The directive issued by the Central Office of the Chinese Communist Party on May 25, 1948, is quite clear on this point. Such, then, was the state of the alliance between the Communist Party and its closest allies, the peasants and farmers. The contradictions which it contained could only lead to conflict.

Next in importance after the peasants and farmers come the petits-bourgeois. These members of the alliance were also extremely numerous, and many of them were Party members.* The petits-bourgeois, who have influenced many 'pure proletarians', both inside and outside the Party, have always been – and still are – an important class, and an important section of the Chinese community. As far as the Chinese Communist Party is concerned, they are something of a mixed blessing, for although they are considered capable of joining with the

* Mao Tse-tung also includes the small farmers among the petits-bourgeois. For purposes of this study I have dealt with them in conjunction with the peasants and kulaks.

proletariat in revolutionary activity, they are also thought to have an inherent bias towards capitalism. But it is not only the dual nature of the petite-bourgeoisie that has impressed itself on the Party. It has also been noted that the philosophical arguments advanced by the members of this class have led to both left and right wing deviationism within the Party. Not surprisingly, therefore, the Chinese Communist Party regards the petits-bourgeois as a 'transitional class'. It is prepared to tolerate them for the sake of the united front, provided they do nothing to impede the prosecution of the struggle against the class enemy. At the same time the Party warns its members not to be misled into thinking that the non-proletarian petits-bourgeois share the fundamental convictions of the workers or their Party, and it reminds them that these petits-bourgeois have often adopted an antagonistic attitude to the proletariat in the past. It also points out that they have acquired, or retained, a penchant towards liberalism, reformism, anarchism, dogmatism, empiricism, adventurism, sectarianism, escapism, individualism, officialism, authoritarianism, corruption and similar non-proletarian practices, and that they will inevitably try to impose their own ideas on the Party and usurp the power of the leadership. Consequently, the Party has advised its members that they must be prepared, both to combat the petits-bourgeois, and to re-educate them.

However, the vast majority of Party members come from the ranks of the petite-bourgeoisie or the semi-proletariat; this is as true today as it was at the time of the agrarian reform. It is difficult to see, therefore, how these men – peasants, small farmers and intellectuals – are to be re-educated by the 'pure' elements, i.e. the proletarians, who represent only a tiny minority and who have, to some extent, themselves been influenced by bourgeois ideas. This is why there has been such a spate of left and right wing deviationism. The roots of these errors can be traced back to 'petit-bourgeois egoism' and 'petit-bourgeois subjectivism'. The only way of overcoming them is to combat petit-bourgeois elements in the Party, starting with a campaign to correct mental attitudes. And so the tiny minority of pure elements in the Party must re-educate not only the rest of the Party but the whole of the Chinese population. The repeated attempts to achieve this objective reached their peak in the cultural revolution.

If we consider the speed with which the Chinese Communist Party expanded its membership we can understand the seriousness of the problem for the present leadership. When the original national front was formed in 1937 there were about 40,000 Party members in China. By 1940, due to the popular appeal of its anti-Japanese policy, these had doubled; by 1945 the Party had a membership of 1,210,000, and by 1948 this had risen to over 3 millions. But these members were not all of the same calibre. The original hard core of 40,000 were fully trained, but the 3 million newcomers, who had been recruited so quickly, were not. They all had to be re-educated. This was why Mao Tse-tung conceded in 1948 that 'impure elements, impure attitudes and impure working methods' were by no means uncommon in the Party. It should be remembered in this connexion that more than half of the new members joined after 1945, following the successful educational campaign conducted by the Party between 1942 and 1944, in which orthodox Marxism had been revised in the light of the special conditions obtaining in China, thus establishing 'Maoism' as the official doctrine of the Chinese Communist Party. During this campaign the uneducated and half educated Party members had been required to study Marxism (as expounded by Chinese authors) whilst the intellectuals were sent to perform manual work and acquire practical experience on the land so as to become genuine proletarian intellectuals. After 1949 a further educational campaign had to be conducted in the Party, due to the continuing rapid growth of the membership, which had risen to more than 5 millions by 1950. In the early days – i.e. from the outbreak of the Sino-Japanese war in 1937 to the establishment of the People's Republic in 1949 – Party policy was, for the most part, designed to promote reconciliation between the classes. Extremist views were dismissed by the leadership as the products of an impure ideology. Subsequently, the Party line was reversed. Thus, from the late 1940's onwards, all Communist Party members have been taught to regard Party policies at any given time in the light of the political conditions obtaining at that time, and to confuse tactical measures with ultimate aims, or yesterday's tactics with today's, has always been – and still is – regarded as a form of deviationism and as a sign of inadequate ideological under-standing. Since the vast majority of Party members in the late 1940's were peasants, many of whom could neither read nor write, these requirements posed difficulties which were com-pounded by the fact that prior to 1949 China was not a homogeneous state. Mao Tse-tung had his central head-quarters in Yenan, but the 'liberated areas' were scattered throughout the length and breadth of China, and were en-circled by Japanese or Kuomintang troops. There were times when the only form of communication between the central headquarters and outlying Communist bases or between the various Communist areas was by army runner. And because communications were so bad, each area had to be given a certain degree of autonomy in the day to day running of its affairs, which meant that area policies did not necessarily reflect the changing tactics adopted in Yenan. This relative independence, which the leadership was obliged to sanction for as long as the fighting continued, created a situation in which 'evils' such as 'the formation of cliques' and 'the sabotage of orders from above' were all too easily encouraged. This con-flict between yesterday's needs and tactics and the new policies of today was also a factor giving rise to the cultural revolution.

To complete the picture of China at the foundation of the People's Republic we must now briefly consider the state of the army and the administration. As far as the army is concerned a few simple statistics tell us all we need to know. Thus, be-tween 1946 and 1948 the People's Liberation Army increased its strength to 2,800,000 men by enlisting some 800,000 Kuomintang prisoners and 1,600,000 Chinese peasants and farmers,[9] which means that all the conflicts that had beset the anti-Japanese united front were transferred to the army. Things were much the same where the administration were concerned. In 1948, the Party planned to provide 30,000 to 40,000 functionaries by the following year to take charge of military, political, economic, financial, educational and Party affairs in an area with an estimated population of between 50 and 100 million people. Clearly, a mere 40,000 to 50,000 men could not hope to administer such a large territory. But in order to find even this modest number of functionaries, the Party had had to enlist former Kuomintang officials and em-ployees with administrative experience in economics, finance, culture and education. According to Mao Tse-tung, the liberated territories in October 1948, when these plans were announced, embraced 29 per cent of all Chinese towns and approximately 35 per cent of the Chinese population (168 million people). By the end of 1949 it was anticipated that this population would increase by a further 200 million, thus bringing 50 per cent of the Chinese population into the Communist fold.[10] But then in October 1949, just one year after the announcement of these plans, the People's Republic of China was proclaimed in Peking. It goes without saying that the only possible way in which the regime could provide an effective administration for the new republic was by adopting the major part of the former Kuomintang officials and employees and using them in all branches of local administration. Inevitably, these adopted 'functionaries' were ideologically and politically suspect in the eyes of the Party leadership, which soon came to regard them as completely unreliable.

And so, at the time of the foundation of the new republic, Chinese society was full of contradictions. These were subsequently enumerated, by Mao Tse-tung himself. In a philosophical treatise written in 1957 he referred, not only to the internal conflicts within the various classes, but also to the conflicts between the workers on the one hand and the peasants and farmers on the other; between the workers, the peasants and farmers, and the intellectuals; between the interests of the state, the collective, and the individual; between democracy and centralism; between those who lead and those who are led; and so on. Mao Tse-tung readily conceded that such conflicts of interest might easily lead to antagonism, but only if the leadership pursued false policies. However, it would seem that, given the nature and aims of the Chinese revolution, such conflicts must inevitably lead to antagonism. For the conflict between tactics and ultimate aims, between a united front and the continuing revolution, appears irreconcilable. The whole object of the united front is to bring all classes and sections of the community together under the leadership of the Communist Party so that they can combat the common enemy under the same banner (which in China has been the banner of democracy). But in the continuing revolution some of these classes and sections of the community are gradually isolated and antagonized; and since the majority of Party members come from these classes and sections of the community, it follows that the Party must eventually become ensnared in internal battles. This prognosis is borne out by the whole social, political and ideological development of China to date. The peak of this development was, of course, reached in the cultural revolution, in which all conflicts, both implicit and explicit, came to a head.

The first attack on the Party came in a film entitled *Wu Hsun Chuan* which was supposed to have slandered the revolutionary tradition of the Chinese people, and to have disseminated reformist and capitulationist ideas. Significantly, the members of the team which produced this film had supported the Chinese Communist Party during the period of Kuomintang rule, and after 1949 were rewarded by Peking with important positions in the cultural life of the new republic. The film itself was so popular, and was so warmly acclaimed by all sections of the community, that Mao Tse-tung himself had to write a leading article for the *Renmin Ribao* before it could be withdrawn from the national circuit. During the cultural revolution the makers of this film were accused of engaging in anti-Party activities, and became victims of the general purge. Their fate is still unknown.

In 1952 the Party leadership went on to the offensive, launching a two-pronged campaign against the adopted officials and employees working in the local administration, the urban petits-bourgeois, the national capitalists, and a small number of Party members. This campaign was known as the 'Anti-Three-Evils' and the 'Anti-Five-Evils' movement. The three evils were corruption, extravagance, and officialism; the five evils were bribery of government officials, tax evasion, theft of state property, fraudulent practices in the execution of state contracts, and economic espionage. But in 1953 the leadership was forced back on to the defensive by adversaries within the Party. This was an important year. It was the first year of the first five year plan; and it also saw the introduction of the collectivization of agriculture, and of the socialization of craft workshops and factories. However, there was opposition to these measures amongst the classes affected by them, which had to be dealt with before they could be implemented. One way and another, therefore, the leadership was very much preoccupied, and two of the top functionaries in the North Eastern Bureau of the Central Committee, Kao Kang and Jao Sou-shih, chose this moment to make a bid for power. But their plans were discovered and at the seventh plenary session of the fourth Central Committee in 1954 they were 'criticized'. Shortly afterwards both men committed suicide. Between 1954 and 1957 the leadership was extremely active and constantly on the offensive. It was during this period that it launched a national campaign against the ideas propagated by Wu Shih, one of the leading figures in the 'May 4th Movement', which had been dedicated to the reform of Chinese culture and from which the Chinese Communist Party had emerged. A second national campaign conducted at this time was the 'counter-offensive' mounted against the 'anti-revolutionary' Hu Feng group. Hu Feng, a Chinese writer, had submitted to the Central Committee a memorandum criticizing the literary principles established by Mao Tse-tung, whereupon he and his 'clique' were exposed as enemies of the Party. In 1955 and 1956 the collectivization of agriculture, and the socialization of industry and crafts, were suddenly speeded up so that by the end of this two year period, and despite repeated statements by the Party urging caution and patience, China had become a socialist state in all essential respects. Imbued with a deep sense of satisfaction, and in the confident expectation that its proposals would meet with general approval and conformity, the Party then launched its 'Hundred Flowers Campaign'. Immediately, it was subjected to criticism that was so outspoken, so violent and so fundamental that for a full two months it simply did not know how to react. In 1957 the exhortation to 'let a hundred flowers blossom, let a hundred schools compete with one another' was abandoned, and the net result of this campaign was the suppression of 'bourgeois right wing elements'. Thinking, no doubt, that this action had finally broken the opposition of the Chinese intellectuals, and that the masses would conform to the Party line, the leadership suddenly took a further fateful decision by announcing the 'Great Leap Forwards', which involved the setting up of people's communes. This measure was a matter of concern, not only to the intellectuals and the bourgeoisie, but to the whole community. We are told that opposition to this policy was widespread amongst both the rural and the urban populations. The conflict even made itself felt within the leadership, where Mao Tse-tung's policy was censured by the Minister of Defence.

Opposition within the Party reached its peak at the conference of Lu Shan, where Mao Tse-tung was attacked in his personal capacity as Chairman of the Central Committee. However, this internal opposition group was quickly suppressed, and its members were repudiated as 'right wing opportunists'. Opposition in the countryside was not so easily dealt with; and far from being suppressed, the peasants and small farmers had to be granted special concessions at this time to help them over the economic crises and the food shortage. The years 1959 to 1962 were extremely difficult ones, and the Party leadership had to brace itself and submit to many indignities in order to survive. Once again, the intellectuals expounded independent views. But these were not the intellectuals who had been purged following the 'Hundred Flowers Campaign' in 1957. They had been members of the petite-bourgeoisie or the bourgeoisie, in other words members of the national front, whereas this second group consisted largely of Party members, who had either had connexions, or sympathized, with the opposition group suppressed after the Lu Shan conference, and who to some extent enjoyed the protection of Liu Shao-chi, the Chinese President later deposed by Mao Tse-tung. During this period the Party intellectuals expressed heretical opinions on philosophy, political economy, history, literature, education and the press. Just how powerful the opposition had become can be judged from the length of time it took Mao to retaliate. In September 1962 he insisted that the *class war* must not be forgotten. In 1963 and 1964 he warned the Party that feudalistic, capitalistic and revisionistic attitudes were still rampant, and that the Chinese intellectuals must be subjected to further searching criticism, and must then be re-educated so as to ensure that they did not stage-manage a revolt in China similar to that mounted in Hungary. But it was not until September 1965 that Mao Tse-tung felt strong enough to launch the cultural revolution which, incidentally, appears to have been planned on a relatively small scale and only developed into a great national campaign at a later stage. By then even the Party was threatened, for its members were openly attacked, and either did not dare, or were not allowed, to fulfil their functions. Eventually, the whole community was embroiled in a conflict such as it had never known before. To understand the nature and significance of this conflict, we need

32

to investigate the individual conflicts amongst, and between the youth, the intellectuals, the workers, the peasants and farmers, and the Party leadership, which were thrown into relief by the cultural revolution. We also need to discover how, or whether, the general conflict unleashed by the cultural revolution was resolved. Finally, we need to establish how the theory and practice of Chinese Communism were adapted to meet the new conditions obtaining in China after this tremendous upheaval. In order to deal with these different aspects I have divided this study into three parts. The first part deals with the conflicts already present in Chinese society before the cultural revolution; the second part deals with the conflicts which emerged during the revolution; and the third part deals with the conclusions which I have drawn from those conflicts and which will, I trust, show Chinese Communism in a new light.

PART I

Contradictions in Chinese Society
before the Cultural Revolution

CHAPTER I

THE YOUTH OF CHINA

*The world is yours, and it is also ours, but ultimately it is your world.
You young people, vigorous and aspiring, are the budding life, you are
like the sun at eight or nine in the morning. Our hopes reside in you.
. . .
The world belongs to you, China's future belongs to you.*

MAO TSE-TUNG

Although there is nothing very original about the motto which
I have chosen for this chapter, it shows that the youth of China
have occupied an important position in the overall development of Chinese society. In this chapter I have treated persons
between fifteen and twenty-five years of age as young people,
these being the official age limits for the Chinese Communist
Youth League. The reason why these particular age limits were
set is quite simple. By the time he is fifteen a young Chinese will
have had eight years' schooling, which means that he will have
acquired sufficient knowledge, and sufficient understanding and
judgement, to enter upon the first stage of adult life; and for the
next ten years he will, as a general rule, still occupy a relatively
junior position in his occupational sphere, and so remain amen-
able to influence. Since educational policy in the Chinese
People's Republic is specifically designed to produce technological, scientific, economic, educational, Party and administrative functionaries (this having been the primary need in
China to date), I have tended to concentrate in this chapter on
schoolchildren and students.

1. Young People Prior to 1958

The People's Republic of China has been in existence since
1949, and the people who were in their late 'teens or early
twenties at that time have long since established themselves as
peasants, workers or functionaries in the new society. In order
to avoid confusion it would appear advisable, therefore, to
divide the period under discussion into two roughly equal sections. 1958 seems the most appropriate point at which to draw
the dividing line, for by then most of those classified as young

people when the new regime was launched had already entered state service; moreover, during the Hundred Flowers campaign of the previous year China had witnessed the first eruption of hostility on the part of the intellectuals and students; and, finally, 1958 saw the introduction of a new policy designed to bring about rapid progress in the political, economic, technological, cultural and educational spheres, and so usher in a new stage in the 'socialist revolution'. At that time there was already talk of a cultural revolution.

The State of Chinese Education from 1949 to 1952

It is generally acknowledged that the education of young people depends on two principal factors: the family and the school. To assess the significance of the part played by the family in Chinese education would, of course, necessitate a general study of the whole of the Chinese population. This would not only far exceed the scope of this book, it would also involve a certain amount of repetition, for the different classes and strata of the Chinese population have been considered in other chapters. Consequently, I have confined myself in this present chapter to an analysis of the education provided by Chinese schools.

In c. 1922 China adopted the American system of education. From then onwards her university teachers received a 'bourgeois' education, either in China or – in the majority of cases – in the USA or Europe. These university teachers then trained the secondary and primary school teachers. As a result, nearly all Chinese educationalists came to acquire a 'bourgeois' mentality; they admired the 'bourgeois' culture of America and Europe for its economic, technological and scientific achievements, and its political freedom. After 1949 the state assumed control of all schools together with their teaching staffs. At that time there were approximately two hundred universities in China; 41 per cent of these were still privately owned, as were 56 per cent of secondary schools.[1] The first thing that had to be done was re-educate the teachers, and in 1950 some 200,000 'bourgeois' intellectuals were given political education. However, in 1951 the Deputy Minister of Education, Chien Chun-yui, complained that the majority of university teachers were still clinging to their old ideas. This then was the state of affairs in the Chinese educational institutes after 1949: the labels on the bottles had been changed, but the wine inside them was still the same.

This state of affairs could not be allowed to continue. A socialist education programme is not designed to produce bourgeois intellectuals. This was made perfectly apparent in the new educational policy which, up to 1952, was conceived in terms of the 'New Democracy'. This policy was based on the need for national re-construction. It was designed to provide large numbers of efficient and healthy functionaries to meet the heavy demand for skilled personnel in all branches of the economy, industry, and the educational, state and administrative services. Political education also played a part in the new curriculum; the students were taught to love their homeland and the people, and to support the government and Chairman Mao. Their blind respect for European and American culture had to be eradicated and replaced by self-respect and self-confidence, so that they could play an active part in the re-construction of China, and serve the people. The teachers at the government's disposal at that time were incapable of providing 'correct' ideological instruction for their students and pupils, although they could have furnished them with adequate professional training. This did not happen, however. The total restructuring of the educational system affected not only the organization of the schools and universities but also their teaching methods. New curricula were introduced based on Soviet models.[2] The regular classes were supplemented by special short courses, and the majority of the textbooks in use during this initial period were translations from the Russian. The Chinese teachers had to absorb a vast amount of new material and impart it at one and the same time. The result was inevitable. The young functionaries trained at that time were neither politically 'virtuous' nor professionally competent. This will become quite apparent on a later page.

One particularly glaring contradiction emerged in the ideological sphere. In order to strengthen their sense of national identity and solidarity the students were told that the Chinese were an *élite* people with a world-wide reputation for industry and courage, a splendid revolutionary tradition, and a glorious history; and in order to undermine the admiration of American culture and the fear of American strength felt by students and teachers alike they were told that this image of America was ideologically false.[3] However, they were also told that they must love, and learn from, the Soviet Union. And so, one foreign culture having been rejected because it undermined the Chinese sense of national identity, it was promptly replaced by another. Later, when the Soviet Union had been rejected in its turn, there was antagonism between those young people, who had been taught to admire the Soviet Union, and the leadership which insisted that it had become the homeland of revisionists and 'socialist imperialists'.

From 1949 to 1952 the development of the Chinese economy, and of Chinese education, was determined by the need for national re-construction. By the end of this period both of these sectors had consolidated their positions. All schools had been nationalized and reorganized. The normal secondary schools had been supplemented by special schools providing a three-year course, and short courses had also been introduced at the universities. The number of students taking technological courses rose to 35·4 per cent[4] of an overall total of 219,700.[5] Judging by the number of students registering at Chinese universities in 1949, it would seem that some 130,000 young people were trained to graduate level during this three year period. Class affiliations also improved: by 1952 20 per cent of all students and 60 per cent of all secondary school pupils came from workers' or peasants' families. All in all, it seemed as if the educational sector was well prepared for the start of the first five year plan, and would be able to provide the trained functionaries that would be needed for the next, and more intensive, phase of the revolution, namely the construction of socialism.

Educational Policy and Student Hardship

For a Marxist-Leninist the education of young people is not just an end in itself. It is also a means to an end. With the intensification of national re-construction at the beginning of the first five year plan the industrial and economic sectors needed more and more technical personnel, who had to be provided by the different institutes of education, i.e. the universities and technical colleges. But demand always exceeded supply; and this produced a vicious circle which had an extremely adverse effect on the students and secondary school pupils. In 1953 58,000 pupils at normal and special (i.e. three year) secondary schools passed their university entrance examination.[6] But if the universities were to come anywhere near to fulfilling their quota, they had to have a student intake in 1953 of 81,000.[7] Inevitably, this sudden quantitative expansion was accompanied by a drop in student quality. As early as 1951 Ma Yin-chu, a well-known scholar at Peking University, complained that student graduates were incapable of applying their knowledge in practical situations. At the time the teachers were blamed for this deficiency. Later, however, Chang Chung-lin, who was the Director of the Planning Committee at the Ministry of Education in 1951, reapportioned the blame. Writing in 1955, he maintained that the reason why student graduates had been unable to meet the requirements of the reconstruction programme was that they had not possessed adequate technical knowledge. Because of this, the industrial concerns had not known how many new technological workers to apply for. Acting on the assumption that quality could be replaced by quantity – in other words, that two low quality workers would succeed where one had failed – the concerns had asked for more skilled personnel than they had actually needed. In order to meet the growing demand for graduates, Chang said, the universities and technical colleges had recruited more and more students, with the result that standards had continued to decline. Paradoxically, Chang Chung-lin also accused the universities and technical colleges of having pursued over-ambitious curricula and of having over-worked the students in the process. He considered that instead of concentrating exclusively on the technical knowledge required for employment in industry, these institutes should have combined specialist training with a general course of study similar to that provided at secondary school level. But be that as it may, the hard fact of the matter was that the universities needed more students than were available in the way of secondary school leavers. And even these school leavers were of dubious quality. Although they had passed their university entrance, a fair proportion of them – those who had attended special schools – had received only three years secondary education. Moreover, because of the great shortage of students at the universities and technical colleges, the schools had to increase their output of university candidates, which means that they were subject to the same pressures as the universities themselves. And on top of all this, they were suffering from an acute shortage of teachers. The special schools were particularly vulnerable to such pressures, for their curriculum was more adaptable than that of the normal schools, and they often accepted pupils who were above the official age limit. Consequently, the quality of the university entrants who came from these special schools was particularly suspect. In fact, the universities are said to have accepted applicants at that time who were completely unsuitable: people in a poor state of health, with little or no political awareness, and with quite inadequate educational qualifications.[8] But then, to a greater or lesser degree, all university candidates were ill prepared; and this, coupled with the excessive demands made on them by the overambitious curricula, and the inability of the university lecturers to adapt their material to the reality of Chinese life, resulted in a poor class of graduate.

The conflict between quantitative and qualitative considerations imposed an enormous strain on the students. In the academic year 1953–1954 7,000,[9] out of a total intake of 81,000,[10] had to give up their studies,[11] mostly for reasons of health but in a number of cases for 'ideological reasons'. Moreover, many of those who stayed on failed their intermediate examinations and could not be promoted, and some had to be put back a whole year. The difficulties of undergraduate life are well illustrated by an article written by a university student and published during the Hundred Flowers campaign; the statements made in this article tally in all essential respects with the official documents which I consulted in connexion with my analysis of the quantitative increase and qualitative decline of Chinese undergraduates:

'University students really are overworked. We even work on Sundays ... Many students spend their weekends in libraries. Many carry their books or Russian vocabulary cards with them at all times, even when they go to the toilet, or when they are riding in omnibuses or trams. The period immediately preceding examinations is even more taxing. Because of the tremendous stress, students suffer constantly from migraine, fatigue, insomnia and neurasthenia; and with every day that passes their symptoms become more severe. Most students suffer from loss of appetite and consequently are underweight. An even worse phenomenon is the incidence of fainting fits in the refectories and libraries, and even in the examination rooms. Many students are so tense by the time they come to sit their examinations that they can't even read the questions. The examinations take a long time to complete, and during this strenuous period many students are taken ill; sometimes whole classes are affected. For example, of the 27 students taking the first year course for nursery teachers in the Teachers' Training Department only 9 completed the examination; and of those taking the second year course there was scarcely a single examination candidate who was able to complete all of the papers. The further the students progress with their studies, the worse their state of health becomes. By the time they graduate, both the men and the women students show definite signs of ageing. Nervous debility and poor vision become more pronounced year by year.

. . .

'Time and again you hear students complain that "our Teachers' Training Department is like a department store; it has everything, but everything is of poor quality". There are people in our department who have studied pedagogy but who can't write about an educational project; and there are others who have studied psychology but who can't make a psychological analysis. This "department store" character is due partly to the enormous size and complexity of the curriculum, and partly to the inability of the teaching staff to relate their material to real life conditions. Take the pedagogy course! In their first year the students on this course have to study eight subjects and attend lectures for twenty-six hours each week. Their main subject is psychology, which involves five hours of lectures; the remaining seven subjects are given over almost exclusively to political theory and cultural history. Not even the teachers know why these subjects have been included in the curriculum.

. . .

'It is not only that the students have little or no general knowledge and lack the ability to work independently, they also find the material presented to them in the majority of their courses completely alien. On psychology, for example, they have not even heard of concepts such as "sensation", "intellectual capacity" and "memory", let alone Pavlov's theories or the philosophical premises of psychology. In order to cater for the students' standards the teacher has to begin by defining basic concepts . . . But this does not fit in with the curriculum so that the teacher is forced to speed things up, and even has to continue his lectures in the break periods if he is to have any hope of keeping to his timetable . . . So whether the students understand his lectures is largely a matter of chance. There are times when they don't understand a word.

. . .

'The attitudes, teaching methods and knowledge of some of the lecturers are unsatisfactory. In the "Logic" course last year the lecturer simply read from his notes, and the students wrote down every work like robots. After his two hour lectures a number of students had to spend even more time checking and correcting their notes . . . The lecturer giving the course on "Revolutionary History" simply read out newspaper articles and passages from books instead of providing a historical analysis. And then there was the psychology lecturer who quoted at inordinate length from the classics. The students felt that he was trying to explain the unknown by reference to the incomprehensible.

. . .

'The subjects presented for discussion (after the lectures) are too wide-ranging and too formal . . . Too many restrictions are imposed, and the conclusions are drawn prematurely. We are not allowed to discuss matters which are not included in the [lecturer's] notes or which the lecturer considers to be unimportant. For each colloquy the lecturer provides a conclusion. But no sooner has a problem been mooted than he produces this conclusion. He wants to announce the conclusion whilst the discussion is still going on. The "Politics" lecturer is the most obvious [offender] in this respect.

'A lot of time is wasted with very little to show for it. As a rule, it takes six hours a week to prepare for each course, although it can take as much as twelve, and sometimes more. And what is the result? During the discussion some of the students are so bored that they sit there yawning. And after the [lecturer's] conclusion they are often heard to remark: "Ah, the same as usual . . ."[12]

This student's article also tallied in all essential respects with the report presented by the Minister of Education Yang Hsiu-feng at the third plenary session of the first National People's Congress on 20 June 1956. Yang, too, referred to the pressures of university life, which left the students no time either to assimilate what they were taught or to relax from their studies, and which consequently undermined their health. The 'student illnesses' were tuberculosis, stomach and intestinal disorders, neurasthenia and high blood pressure. The Minister of Education even mentioned the 'improper pressure' brought to bear by the universities that tried to urge their students on to still greater efforts by encouraging competition. These observations show the kind of tension that was created as a result of the conflict between the personal needs of young people and the requirements of the educational programme. They also help to demonstrate the further conflict that existed between the students and the universities, or to be more precise between the students and those responsible for educational policy, which was of course binding on all educational institutes. In fact, it would seem that young people in general were dissatisfied with the government's educational policy. Since the proposals for improving the educational system made in the student's article from which I have quoted were addressed to the 'Ministry of University Education and the Ministry of Education' – which are separate ministries – it must be assumed that the Chinese youth knew perfectly well who was responsible for the abuses. The implication would seem to be that there was a general conflict at that time between the young students of China and the government.

The Ideological Attitudes of Chinese Youth

But this was not the only conflict with which the young people of China had to contend. Even in the early 1950's there were difficulties on the politico–ideological front. True, there was no lack of political courses at the universities. But judging by the student's article quoted above, it would seem that one reason why the students attended these courses was in order to obtain a good report from the university authorities. The situation in the secondary schools seems to have been much the same, for if we consult the 'Regulations for Secondary School Pupils'

45

published in 1955 we are immediately struck by their lack of political content. Only two of the eighteen paragraphs are in any way concerned with political matters. Thus, secondary school pupils were told that they must be prepared to serve their country and the people; they were also required to show respect for the Chinese flag, and to honour and love their national leader. But that was all. The other sixteen paragraphs were given over in their entirety to student behaviour during and outside school hours. And if we further consider the directives issued by the Communist Youth League, the organization primarily responsible for youth work in China, we can also see the relative lack of emphasis placed on political activities. There were three of these directives in all. The first two dealt with the various ways in which the members of the League could help their fellow pupils to become more interested in their studies, and to acquire greater powers of self-discipline and a capability for independent thought. Only the third directive called upon the members to encourage all secondary school pupils to engage in 'voluntary social and welfare work'.

In 1956 the Chinese press[13] reported that although both the number and length of the political courses held at universities and technical colleges had been greatly reduced, the students were still discontented. It seems that they were interested only in their professional training. Apart from that they wanted to be free to do as they pleased, and so they cut the political lectures. The worst offenders in this respect were the students in the technical colleges and medical faculties. The ideological attitudes of the technical students became so suspect that a number of factories and mines were loath to allow them to complete their practical training on their premises, and equally loath to employ student graduates. In a speech delivered to the first National People's Congress Yang Hsiu-feng, the Minister of University Education, enumerated the abuses obtaining in the universities and technical colleges. Some of the students, he said, had been corrupted by bourgeois ideas. He considered that such young people were morally degenerate, and had led a decadent life; they had banded together, broken the law, and undermined discipline; others were fully-fledged reactionaries, who had spread anti-socialist views and founded secret organizations. According to the minister, counter-revolutionaries, the children of former estate owners and capitalist agents had infiltrated the universities, where they had committed arson, poisoned the minds of innocent dupes, stolen official documents, damaged or destroyed machines and technical installations, and displayed reactionary posters. Even before the Hundred Flowers campaign the students' suspect ideological attitudes had been patently obvious. Nor were they at all surprising, for at that time 80 per cent of Chinese students came from non-proletarian backgrounds.[14] The secondary school pupils were also restive and rebelled in their own way. Even members of the Communist Youth League, from which the next generation of Communist Party members would emerge, failed to conform to the Party line. They complained that both the structure and the discipline of the League were too rigid, they boycotted its conferences and political meetings, neglected their League duties, and when they left school refused to accept the posts allocated to them. The young workers were not much better, for on occasions their behaviour was far from proletarian. In Shanghai there were instances of young workers hiring dance halls, and dancing girls to go with them. They are also said to have loitered near girls' schools, and to have accosted the schoolgirls in the hope of persuading them to go dancing.

Clearly, the ideological attitudes of young people in China, especially those attending schools and universities, were suspect. Many were dissatisfied with the state of Chinese education, politics and professional life. They often found it difficult to obtain employment, and in some cases the posts allocated to them by the State were entirely unsuitable. For example, philosophy graduates would have to work as librarians, law graduates as bookkeepers, chemistry graduates as language teachers, and engineering graduates as history teachers. It is not surprising that the contradiction between the youth and the leadership was serious, particularly in view of the fact that 80 per cent of students and 40 per cent of secondary school pupils came from bourgeois environments and were still subject to the bourgeois influences of their old class affiliations. All these factors helped pave the way for the emergence of the second pan-Chinese students' revolutionary movement. The first had been the 'May 4th Movement' of 1919, in which pupils and students had rebelled against the government, undermining the traditional authority of Confucianism, and laying the foundations for a new culture.

Although the conflicts which broke out between the youth and the government constituted only one aspect of the 'Hundred Flowers Campaign', it was a very important aspect. After all, today's youth are tomorrow's leaders. Moreover, the Party knew from the events of 1919 that the students were a force to be reckoned with. The ideological basis of the 'Hundred Flowers Campaign' was provided by a speech of Mao Tse-tung's entitled 'On the Correct Way of Dealing with Popular Conflicts', which was delivered to a closed session of the State Council (the Chinese cabinet) on February 27, 1957. On April 30 of the same year the Chinese Communist Party took steps to rectify the working methods employed by its functionaries, and asked its followers to help it achieve this objective. The 'anti-Party revolt' was a direct result of this initiative. It continued until June 8, 1957, when the *RMRB* – the *People's Daily* – began to expose the members of this revolutionary movement as right wing deviationists. These denunciations were followed by a radical purge. But in the case of the students the revolt was more protracted. 1957 was a particularly bad year for Chinese education. Both the junior and senior secondary schools, and the universities, were overcrowded, and it is claimed that some 4 million primary school pupils, 800,000 junior secondary school pupils, and 90,000 senior secondary school pupils were unable to continue their education.[15] Although these figures come from an English source and so cannot be regarded as entirely authentic, there can be no doubt about the fact that the prospects for both pupils and students were most unfavourable. This was conceded by Chou En-lai in the report which he submitted to the National People's Congress. Speaking on June 26, 1957, the Premier claimed that the student intake at the Chinese universities and technical colleges had been abnormally high in previous years and that consequently the number of pupils and students entering the secondary schools, universities and technical colleges in 1957 would be reduced. He then went on to say that those who failed to obtain places at these higher institutes would be absorbed into industry and agriculture, and insisted that they should regard their new employment as a great honour. But the secondary school pupils, who suddenly found themselves faced with an uncertain future, did not feel at all honoured. They went on to the streets, beat up their local functionaries, and demanded fair treatment. The anxieties felt by these pupils is well illustrated by the events which took place at the 'First Secondary School' in the town of Hanyang. The revolt there lasted from June 12 to 14, 1957, and was described by the *RMRB* on August 8 as a 'miniature version of the Hungarian rising'. This rising, which had taken place in the previous year, and Krushchev's de-Stalinization speech were two of the principal reasons why the Chinese Communist Party was determined to rectify its members' working methods. The revolt in Hanyang broke out when the pupils discovered that the quota of university places allocated to their school had been fixed at 5 per cent of those who passed their university entrance. The angry pupils demanded that their headmaster should show them the directive in which the quota had been laid down. This he declined to do, but assured them that the quota was actually 26·3 per cent, only to be contradicted on this point by the Assistant Director of the Education Department for the Hanyang district. When this happened, the pupils – who had the sympathy and support of their teachers – banded together and marched on the local government headquarters, where they wrecked a number of offices and demanded that the quota should be published. When they failed to obtain satisfaction from the government, they marched on the offices of the District Committee of the Communist Party. There they were accused of indulging in counter-revolutionary activity, and in the ensuing confusion they seized two Party functionaries, tied them up and carried them off to the school.

The following day a notice was posted in the school informing the pupils that a strike staged by the secondary school pupils in the neighbouring town of Wuhan had been successful. In Wuhan, it was alleged, the quota had been raised from 30 to 50 per cent whereas in Hanyang it had been cut back from 26·3 to 5 per cent. At this a body of some 800 pupils again marched on the local government headquarters, and on this occasion their representatives were received by the mayor. However, far from acceding to their demands, he criticized them for their undemocratic behaviour, whereupon the pupils tried to take him prisoner. They were foiled in this attempt by government functionaries, but succeeded in capturing three of these and taking them with them. Later, when the pupils

49

discovered that three of their own members had been seized by the District Committee of the Party, they marched on the Committee offices and forced their way into the building in order to free their comrades. They captured the Party secretary and were about to tie him up when six or seven hundred workers appeared and drove them out into the street. The pupils later claimed that 146 of their members had been wounded in the fracas, two of them mortally. They then drafted, and reproduced, open letters to the people – i.e. to the population of Wuhan etc. – and planned to take control of the local radio station in order to publicize 'the truth about the way in which the District Committee of the Party called upon the workers to beat up the pupils'. But the following day the pupils were warned by the Party that things had gone too far, and that although the principal culprits were the counter-revolutionaries who had sought to exploit the situation, their strike now involved antagonism between 'the people and its enemies', and had to be called off. The counter-revolutionaries were duly arrested and condemned, and the pupils returned to their classrooms.[16] The fact that the Chinese Communist Party found it necessary to execute these local 'counter-revolutionaries', even though it had taken no action against other 'right wing elements' such as the ministers Chang Po-Chun and Lo Lung-chi, who held high positions in the government and whose names were household words throughout the People's Republic, shows how much importance they attached to the youth problem.

By and large, the secondary school pupils seem to have been concerned with immediate practical problems. Their conflict with the government or, alternatively, the Party was apparently due to the fact that they felt themselves to have been unjustly treated. They made three demands on the leadership: a higher quota of university places for pupils at normal secondary schools, the abolition of the system whereby pupils at the special (three year) secondary schools for workers and peasants were allowed to go straight on to university, and fair treatment for those pupils at normal secondary schools who were refused university places. Most of the demonstrations and disturbances mounted by secondary school pupils took place after June 8, 1957, the day on which the Party launched its counter-offensive. This is significant, for it means that these pupils did not think of themselves in any way as right-wing elements. As in the cultural revolution, so too in the 'anti-Party revolt', the pupils in different secondary schools tried to establish liaison with one another. Individual schools wrote letters to other schools urging concerted action. These endeavours were not unsuccessful. The secondary schools in Soochow, for example, were undoubtedly influenced by letters received from the secondary schools in Shanghai. A further indication that the majority of the secondary school pupils had no right-wing sympathies is to be found in the fact that they addressed their complaints and appeals to the provincial and national newspapers, to the central political committees, and even to Mao Tse-tung. If this had been the cultural revolution, the secondary school pupils would have been hailed as true exponents of the thoughts of Chairman Mao. But in 1957 they were told that they were being exploited by right-wing elements, and were engaging in activities inimical to the Chinese people. And, of course, their demands were rejected. Far from being granted more university places, they were told by Chou En-lai that they should regard their future employment in industry or agriculture as a great honour. But conflicts of this order cannot be resolved by directives from above. After all, it was not just a question of a few young people being denied further training; about a million secondary school pupils were unable to proceed to university, and as many as 4 million primary school pupils were being deprived of secondary education.[17] When the former secondary school pupils were finally forced to assume their new status as 'educated workers and peasants' the conflict between them and the government continued unabated, albeit in a different form.

Where the Chinese students were concerned the conflict with the leadership was much more profound and much more complex. Although they undoubtedly felt a sense of grievance over the way in which they were treated by the authorities, the students were not really concerned with day to day issues. Theirs was essentially an ideological conflict. Not surprisingly, perhaps, the 'anti-Party revolt' was initiated at Peking University which had a long revolutionary tradition. It was the students of Peking who had launched the 'May 4th movement' in 1919 by demonstrating against the pro-Japanese government of the day and burning down the house of a disloyal politician. Many of the professors at Peking University had been founder members of the Chinese Communist Party, and it was in Peking that Mao

Tse-tung first made contact with Marxism. In 1957 the Chinese students criticized the Party in the belief that by doing so they were perpetuating the spirit of the 'May 4th movement'. At Peking University the students built a 'democratic wall' in front of the refectory, and on May 19 the first wall newspaper was posted there, thus initiating a new era of mass communication which reached its peak in the cultural revolution. This publication, which bore the signatures of a group consisting of members of the Communist Youth League and other young people, called upon the committee of the Youth League in the university to state whether it had sent a delegation to the third National Congress and, if so, to explain how the composition of that delegation had been decided upon. Subsequently, countless wall newspapers were posted, and the students also set aside five hours each evening – from 17.00 to 22.00 hours – for discussions. They even proposed that classes should be suspended so that they could concentrate exclusively on their political activities, a proposal which was actually put into effect during the cultural revolution. Many of the wall newspapers drew attention to the undemocratic situation whereby students who were Party members or members of the Youth League enjoyed special privileges: they were the only students allowed to go abroad, and they were given the best posts when they graduated, posts in remote and isolated districts invariably being allocated to non-members. In other wall newspapers the students argued that political courses should be optional, that the Party Committee at the University should be 'liberalized', and that the academic administration should be responsible for the academic curriculum. As time passed and the students became more outspoken, the political content of their newspapers increased. Excerpts from Krushchev's de-Stalinization speech were reproduced together with the comment: 'The Americans have been given the translated text of Krushchev's speech. Why haven't we?' In their publications the students also questioned the legitimacy of many of the purges of 'right-wing elements' carried out by the Party in the past.

What seems to have happened in 1957 is that, after seeing that their well-meaning criticisms of the methods used by the Party had made absolutely no impression on the leadership, a number of the students at least decided that further criticism of this kind was useless unless the whole system of government in

China was modified. For the first few weeks of the 'anti-Party revolt' no reference was made to the basic structure of the Chinese social system. But when the Party launched its counter-offensive, special student organizations and societies were founded, and these published magazines in which the existing socio-political system was criticized with all the revolutionary fervour that had characterized the 'May 4th movement'. These student groups wanted to start 'a movement for the promotion of freedom and democracy, and the reform of the political system'. They regarded the existing system as outmoded and considered that 'the masses would withdraw their support' unless changes were made. They also condemned the Party's rejection of western civilization, and called for a reappraisal of capitalism.[18] At Peking University there were at least four student organizations of this kind: 'The Hundred Flowers Society', 'The Hundred Flowers Tribune', 'The Chang-Shen Poets Group' and 'The Free Tribune'; at the Teachers' Training College in Peking there were two groups: 'Bitter Medicine' and 'The Mouthpiece of the Lowest Social Class'; and at the Peking Institute for Geology and Petroleum there was a subsidiary branch of the 'Hundred Flowers Society'. At Tientsin University in the city of Tientsin there were eight student organizations: 'The Trumpet', 'Spring Thunder' etc. At Wuhan University in the industrial town of Wuhan the students published a magazine entitled 'Flames' whilst their counterparts at the Teachers Training College in the provincial capital of Kweilin published a similar magazine under the title 'Battle-cry'. Student unrest was widespread in 1957, and there can hardly have been a university town in China where disturbances did not take place. In Peking there was at least one bomb outrage. Student demonstrations were commonplace, and clashes between students, police, and peasants and workers by no means rare. In reporting such incidents the Chinese press always represented them as spontaneous demonstrations of peasants and workers in defence of the interests of the Communist Party. Such spontaneity may, perhaps, be doubted, for in the course of the cultural revolution it became clear that Party functionaries made a regular practice of organizing the peasants and workers as a means of controlling the youth of the country.

Like the 'May 4th movement' and, to a lesser extent, the

proletarian cultural revolution of a later date, the 'anti-Party revolt' was essentially a protest on the part of Chinese youth. In the 'May 4th movement' of 1919 the youth protested against Confucianism and its timeless maxims. They fought against the intellectual aridity of an era, in which people preferred to quote from Confucius, Menzius and other traditional authorities, whose teachings were generally held to be incontrovertibly true, rather than evolve an independent philosophy. They destroyed the sacred cows of Chinese tradition, and demanded proof instead of quotations. In the 'Hundred Flowers Campaign' of 1957 the students and young people consciously sought to revive the spirit of the 'May 4th movement'. To some extent, they even revived the terminology used by their predecessors. Thus, they spoke of freedom, democracy and reason, of independent thought and the abolition of dogmas. The only essential difference was that they protested against Marxism and the thoughts of Mao Tse-tung. In 1957 it was by no means rare to discover in student publications statements such as 'Marxism–Leninism must be modified', 'Marxism has not developed since 1895 [the year of Engel's death]' or 'Mao Tse-tung's thoughts are a mixture of metaphysics and dialectics, and were formulated in order to mislead the people'. The youth demanded a wide range of rights and freedoms, including personal freedom, freedom of the press, freedom of opinion, and the right of assembly. The young people of 1919 had criticized China's pro-Japanese policy on the grounds that it constituted an abject betrayal of national sovereignty, and the young people of 1957 criticized the Chinese Communist Party's pro-Soviet policy on precisely the same grounds. In 1957 the students also demanded that their personal files – which were kept by the Party Committees at the universities and were referred to in student circles as the 'black list' – should either be made available for public examination or should be destroyed. Another point which the members of the 'anti-Party revolt' had in common with their predecessors of the 'May 4th movement' was their realization that, if it was to be successful, their enterprise must be broadly based. Consequently, they not only made contact with the students in other departments of their own university or college, they also sent representatives to establish a liaison with other universities or colleges in both their own and other towns, a practice subsequently adopted by the Red Guards in the cultural revolution. They even made approaches to the general populace in an attempt to gain their sympathy, if not their support. They stuck posters on the walls of newspaper offices and Party Committee buildings, and sent representatives to the workers and peasants to tell them about the abuses in Chinese society. At the same time, Party functionaries were hard at work organizing resistance to the students amongst the workers and peasants. We find references in the Chinese press, not only to the clashes which took place between the students and the populace, but also to the sympathy felt for the students by members of the workers' and peasants' communities. Such people were described as right wing elements, counter-revolutionaries or dupes.

Class Affiliations of the 'Anti-Party Rebels'

The young people who took part in the 'May 4th movement' of 1919, the cultural revolution of 1965, and the 'anti-Party revolt' of 1957 all criticized the social system in which they were obliged to live. And yet, to a greater or lesser degree, they were all products of those systems. It is perfectly true that the youth of 1919 were very much exposed to western influences, and the majority of the young rebels in 1957 could not have been more than fourteen at the time of the establishment of the People's Republic. But at fourteen people are still malleable, and we have already seen that from at least 1952 onwards ideological training was certainly not neglected, even though it was not always combined with manual labour at that time. None the less, many young people of China rebelled against the tutelage of the Party and the Youth League. According to the testimony of a 'rightist group' at the Linchuan Teachers Training Institute, the average age of the rebels in 1957 was between nineteen and twenty, and the oldest rebel was only twenty-two. Not surprisingly most of the rebels came from non-proletarian homes, their parents having been estate owners, big farmers or members of the bourgeoisie. In fact 80 per cent of all Chinese students came from non-proletarian backgrounds. At the University of Wuhan in Central China one of the third year classes in the Sinological Department was composed in its entirety of the members of a 'rightist group'. (In China the universities are organized in the same way as schools, which means that the students in each year are divided up into different classes.) Of the thirty students in this class – or rightist group – twenty-five were children of estate owners, big farmers or members of the bourgeoisie. According to a report in the *RMRB*, many of their relatives had incurred the wrath of the Party, and had been suppressed, or interned, or kept under surveillance. It was suggested in the *RMRB* report that it was for this reason that the members of the group had been discontented with the Party and the social system. And yet these students had had no thought of revenge, and had not called for the withdrawal of the measures which had brought such hardship both on themselves and on their relatives. What they wanted was the right to think their own thoughts instead of subscribing to dogmas. In the 'anti-party revolt' of 1957, as in the 'May 4th movement' of 1919, every Chinese university produced several student newspapers, and on July 24, 1957 the *RMRB* subjected the editorial staff of one of these newspapers – the 'Public Forum' published by the students of Peking University – to a detailed analysis in terms of class affiliations. Of the fifteen members of the staff, eleven – about 75 per cent – were the children of large estate owners, bureaucrats or capitalists. It should be noted in this connexion that people denigrated as 'bureaucrats' at that time were quite likely to be government or Party functionaries; 'bureaucracy' was a mental attitude developed by the mandarins which the Party found undesirable and which Mao Tse-tung hoped to correct through the 'Hundred Flowers Campaign'. Seven members of the editorial staff of 'Public Forum' were investigated at greater length in the *RMRB* article, and the composition of this smaller group is particularly interesting. The first of the seven was supposed to have served a term of imprisonment for counter-revolutionary activities, the second was supposed to have served eight months for theft and was also said to have been found in 'a lady's toilet on two occasions', the third was a Party member, the fourth a 'book thief', the fifth a former soldier who had fought on the Korean front, the sixth a member of the Youth League, and the seventh a member of the reactionary bourgeoisie. This is a significant and intriguing list. The ideological reforms carried out by the Party cannot have been entirely successful if a former counter-revolutionary was able to relapse in this way. And it is curious that the *RMRB* should have seen fit to inform its readers that one of the two thieves had been found in 'a lady's toilet on two occasions' but had not thought to provide further information on the circumstances of the alleged thefts. In the case of the 'book thief', certainly, one would have expected a more detailed account. But the most serious factor of all from the Party's point of view was that a Party member, a member of the Communist Youth League and a former soldier had all been corrupted, for the Party relied on the members of these three groups to propagate communist ideas amongst the youth of the country. But then the ideological attitudes of many Party and League members were bound to be suspect if they had not joined until after 1949. We know from the events of the Hundred Flowers' campaign that some of them at least had become members simply in order to improve their career prospects. It is an established fact that there was no shortage of 'rightist elements' in the Youth League. These rightists maintained that, since it was simply a satellite of the Party and, as such, could be suppressed at any time, the League had no real *raison d'être*. They disagreed with the Marxist–Leninist ideology, and criticized the system whereby young people were required to attend politico-ideological courses. They also objected to the investigations carried out into the class affiliations of Chinese youth, and they condemned the relationship that had been established between the League and the youth as a 'cat and mouse game'. Even in the special schools run by the League for training their own functionaries newspapers were sometimes found posted on the walls bearing slogans such as 'Down With Communism', and numerous branch associations of the Youth League were rendered completely ineffectual, due to the activities of their rightist elements. Nor was it only the lesser lights in the League who joined in the protest; some of the leading functionaries in the League's Central Committee were also involved.

The most celebrated of the rightist elements amongst the Chinese youth was a girl student named Lin Hsi-ling, who joined the Red Army at the age of fourteen, and later studied at the People's University in Peking, which accepted only proven revolutionaries and their children. But despite her background, Lin was more active and more outspoken in her opposition to the Party than any of her colleagues. Her views were widely reported, and many young people looked upon her as their spokesman and champion. In fact, her influence was so great that the Peking Students' Union found it necessary to publish a selection of her speeches and articles in a brochure entitled 'Look! What Sort of Speeches are These!' and distribute it to the students so that they could analyse Lin's views for themselves. The object of this exercise was to persuade the students that her views were mistaken in the hope that they would then mount a mass anti-Lin campaign. In actual fact, however, the ideas of Lin Hsi-ling – some of which were put into practice during the cultural revolution – were more or less in line with the views held by the majority of dissident students. Because she played such an important part in the 'anti-Party revolt' I now propose to deal with her ideas in greater detail. Lin considered that the demands formulated by Hu Feng, one of the right-wing elements exposed by the Party, were essentially valid, and she argued – quite plausibly – that the Party had subsequently based its 'Hundred Flowers Campaign' on those demands. There would be nothing surprising about such a volte-face, for the Chinese Communist Party has displayed a rare talent for disposing of its critics by branding them as right-wing deviationists whilst taking careful note of their criticisms for possible future use. Thus, some of the criticisms levelled against the Party in 1957 were acted upon in the cultural revolution. Lin also considered that both the Chinese and Soviet forms of socialism were bogus since both had been built up on a feudal and imperialist basis. Consequently, she insisted on the need to continue the struggle for a genuine and democratic form of socialism. This, of course, was partially realized by the introduction of general mobilization and the setting up of revolutionary committees during the cultural revolution. Lin conceded that the Communist Party had fought on the side of the people against the Kuomintang but maintained that, once it had assumed power, the Party had oppressed and deceived the people. She also complained that too many guardians had been appointed to watch over the Party and preserve its ideology, and that the people entrusted with this office were mere opportunists, who used their power to further their own careers, even though that power had been bought with the blood of China's martyrs. This abuse was also partially remedied in the cultural revolution by the assault on the functionaries. Another criticism of Lin's subsequently endorsed by the Red Guards concerned the interest that was still being paid to the former owners of industrial concerns on their original investments. This, she insisted, should be discontinued. Lin Hsi-ling further accused the Party of judging people not on their merits or abilities but on whether they belonged to the Party or the Youth League. This practice, which placed a premium on Party or League membership and so tended to attract recruits who were essentially career-minded, was equally abhorrent to the Red Guards. Lin also maintained that the three great evils of bureaucracy, subjectivism and sectarianism – which the 'Hundred Flowers Campaign' was specifically designed to remedy – had their roots in the hierarchical organization of Chinese society. It will be remembered in this connexion that even before the cultural revolution was mounted the army did away with all visible marks of rank in order to play down its authoritarian structure. Another point seized upon by Lin Hsi-ling was the abject attitude adopted by the Chinese Communist Party towards the Soviet Union, which she compared with China's adulatory attitude towards foreigners in general, and Americans in particular, prior to 1949. This pro-Soviet attitude was, of course, reversed long before the cultural revolution. Chou Yang, responsible for art and literature in 1957, came in for particularly heavy censure from Lin, who claimed that he had imposed a dictatorship on China's artists and writers. Chou Yang was brought down in the cultural revolution; but so too were many of China's artists and writers. Lin also drew attention to the fact that people who did not hold positions of power simply did not dare to argue with the Party, and she urged that all members of the community should be encouraged to express their opinions openly and freely. The Party, she said, should not expect to receive endless hymns of praise from the people; on the contrary, it should also be receptive to criticism. Moreover, instead of trying to convince the people that they were living in a perfect society run by a perfect government, it should take the people into its confidence and openly discuss any difficulties that occurred. Within the limits imposed by the system, these demands were also met by the Party at a later date. Throughout Chinese history revolts staged by young people have always ended with the leaders being suppressed or bribed. The leaders of the 'May 4th movement' were 'bought off' with positions of power. Irrespective of whether they joined the Kuomintang or the Communist Party, they became part of the establishment and soon forgot their revolutionary ardour. The young people who took part in the 'anti-Party revolt' of 1957, on the other hand, were suppressed as counter-revolutionaries and rightists or else were told that they had been suborned. The fact that many of their ideas were later implemented was beside the point. But conflicts cannot be resolved by suppression. The young people who were directed into industry or agriculture brought their conflicts with them into their new environment, where they assumed a new form but lost none of their old potency. And the fundamental conflicts enacted between the youth and the leadership of 1957 were inherited, and developed, by the following generation.

2. Young People After 1958

We have seen that the demands made by the secondary school pupils for a larger allocation of senior secondary school and university places were rejected by the Party on the grounds that the expansion of higher education had proceeded too rapidly in the past, which would suggest that by 1957 the Party was opting for quality rather than quantity. But with the introduction in the autumn of 1958 of the 'Great Leap Forwards', i.e. the policy of rapid socialization, China's educational policy underwent a sudden transformation.

The Educational Revolution

The educational developments that had taken place prior to 1958, according to the leadership, had been purely evolutionary; it was only after the introduction of the 'Great Leap Forwards' that Chinese education entered upon its revolutionary phase. The new educational policy was designed to eradicate the distinction between mental and physical work, and so enable the intellectuals to acquire a working class outlook, and the workers a capacity for intellectual thought. This meant that every aspect of education was to be political.

The schools and universities were to set up factories and farms, the industrial concerns and communes schools for all grades of pupils. For the youth of China this revolution meant that they were to be educated to serve 'the working class and the cause of socialism'. If this was to be achieved, the Party insisted, the social awareness of the younger generation would have to be strengthened, and the right way of doing this was by combining mental and physical work. The leadership hoped that the Chinese pupils and students would undergo a spiritual transformation if they performed manual tasks and came into contact with peasants and workers. By exposing them to such influences, it was hoped that they would adopt a proletarian outlook.

The educational revolution was accompanied by a sudden and significant increase in the number of students attending universities and colleges: from 440,000 in 1957 to 660,000 in 1958. On the face of it, this would suggest that the demand for a larger quota of university places made by the secondary school pupils in the 'anti-Party revolt' had been met. But this was not the case, for in the same period the number of secondary school pupils rose from 7 to 12 millions,[19] of whom 8.52 millions attended normal secondary schools. The students' earlier demand for a reduction in the number of political courses or, preferably, their complete abolition was also rejected in 1958. In fact, political education was intensified. This was inevitable, for the educational revolution was conceived as an extension of the ideological revolution, i.e. an extension of the campaign launched by the Party in order to change the working methods employed by its members, and to expose right-wing deviationists. As for manual work, which the students were required to carry out in addition to their academic and political studies, this served a dual purpose. On the one hand it enabled large numbers of students to help to boost production – during the 'Great Leap Forwards' 90,000 students and young technological lecturers were sent to work in the steel industry, and 'several hundred thousand students, several million secondary school pupils, several tens of thousands of primary school pupils, and several hundred teachers' in general industry and agriculture – whilst on the other hand, it ensured the integration of intellectual and manual work in the school curricula. The fact that this manual work was especially designed to promote proletarian attitudes amongst the students made things much more difficult for them than they would otherwise have been. It would have been logical for students specializing in a particular branch of technology to perform their manual work in industrial concerns where their theoretical knowledge could have been put to practical use. But the Party leadership saw ideological dangers in this sort of arrangement. It considered that students who were allowed to perform their manual work in this way might think that the sole object of the exercise was to improve their practical skills, in other words that manual work in China was no different from workshop practice in the bourgeois democracies This, it was felt, would have destroyed the ideological character of manual work, and reinforced the bourgeois attitude adopted towards it by many of the students. And so the leadership decided that, as a general rule, the students should be asked to perform heavy physical work which had no direct connexion with their university activities. The more menial the task, the better it suited its ideological purpose, and since agricultural labouring was generally regarded as the most menial task of all, the students were sent to work in communes whenever possible. It was by no means rare for both students and pupils to go with the peasants to collect dung.[20] The period of time spent on manual work varied from three months to a year.

In the autumn of 1958 the Party leadership was distinctly optimistic, even though it conceded that the educational revolution was not without its adversaries. But these adversaries, it was claimed, consisted entirely of bourgeois teachers and students from capitalist homes. It is perfectly true that the Party had grounds for optimism. By then 70 per cent of all secondary school pupils and 62 per cent of all students are said to have come from working class homes.[21] In April 1959 the Minister of University Education warned that the students should not be overburdened with physical work, lest it impair their health and prevent them from keeping up with their studies. (We have already seen that poor health and reduced powers of concentration had been student bugbears for years.) In 1960, it is true, the same minister was still advocating an intensification of manual work for the pupils at secondary and primary schools; but he also warned that the Chinese educational system was not meeting the requirements of national reconstruction, and insisted that what was needed was a balanced programme that would take due account of both manual work and the need for relaxation. Clearly, if the Minister of University Education was prepared to issue such a warning, there must have been widespread discontent both inside and outside the Party. But the real extent of this discontent, and the real mood of Chinese youth, only became fully apparent from 1961 onwards.

Discontent of the Youth and the Lack of Unity Amongst the Leadership

At the beginning of 1961 the Communist Youth League was instructed to revive the 'Yenan method' and propagate it amongst the youth of the country. (Yenan, it will be remembered, was the headquarters of the Chinese Communist Party during the struggle with the Kuomintang.) The object of this campaign was to enlighten the youth about the nature of the class war and the needs of the production programme, and it was prompted by the desire to remove the dissatisfaction felt by both the leadership and the youth. The younger generation had not experienced the revolution and had no first-hand knowledge of the class war; and because of this it could not understand why the Party found it necessary to intensify the class war in peace-time or to attach such importance to the construction of socialism. This did not only apply to the children of capitalist families; the sons and daughters of the Chinese workers had also been influenced by bourgeois ideology. The bourgeois leanings of young people at that time are well illustrated by a reader's letter published in *Llongguo Quingnian*, a fortnightly magazine for young people. This young correspondent said that he could not understand why it was that in 1961 the revolution should still involve such great hardship, since the Chinese economy had reached a point where it would be perfectly feasible to raise the general standard of living. What the students wanted, he said, was to complete their academic training, and he could see no good reason why the Party should send them to the countryside to become farmers. In replying to this letter the editor stated that individuals should follow all directives issued by the Party and sacrifice their personal ambitions for the good of the community. But the complaints made by this correspondent were not so unreasonable, for the lot of the young people who were sent to work in the communes was far from easy. Consider the case of Lapei, a town near the Russian border. In 1955 this town had a population of 10,000 people. By 1961 it embraced no less than 61 different settlements, and had a population of 60,000 people, who spoke many different dialects. The young people who worked there had cleared 17,000 Mou (one Mou = 670 square metres) of land and made it ready for cultivation, and had erected buildings on a further 3,000 square metres. It is quite clear from these statistics that the young people sent to Lapei had to work very hard; and it is equally clear from the statistics for Party and League membership in Lapei that they were far from enthusiastic about their project: eighteen joined the Party and twenty-two joined the Youth League.[22] The fact that the youth objected to Party policy is understandable, although if the leadership had been united, they would have been quite powerless to change it. However, there were also conflicts within the leadership.

Speaking for the Central Committee of the Chinese Communist Party, the Foreign Minister Chen Yi discussed the respective roles of politics and professional studies at Chinese universities in a speech on August 10, 1961. Chen Yi gave a completely new appraisal of the relationship between politics and professional studies, thus revising the policy formulated during the educational revolution of 1958. He insisted that the *first* and *most important* task for students at universities and technical colleges was to acquire adequate professional knowledge. Consequently, he said, they should *not* spend very much time on politics or manual work lest this should have a prejudicial effect on their studies and so retard the development of Chinese science and culture. According to Chen Yi, even those students who evinced no interest whatsoever in political matters should not be condemned, provided they made progress in their professional studies. The Party, he said, *did not expect* the students to be ardent Marxists, and would be perfectly well satisfied as long as they obeyed its directives and did not rebel; only Party members, members of the Youth League and Communist functionaries would be required to pursue an intensive course of political study, and engage in political activities. In order to illustrate this new ideological approach Chen Yi held himself up as an example. His own attitude, he said, was not ex-

clusively Marxist–Leninist. On the contrary, he also subscribed to some of the conceptions of Confucius and Menzius,
and to certain bourgeois ideas. Over and above all this, Chen
Yi suggested that it would be wrong to attach too much importance to the original class affiliations of young people, and
in this connexion he pointed out that many of the Party leaders
had not come from working class backgrounds. This was the
first time that the non-proletarian origins of the leadership had
been officially revealed. The net result of Chen Yi's speech was
that educational policy reverted to its pre-1958 condition.
Henceforth, ideology was officially recognized as being less
important than professional training. In early September, 1961
– i.e. within a month of Chen Yi's speech – the timetable at
Peking University was revised so that the students had more
time for their professional studies, and had their weekends
completely free. The Chinese press then tried to justify this
new line in Marxist terms. The *RMRB* maintained that every
new cultural or scientific achievement – including Marxism –
had come about as a result of a general accumulation of
knowledge, and from this it concluded that if they wished to
be ideologically progressive, young people must first devote
themselves, seriously and energetically, to the acquisition of
knowledge. The members of the Youth League were told that
they must set a good example by applying themselves to their
studies with even greater diligence than their colleagues. The
teachers were even urged to model themselves on Confucius
by devoting more of their time to their talented students.[23]
Finally, there was general recognition of the fact that teachers,
students and pupils needed long vacations in which to re-
cuperate.

This appears to have been the first occasion on which conflicts between the youth and the leadership were successfully
resolved. But although it had granted concessions, the Party
continued to exhort the youth to greater efforts. In attempting
to direct Chinese youth on to the socialist path, it even went
so far as to quote from the sayings of Confucius. Thus, young
people were told that 'a man whose desires are not self-centred
is a strong man', and they were urged not to concentrate all
their efforts on the need to provide themselves with enough
'food and clothing', or to try to cover up their ideological
shortcomings and pass themselves off as 'perfect young men

and women' in order to obtain personal advantages. These exhortations were directed at the whole of Chinese youth, and they give a clear indication of their 'bourgeois outlook and way of life', and of the way in which they had reacted to the corrective measures taken by the Party.

By then the situation was critical. In the towns young workers and secondary school pupils – many of them no more than fifteen years of age – spent their evenings in dance halls. In the country districts things were even worse. When the young peasants married, the wedding celebrations went on for days, and the crops were often allowed to rot in the fields. Moreover, in rural areas feudal customs still prevailed. For example, marriages were arranged by the parents, and if female functionaries tried to make contact with the local male population they were simply ridiculed. The threat which this state of affairs posed for socialist ideology becomes immediately apparent if we consider that such incidents were still being reported after the communization of rural China. But no effective remedy could be applied whilst the Party leadership was divided and continued to issue contradictory directives. Faced with this ambivalent situation the young functionaries did not know which way to turn, and the 'bourgeois outlook and way of life' adopted by the young people in all sections of the Chinese community continued to flourish.

Mao's New Directive and the Reaction of Chinese Youth

The ideological *détente* was brought to an end when Mao Tse-tung called for a renewal of the class war at the 10th plenary session of the 8th Central Committee in September, 1962. In his speech Mao impressed on the youth that democracy was only a means to an end, and that freedom must go hand in hand with discipline, and would be granted only to those who supported the cause of socialism. Critics of the new policy were promptly suppressed on the grounds that they constituted a threat to the State, and the people were told that the country was faced with a straight choice between a bourgeois and a proletarian dictatorship. On February 15, 1963, the Central Committee of the Communist Youth League issued a directive informing the youth that they must learn from the example set by 'Lei Feng'. Particular importance was attached to this campaign by the leadership, and Mao Tse-tung himself composed a title for an article on Lei-Feng, which was published on March 2, 1963, in a special edition of the magazine 'Chinese Youth'. The object of the campaign was to teach young people that they must serve the interests of the people, help their neighbours, submit willingly to hardship, and live economically. They were urged to perfect themselves, both ideologically and professionally, by studying and acting upon the thoughts of Chairman Mao. Throughout China, mass meetings and discussions were arranged, plays were put on, and special wall newspapers were posted, all dealing with the life of Lei Feng, who had been so dedicated to his work that he had died as a result of his prodigious efforts. But Lei Feng had kept a diary, and the young people of China were now advised to study his writings so that they might learn from him. Above all, they were urged to take note of the fact that Lei Feng had been a serious student of the works of Mao Tse-tung, and that it was due to his almost constant pre-occupation with these works that he himself had become a model for the whole of Chinese youth. As a result of this campaign, Chinese education was again based primarily on the requirements of the class war. Once again, the Party leaders insisted that young people should be given intensive ideological education so that they would be in a position to continue the class war until such time as a Communist State had been established. This, they said, was an essential measure, because the youth of 1963 had never experienced capitalist exploitation and consequently had no first hand knowledge of the class war.

Accordingly, academic education at schools and universities was cut back to allow more time for ideological instruction, and pupils and students were also expected to attend ideological classes during their leisure time. In addition, manual work was increased and its administration centralized. In Peking, for example, contact was established with the people's communes in the surrounding districts, and firm arrangements were made stipulating when, and in what capacity, the students attending 47 different colleges in the city were to perform their manual work. As for the secondary school pupils, their manual work was arranged by the government Education Department, which means that it was even more tightly controlled. These pupils had to spend a minimum of two weeks every six months on the land, and were also expected to help out in local factories during their leisure hours. But, above all, the young people of China were to be brought into contact with the peasants; they had to live with them, and take their meals with them.

The Youth and China's Future

In 1962 Mao Tse-tung became concerned about the future of Chinese Communism,[24] and his concern was dictated in part by the ideological dispute that had broken out between China and the Soviet Union. Mao felt that if capitalism could be restored in the land of the October Revolution, it could be restored in China. After all, in China the feudal system had held sway for thousands of years, and the bourgeois system for over a hundred years, whilst Marxism–Leninism had been completely unknown until the 1920's. Moreover, the youth of China were politically naïve, and had been influenced by bourgeois ideas. They believed in brotherly love, and had a horror of war; they attached immense importance to their professions, and very little to politics. And, of course, in every part of China class enmity was still rife. '*Old* and *new* bourgeois elements, and *degenerate* and *disaffected* Party members' were trying to restore the capitalist system, and numerous branches of the Party and the Youth League had already been corrupted. The age of the junior functionaries also gave cause for concern, for like the Party members, their average age was forty. Unless suitable successors could be found, it was to be feared that Red China would not be red for very much longer. Young recruits joining the Party or the Youth League were expected to fulfil certain requirements, which were defined by Mao Tse-tung himself. There were five of these in all: 1. they had to be prepared to carry on the class war, and to study the 'thoughts of Mao Tse-tung'; 2. they had to keep their sights fixed on the world revolution at all times, and never try to pursue personal or national interests; 3. they had to learn how to win over anti-communists and those corrupted by them, and never allow themselves to become estranged from the people; 4. they had to follow the general Party line and support the principle of democratic centralism; 5. they had to be humble and cautious.

Curiously enough, the younger they were at the foundation

of the People's Republic, and the more frequently they had been given a proletarian education, the more refractory the youth tended to be. And it was not just the children from capitalist families who refused to conform. It will be remembered that in the 'anti-Party revolt' of 1957 the rightists and those whom they had suborned did not always come from bourgeois backgrounds, and by 1961 it was openly conceded that boys and girls from working class families had been influenced by bourgeois ideas. Two years later, it was reported in the *RMRB* that the children in a number of urban secondary schools, 90 per cent of whom were working class, possessed no political or ideological knowledge whatsoever.[25] Also primary school pupils, even those from working-class homes, had failed to realize how 'fortunate' they now were. According to another report, the strongest opposition to the Party's educational policy came from those secondary school pupils who had 'read a few books and so thought themselves superior'.[26] At that time approximately 80 per cent of all secondary school pupils came from working-class homes, and only 18 per cent of those who completed their secondary school courses were allowed to proceed to higher institutes.[27] Those forced to become manual workers complained that they had no hope of promotion, that their work was tedious and unrewarding, and that their years of study had been wasted. The Party responded with the charge that young people from working-class homes who objected to manual work were denying their origins. In a country like China, where great importance is still attached to the family, this charge was both grave and insulting.

The most remarkable of all the newspaper reports on the activities of Chinese youth appeared in 1964. It seems that in major cities like Shanghai and Peking, and even in distant provinces such as Shensi and Shansi, numerous young people were going about with long hair, pointed shoes and tight trousers. The situation was so bad that the leadership found it necessary to convene special conferences for tailors, hairdressers, etc. in order to impress on them that they must abandon this new trend. But the conferences were not an unqualified success, for some of the participants appeared in western dress. Other aspects of western culture also found favour with a section of Chinese youth at that time. Photographs of 'indecently attired actresses' could be bought over the counter in any major city. So too could 'ideologically unhealthy' records, although these were suitably disguised with proletarian titles. It seems that young Chinese girls took pleasure in standing in front of their mirrors striking poses copied from those foreign actresses, and on occasions pin-ups were even found in books belonging to primary school pupils. By and large, the children of former capitalists did not follow the western fashion; they were always suspect, and so could not afford to expose themselves in this way. And, in fact, it was the young people with socially acceptable class affiliations – above all, the sons and daughters of senior functionaries – who flaunted their bourgeois and western tastes. These young people had become 'degenerate, disaffected' and politically unreliable. Not that the ideological attitudes of the children of former bourgeois and petits-bourgeois families were any more reliable. Many of them objected to being classified as members of the exploiting class, maintaining that it was only because their fathers had worked hard and saved their money that they had been able to buy up land or build factories. Others argued that since the bourgeois regime had been overthrown and its supporters reformed, there was no point in retaining the old bourgeois classification. But their arguments were not accepted. Information about former class background still had to be entered on all official questionnaires.[28]

We see, therefore, that the young people from capitalist backgrounds had been alienated by the discriminatory treatment meted out to them whilst those from working-class homes were not always very reliable. But there was a third group of young people which was even more embittered. This group consisted of former secondary school pupils who had been refused university places and directed into industry or, more particularly, agriculture. Twenty million young people were put to work on the land by the end of 1961, and a further 20 million by September 1963.[29] They were the 'educated peasants' who, it was hoped, would raise the cultural level of the rural population, thus hastening the day when the peasants would share the cultural attitudes of the workers, and so be prepared for a speedy transition to communism. At the same time, these former pupils were supposed to play a leading part in the modernization of Chinese agriculture. They were to drive the tractors, and service the mechanical and electric pumps and agricultural machines. It was estimated that at that time 80 per cent of all 'specialist workers' employed in agriculture were young people. By 1963 some 10 million young people also held administrative posts – as book-keepers, clerks, etc. But not everybody could be given one of these better jobs. In 1963, China possessed 100,000 tractors, 4 million mechanical pumps, and a limited number of electrical pumps.[30] Between them, these provided work for 5 million young people; and if we add these 5 million drivers' and mechanics' jobs to the 10 million administrative jobs, it still leaves 25 million young people unaccounted for. They were expected to work as ordinary peasants, and to double as Party propagandists and teachers in their spare time. In fact, all young people sent to work on the land were told that they must not only learn from the local peasants, but teach them as well. They were also told to submit reports on them to their local Party committee.

The decision to direct young people into agriculture was to some extent forced upon the Party by political necessity. In 1962 an enquiry was carried out in a district in the province of Shansi to discover the career pattern of the local schoolchildren. The results of this enquiry were shattering. It seems that in the period 1949 to 1962 only 9 out of a total of 10,000 primary school leavers went to work on the land. The ratio for junior secondary schools was much the same: 1 out of a total of 1,554.[31] Whether the young people directed into agriculture appreciated this necessity was not considered under the terms of this enquiry. As for the press accounts of their reactions, they were more or less stereotyped. When they first set out, it was said, the young people were full of enthusiasm, and although they tended to lose heart when they discovered just how backward the villages were, once they had taken things in hand they soon threw off their depression, and from then onwards were quite contented with their lot. Occasionally, the Chinese newspapers also reported the grievances aired by the 'educated peasants'. Above all, it seems, they felt it was a waste of talent to ask secondary school pupils to perform tasks which could be accomplished equally well by illiterates and insisted that they should be given skilled employment in one of the branches of modern technology. They also complained that by the time Chinese agriculture was modernized, they would be too old to benefit, and asked why the Party had bothered to send them to school if the only work it had for them was manual labour of the most menial kind. Finally, they pointed out that since the government had to spend between 300 and 400 yen per year on every secondary school pupil, their education had been a complete waste of public money. Faced with such charges, the Party leadership told these young people that they were adopting a shortsighted attitude and would be better advised to think in terms of the future.

In conclusion, I would like to deal briefly with the Communist Youth League, which was largely responsible for the implementation of the leadership's youth policy. Between 1949 and 1953 the membership of the League rose, by an average of 2,202,500 per year, from 190,000 to 9 millions. By 1957 it had risen to 23 millions, which gives an annual growth rate of 3·5 millions for this four year period. In the following year League membership rose to 25 millions, after which it remained more or less constant. In 1959 and 1961 there was no fluctuation at all. Out of the total membership of 25 millions, 10 millions lived in the countryside; but out of a total youth population of 130 millions, 100 millions lived in the countryside.[32] This means that nearly 50 per cent of urban youth belonged to the League compared with only 10 per cent of rural youth. It also means that the class affiliations of the members were far from ideal. This was confirmed by Ho Jao-pang, the chairman of the League, in 1964 when he publicly conceded that the League had been receptive to bourgeois and other non-proletarian ideas, and had been infiltered by class enemies and 'bad elements'. According to Ho, this was due to the fact that the members came from different social backgrounds. Ho also admitted that the 'degenerate elements' in the League had suborned a number of their comrades. Even the loyal majority – who were motivated by lofty ideals – came in for their share of criticism. It appears that they had shown little enthusiasm for their routine duties and executed them in a slipshod manner. Finally, Ho complained that the higher echelons in the League had lost contact with the small provincial committees.

Clearly, the ideological attitudes espoused by the membership of the Youth League were suspect. Moreover, it is quite evident from the membership statistics quoted above that after 1958, the year of the 'Great Leap Forwards', the League held little appeal for the young people of China, for it gained virtually no new members.

Ideological Attitudes of Chinese Youth Immediately Before the Cultural Revolution

Ho Jao-pang also cast considerable light on the ideological attitudes of Chinese youth in the period immediately preceding the cultural revolution. In the report which he submitted to the Ninth Congress of the Communist Youth League he pointed out that the struggle between the proletariat and the bourgeoisie for the support of Chinese youth constituted one important aspect of the class war during the socialist phase of the revolution. The enemies of the revolution, he maintained, would do anything to entice young people into the non-revolutionary or counter-revolutionary camp, and he reminded his audience that a large proportion of China's youth came from non-proletarian backgrounds and were still influenced by false ideologies. Since they had grown up in a period of peace and stability, Ho said, they were liable to attach excessive importance to the concept of peace, and to hanker after a life of ease and comfort; and since they had not undergone the acid test of fighting in the revolution, they lacked the necessary understanding for the complexity and hardships of the revolutionary process. According to Ho Jao-pang, a number of new bourgeois elements and revisionists had emerged from the ranks of Chinese youth, due to the corrupting influence of the traditional bourgeois ideology. It was, he said, a dangerous error of judgement to assume that people who had been brought up in the new society must necessarily have a 'red heart' and could assume responsibility for the further prosecution of the revolution without first receiving revolutionary, i.e. Marxist–Leninist, training, without being hardened in revolutionary campaigns, and without completely revising their attitudes. In Ho's opinion, the young people of China were in a precarious situation: by Maoist standards, those from capitalist backgrounds were still regarded as unreliable whilst those who had been classified as reliable had none the less produced a number of 'new bourgeois elements and revisionists'; and all the time anti-Maoist elements, both inside and outside the Party, were trying to lure young people into the anti-Maoist camp. In actual fact, the original Maoist educational programme, which had been reintroduced in 1963, suffered a serious reversal on the eve of the cultural revolution. As early as March and April of 1964 China's major cities and provinces began to press for a reduction in all extramural activities at Chinese schools and universities so as to allow the pupils and students more time for their academic studies. It was also hoped that the implementation of this proposal would improve student health and foster a more positive attitude towards the Party. It seems likely that this recommendation was inspired by the decision taken by the Party committee in Peking to reduce the pressure of work at schools and universities in the capital, and to allow pupils and students to spend their leisure time as they wished. In July 1965 the Maoists were actually accused of having failed to show a proper concern for the needs of young people: because they were given no time for relaxation, it was argued, their health was being impaired; and although revolutionaries might reasonably be expected to lay down their lives for the revolution, until such time as they were required to do so it was better that they should be kept healthy, for healthy people were of greater use to the state. It was also argued that young people in a poor state of health were likely to lose heart, and it was recommended that girls, and any boys or young men whose health was suspect, should be excused manual work.[33] Maoist educational policy was even subjected to a critical reappraisal in an editorial in the *RMRB*, the *People's Daily*. In this article it was suggested that the pressure of work at schools and universities might be alleviated by reducing extramural activities to a minimum and increasing leisure time. The writer conceded that, in the final analysis, the educational curriculum must be based on a political conception, but he warned against a formalistic or dogmatic approach, and insisted that the health of the pupils and students should on no account be jeopardized. This reappraisal of educational policy in the *RMRB* was inspired by a resolution passed at a Party conference held in the Ministry of Education and chaired by President Liu Shao-chi, which called for a reduction in manual work and political education at Chinese schools and universities. Exemplary schools were nominated, and exemplary measures taken by the educational departments of different towns and provinces singled out for special commendation. At one school in Shanghai, which was praised both by the educational department of the municipality and by the Communist Youth League, and which was held up as a model for the whole country, the local Party Committee introduced the new anti-Maoist educational system at the end of April 1964. Under this new system the pupils were allowed to use their evenings for private study, and were also given adequate time for leisure activities, relaxation and sleep. In addition, a number of important provisions were laid down for the protection of the pupils. Thus, nobody was allowed to perform manual work without the permission of the Youth League, nobody could be forced to take part in political activities, group study was restricted to academic subjects, the thoughts of Mao Tse-tung could only be taught in political classes, and no mass meetings or conferences were allowed on Sundays or in the mornings, afternoons or evenings of weekdays.[34]

If we consider the whole period from 1949 to the cultural revolution in 1965 it is readily apparent that the conflicts between the Chinese youth and the leadership were never resolved. On the contrary, they were gradually intensified as a result of a whole series of developments: the 'anti-Party revolt', the educational revolution, the new Maoist educational policy and, finally, the vacillating educational policy pursued by the Chinese Communist Party (which was also bedevilled by internal conflicts). Many young people were discontented because they had no time for their studies, no time for leisure, and precious little time for sleep; they also objected to political education and manual work, which neither interested them nor helped them in their academic pursuits; finally, they took exception to the fact that, upon completion of their studies, there was absolutely no certainty that they would be employed in the kind of work for which they had been trained and in which they were interested. In other words, the young people of China wanted a greater degree of personal freedom, which they could not obtain if every line of development was predetermined. To a certain extent, the conflict between Chinese youth and the Chinese leadership was a conflict between a younger generation, which refused to conform, and an older generation, which insisted on conformity and had the power to enforce it. Small wonder, then, that the original hard core of unreliable elements was augmented by a constant flow of malcontents. And one day this younger generation would be taking over control of China. Given these circumstances, is it surprising that Mao Tse-tung should have launched the cultural revolution? It was the only way he could establish a new proletarian educational system and give the youth of the country a revolutionary outlook.

CHAPTER II

THE INTELLIGENTSIA

Ideological reform – especially the political education of the intellectuals – is one of the most important preconditions for the total reform of our democratic system and for the gradual industrialization of the state.

MAO TSE-TUNG

We have already seen, in the introduction to this book, that until the correct ideological superstructure has been set up, it is not possible to proceed with the development of an infrastructure. To a very considerable extent this superstructure is provided and maintained by the intellectuals, who are largely responsible for the cultural development of modern states. And since culture determines human customs and patterns of behaviour, and influences human thought – which in China is regarded as the soul, i.e. the principal motivating factor, of both individual and corporate activities – it is understandable that Mao Tse-tung should have stressed the importance of the intelligentsia and insisted that they must give their 'heart' to the Party. The intelligentsia is composed of teachers (who instruct the young, i.e. the heirs to the future), scientists (who are responsible for the technological development of the state), and artists and writers (who influence the masses). I have already considered the teachers to some extent in my analysis of Chinese youth. Because of this, and because their attitudes are reflected in the activities of their charges, I do not propose to dwell on them in this present chapter. Nor shall I deal at any great length with the scientists. Since the Party depended on their active and willing cooperation, both for the expansion of industry and for the defence of the country, they were seldom disciplined and consequently played only a minor role in the ideological sphere. This leaves the scholars and writers – the 'workers' in the social sciences and the arts – who have not been dealt with before. Because of this, and because they have influenced the thinking of the Chinese people quite as much as the teachers, I shall concentrate on them in this analysis of the Chinese intelligentsia.

1. Early Attempts to Promote a 'New Attitude'

In his report to the National People's Congress at the beginning of 1956 Chou En-lai stated that there were 3,840,000 Chinese intellectuals engaged in scientific research, technology, education, medicine and the arts. We know that 217,000 people graduated from Chinese universities and technical colleges between 1949 and 1956, and a further 595,000 between 1957 and 1962.[1] Clearly, therefore, the vast majority of the intellectuals referred to by Chou were products of the old China. Moreover, if we consider the class affiliations of the Chinese students in the 1950's and early 1960's, it seems highly unlikely that the younger intellectuals, who completed their studies under Communist rule, will have been loyal to the Party. After all, prior to 1962 less than 50 per cent of educated Chinese came from working-class homes. Not that 'pure' descent was any guaranty of ideological correctness, as was clearly demonstrated by the students. But even today it seems probable that the politically unreliable elements among China's intellectuals are still in the majority. This would be the case even if twice as many students had graduated in the 9 year period since 1963 as in the 14 year period prior to 1963; and although the Chinese stopped publishing the relevant statistics in 1962, an increase of this order seems unlikely.

In his report Chou En-lai also said that there were 100,000 'top intellectuals' in China, and that one third of them had acquired this status since 1949. Chou claimed that of these 100,000 45 per cent were favourably disposed towards socialism, 40 per cent were politically neutral, 10 per cent were ideologically reactionary, and the remaining 5 per cent were counter-revolutionary.[2] This optimistic assessment is understandable if we consider that in the seven year period preceding Chou's report the Chinese intellectuals had been given repeated political education. But optimism went by the board after the 'Hundred Flowers Campaign'.

The Ideological Education of the Teachers

A full year before the People's Republic of China was founded the Chinese Communist Party started to combat the bourgeois intellectuals in the 'liberated areas'. This campaign also brought the non-bourgeois intellectuals their first real encounter with re-education and self-criticism, for they were expected to criticize themselves as well as the renegades. After the proclamation of the People's Republic the political education of China's intellectuals was carried out on a nation-wide scale. Political classes were introduced at all universities, and everybody on the staff – from caretakers to professors – was obliged to attend them. After every lecture a discussion was held, and the main points raised during the discussion were recorded and submitted to the local Party Committee in the form of an ideological report.[3] The members of these classes were also shown revolutionary dramas which invariably portrayed the conversion of ideologically suspect characters. Discussions were held after these performances in order to underline the moral. After each political seminar the class members had to subject their ideas to a critical examination, record their findings together with any relevant comments, and show these to the rest of the group. In this way it was possible to assess the ideological maturity of each class member with absolute precision. Political classes of a similar order were introduced at primary and secondary schools, and special political courses for teachers were held during the school holidays. In addition, a number of teachers were sent to courses at 'revolutionary universities'.[4] In June, 1950, Peking reported that the false notion of 'impartiality', which had been so popular in intellectual circles, had been largely eradicated. It also claimed that the intellectuals had learned to hate the USA for its aggressive imperialism, to love the USSR for its peaceful policies, and to serve the people of China. In order to strengthen the teachers in their new ideological attitudes, the Party sent them out into the villages as propagandists for the proposed agrarian reform. They were told to explain the Party's policy to the peasants and to incite them against the estate owners and Kulaks. In this way the Party hoped to start a class war in the countryside, and at the same time to destroy any last remnants of bourgeois ideology amongst the teachers. This measure was also said to have been extremely successful, and we are told that the teachers returned to their posts with a completely different outlook.[5]

And yet in 1951 the deputy Minister of Education stated that all previous attempts to re-educate the teachers had been unsuccessful. He drew attention to three cardinal errors, to which he considered the intelligentsia to be particularly prone, and called upon the Party to deal with them. These errors were: 1. the intellectuals' predilection for the ideology of

'European and American capitalists' and, more particularly, their admiration for the USA; 2. their penchant for individualism and subjectivism; 3. their preference for the western curriculum, to which they had been introduced in England or America and from which they were still teaching.[6] And so the political education of the teachers was stepped up. This time not even the village schoolmasters – whose lessons were restricted to simple arithmetic and the basic symbols of Chinese script – were spared. All teachers had to study, and re-study, ideological pamphlets; they had to attend lectures and listen to speeches given by ideologists and local Party leaders; and they had to subject themselves, and others, to exhaustive criticism. They were expected to join in every ideological campaign, criticizing the renegades against whom it was mounted in order to expose any latent bourgeois inclinations within themselves. Pupils and students were encouraged to coerce their teachers into confessing their faults. On occasions the teachers had to mount the rostrum at a mass meeting and admit to ideological errors, in thought and deed, over and over again.[7] And so the re-education of the teachers was intensified year by year until, in 1956, Chou En-lai felt justified in claiming that only 10 per cent of China's 'top intellectuals' were still reactionary. It is to be assumed that Peking's assessment of the ideological attitudes of the other teachers at that time was much the same.

But let me quote a few incidents to show the sort of conditions with which the teachers had to contend. Kuo Mo-jo, the only eminent intellectual from pre-communist days to have survived the Party purges, once told a Bulgarian newspaper editor that the research work carried out by a Chinese professor had been suppressed by the Party because it contradicted the theories of the Russian scientist Lyssenko.

The following statements, which were made by a professor of political economy, give some idea of the difficulties under which the university teachers had to work:

'Since the Liberation the political functionaries at the universities have assessed the professors in the light of their willingness to submit to discipline rather than on the basis of their academic ability. What this means is that the professors have to teach in accordance with the guidelines [laid down by the functionaries]. We are not allowed to teach anything unless it has been authorized.

We spend most of our time attending political meetings and writing out lectures, which have to be submitted for political scrutiny and authorization. The search for "authorities" is particulary time-consuming. Every single word and every single idea has to be based on an "authority". It goes without saying that the foremost authorities are Marx, Lenin or the top representatives of the political leadership.'[8]

The situation in the primary schools was described in an editorial in *Jiaoshi Bao* (Teachers' Newspaper) on October 9, 1956:

'In their letters to the editor a number of readers have commented on the discrimination to which the intellectuals are being subjected. A clear indication that such discrimination is taking place is provided by the unjust treatment meted out to the primary school teachers. Some functionaries, primarily at district and village level, belittle the work of the primary school teachers, treat them in an impudent and improper manner, subject them to ridicule, insult them, refer to them as anti-Communist elements, and restrict their personal liberty. In many districts the functionaries order the primary school teachers around as if they were their personal servants.'

The Re-education of Writers and Artists (Cultural Workers)

Although the Chinese Communist Party had already started to re-educate those engaged in cultural pursuits before the proclamation of the People's Republic, it was only after the release of the film *Wu Hsün Chuan* in December 1950 that it really took this section of the intelligentsia to task. *Wu Hsün Chuan* was, therefore, the first milestone in the development of Chinese cultural re-education. The historical Wu Hsün was born into a poor Chinese peasant family, as the youngest of seven children, in 1839. Five years later his father died. Because his family was impoverished, he was unable to attend the village school, and as a result of his own deprivation he came to realize the general importance of education. Consequently, he resolved that one day he would found his own schools for the poor. In order to accumulate the necessary capital, he tried his hand at every job that came his way. But far from making his fortune, he was scarcely able to make ends meet; and when he was 16, he was actually reduced to begging. But after 32 years Wu Hsün was finally able to found his first school. In the 1940's every Chinese schoolboy knew the story of his life, and on December 5, 1949 the GMRB commemorated the 110th anniversary of his birth in an editorial entitled 'Learn from Wu Hsün'. The film about Wu Hsün was made by Kun Lun Films of Shanghai, a reputable company with numerous good films to its credit; the producer was Hsia Yun-foo, the director Sun Yü. After its release in December 1950 the film ran for several months and was well received throughout China. Three books and at least 47 articles appeared at the time, in which the historical Wu Hsün, and the film of his life, were both praised. But in the editorial in the *People's Daily* on May 20, 1951 – whose authorship was attributed to Mao Tsetung during the cultural revolution – both the historical character and the film character were repudiated as 'propagandists of a feudal culture' whilst the intellectuals who had praised them were condemned for ideological immaturity and wrongheadedness. This condemnation was followed by an appeal to the Chinese people, published in the *RMRB*, to criticize the story of Wu Hsün and to continue the struggle against the reactionary ideology of the bourgeoisie. As a result of this appeal, the Chinese newspapers and magazines were packed with criticisms of Wu Hsün's life and the film in which it was portrayed, and self-criticisms sent in by people who had praised them. Most of the Chinese dailies devoted a quarter of their columns to this affair whilst a number of magazines published special issues. Meanwhile, the owner of the film, Hsia Yun-foo, 'presented' his film company and over 70 cinemas to the state. The campaign was officially closed on August 8, 1951, by Chou Yang, the 'king' of Chinese culture and literature prior to the cultural revolution, who published an article of enormous length – 15,000 symbols – in the *RMRB*. The object of this campaign was to impress on the Chinese intellectuals that films like *Wu Hsün Chuan*, in which the hero revealed no sense of class loyalty and did not participate in the class struggle, were no longer admissible. On the contrary, they were to be treated as political crimes, for everything – even education and culture – formed part of politics, and part of the continuing revolution. But the 'Wu Hsün campaign' also revealed the differences which existed between the artists and writers on the one hand and the leadership on the other; and it pinpointed the 'political immaturity' of the Party's cultural functionaries, who had failed to detect this 'evil' in time, thus obliging Mao Tse-tung to intervene in person. This is an important point, for these cultural functionaries were one of the groups that criticized Mao's policies from 1958 onwards.

The next peak in the development of cultural re-education was reached in 1954/55. In October 1954 two young students wrote a commentary, in which they attacked the interpretation advanced by Yü Ping-po, an established critic, of the eighteenth-century novel *The Dream of the Red Chamber*. The students claimed that Yü had considered this work from a bourgeois point of view, which had led him to espouse the decadent philosophy of 'art for art's sake'. Far from being an autobiographical work, as suggested by Yü, it was, they said, a symbolic account of the decline of the feudal system. Finally, the two students claimed that literature and literary criticism were ideological weapons and, as such, an integral part of politics and of the continuing revolution. Their commentary was hailed by the *RMRB* as 'the first shot to be fired against the ideology and methodology of the bourgeoisie in thirty years', and it led to renewed ideological education of China's cultural workers. Numerous discussions and public debates were organized by the 'Union of Chinese Writers' and the 'Federation for Chinese Literature and Art', and criticisms of bourgeois methods used in art appreciation were published, which were immediately followed by self-criticisms on the part of those responsible.

It is interesting to note that the students first submitted their commentary to *Wenyi Bao*, the official literary gazette, and that it was only after it had been rejected by this Party organ that they arranged for its publication in the students' magazine at Shantung University. Subsequently, the editors of *Wenyi Bao* discovered that the two students enjoyed the protection of important Party members, and tried to make good their blunder by reproducing the commentary in the gazette. In doing so, they committed an even worse blunder, for the commentary appeared with an editorial note stating that 'in many respects the authors' views are neither well documented nor well considered.' These *faux pas* proved extremely costly for the chief editor, who was exposed as a right wing deviationist. He was accused of having repudiated Marxism–Leninism, opposed Party orders, regarded *Wenyi Bao* as his private property, embraced bourgeois ideology, and suppressed the newly emerging forces of the younger generation. A full scale campaign was mounted against him, which was surprising in so far as he was a long-serving Party member. His past life was scrutinized, and it was claimed that he had once said that, because of the tutelage imposed by the Party, the writers of China could no longer call their souls their own, and that they were haunted by the fear of writing something false, lest it should be construed as a political error. This campaign was almost certainly a piece of in-fighting between different factions within the Party hierarchy, for *Wenyi Bao* was the only literary magazine that had not been under the direct influence of Chou Yang. What is quite certain is that, once the chief editor had been disposed of, and the rest of the editorial staff 'reorganized', Chou Yang had absolute control of all literary and art publications. At the same time, of course, the campaign against the chief editor fulfilled an ideological purpose, for it was accompanied by public discussions and the usual flood of criticisms and self-criticisms, which provided a guide-line, and served as a warning, for China's writers and artists. It is interesting to note in this connexion that, in one of the discussions, Kuo Mo-jo suggested that it was improper for the minority to accede to the wishes of the majority.[9] The minority that he had in mind was the minority of the Party faithful.

We have seen that both of the campaigns mentioned above provided the leadership with a perfect vehicle for ideological training. So too did the campaign launched against Hu Shih. This was actually initiated during the campaign against Yü Ping-po, who had studied under Hu Shih, for in the course of the discussions and public debates convened to consider the rights and wrongs of Yü's critical method, it was suggested that Hu's reactionary ideas should also be subjected to a probing and critical analysis. This suggestion was duly implemented, and in Peking alone 15 critical assemblies were convened between December 1954 and February 1955. In addition, countless articles appeared in the Chinese press, in which Hu's conception of literature and science was branded as bourgeois poison. As a result of the press coverage, the anti-Hu

Shih campaign was taken up by universities and literary associations throughout China. At first sight, it seems rather strange that the Party should have bothered to conduct a further campaign against Hu Shih, for he was not even living in China at that time. But it had its reasons, which were set out in an *RMRB* article in January 1955:

'Hu Shih is a political *intriguant* and an arch traitor who poses as a scholar. The influence exerted by his reactionary ideology has still not been eliminated. It is not just that our intellectuals still subscribe to bourgeois prejudices such as individualism and categorical independence – i.e. the independence of scholarship from politics – and other bourgeois conceptions, . . . the fact of the matter is that his reactionary ideology . . . still exerts an influence on the people, and so impedes the construction of socialism. Consequently, it is of the greatest importance that his reactionary ideology should be exposed, and his insidious influence, both on the intellectuals and on society in general, removed. All those who, consciously or unconsciously, have succumbed to his ideas in the past must participate, actively and courageously, in the ideological battle against Hu Shih in order to re-educate themselves and become genuine socialist workers. There is even a lesson in this campaign for Communists and Marxists. They should regard the propagation of socialism amongst the masses as if it were a military operation, and work ceaselessly in support of the leadership in the ideological sphere so as to ensure the successful outcome, and subsequent consolidation, of our socialist revolution and transformation.'[10]

Although they seemed rigorous enough at the time, these three initial campaigns to correct the ideological attitudes of the Chinese writers, artists and scholars were superficial by comparison with the fourth. The new target was Hu Feng, who had allied himself with the Chinese Communist Party way back in the 1930's. Hu Feng was accused of disseminating bourgeois idealism under the guise of Marxism, and of forming subversive cliques or – in the terminology of the cultural revolution – of 'waving the red flag in order to oppose it'. Although he had been a thorn in the flesh of the literary bosses – i.e. men like Chou Yang – ever since 1949, they took no action against him until he submitted a petition to the Central

Committee in June 1954. In this petition Hu Feng argued that, in actual fact, there was no such thing as an abstract Party viewpoint and that Party policy was simply the sum total of the demands made by the masses re-formulated in a more refined form. He then quoted Mao Tse-tung in support of his thesis that if Marxism is substituted for realism in art, then art must be destroyed. Hu Feng accused the Party's cultural functionaries of projecting their own narrow conception of a 'popular context' and 'popular sociology' on to 'socialist realism', thus invalidating the works of Chinese authors. He held the view that the great works of literature had been created, not because their authors had had a correct proletarian outlook, but because they had observed their environment carefully and accurately. As examples he quoted Balzac and Tolstoi, who had disassociated themselves from their class, and even condemned it for its suppression of the masses. Hu was opposed to the policy directive which stipulated that Chinese writers should deal only with the agreeable aspects of Chinese society. He argued that 'if everybody described the agreeable aspects of life, it would be impossible to continue the struggle for still better living conditions'. Hu also considered that artists and writers should not be forced to subscribe to a set ideology, since this must necessarily inhibit their search for reality and truth. He then went on to accuse the literary 'authorities' of monopolizing Karl Marx, which meant in effect that they were the only people allowed to interpret or apply his ideas.[11]

We see, therefore, that Hu Feng was not opposed to the regime in principle; he just wanted a certain amount of reform, a certain amount of liberalization. (Incidentally, he seems to have been of the opinion that the repressive measures taken against the Chinese cultural workers were initiated without Mao Tse-tung's knowledge, which is interesting in that it reflects a similar tendency in the Kuomintang, where many of Chiang Kai-shek's followers had looked upon Chiang as a good and just leader surrounded by evil and corrupt ministers.) As for the charges brought against Hu Feng by the Party, these appear to have been unfounded. If he really had been a counter-revolutionary, it is hardly likely that he would have shown his hand by openly submitting a petition to the Central Committee. But be that as it may, the essential truth of the matter is that Hu Feng gave expression to the wishes of a large section of the community. This is readily apparent from the fact that, after exposing him and the members of his group, the Party called upon the Chinese people as a whole to examine their thoughts and actions with great care in order to discover, and eradicate, any traces of 'Hu-Fengism'. The anti-Hu campaign was waged from the autumn of 1954 to August 1955. It was a long drawn out affair, not because the Party wanted to prolong it, but because even after Hu had been condemned as a counter-revolutionary, many people, who had not even been members of his group, spoke out in his defence.[12] It seems highly unlikely that this campaign achieved its ideological aim, namely the re-education of the Chinese intellectuals. According to Robert Guillain, who visited China during this campaign, many Chinese intellectuals were quaking with fear at that time, and some even committed suicide.[13] The lesson that the Party leaders ought to have learned from the anti-Hu campaign is that ideological differences cannot be resolved by the use of such tactics. In fact, this lesson was not learned, as we shall see when we come to consider the 'Hundred Flowers Campaign'.

2. 'Poisonous Plants and Weeds'

Looking back on the 'Hundred Flowers Campaign' the chief of the propaganda department of the Central Committee said that rightist elements had tried to usurp the functions of the leadership 'in the democratic parties and in its dealings with writers, artists, journalists, scientists, technicians, lawyers, industrialists and businessmen' so as to establish a base from which to make their bid for power. (Incidentally, when this functionary was deposed by the Red Guards during the cultural revolution, his own activities were condemned in virtually the same terms.) According to the propaganda chief, these rightist elements had tried to incite unrest amongst the youth in the hope that the workers and state employees would join them and so start a general rising. Chou En-lai also summed up the 'Hundred Flowers Campaign' with the statement that the rightist elements had tried to lead the country away from the socialist path and back on to the capitalist path. If we consider the ideological differences between the leadership and the intellectuals from the Chinese Communist point of view, then it must be admitted that both the propaganda chief and

Chou En-lai were fairly near the mark. The fact of the matter is that in the 'Hundred Flowers Campaign' many of the youth and the intellectuals rebelled against the tutelage imposed by the Party, and demanded their independence.

Bourgeois Views of the Teachers

Many Chinese teachers objected to Party policy on two principal grounds: they disliked Party interference in educational matters, and they were dissatisfied with the social system as such. They complained that China's institutes of learning had been transformed into hives for Party drones, whose only contribution to the educational system was the dissemination of Party dogmas. According to university professors, the Chinese universities had become so bureaucratic that they were almost indistinguishable from the yamens – the official residences – of imperial China, and the number of university rectors and heads of department who held no academic qualifications and had been appointed for purely political reasons was quite incredible. These professors cited specific examples. Thus, the History Department at the North Eastern Teachers' Training Institute had no less than 32 heads of department, and the head of the Russian Department at the Teachers' Training Institute in Shenyang – a Party member – could not speak a word of Russian. Nepotism was also a factor. For example, the head of the History Department at Shenyang created a second chair in his own department for his wife.[14] The university professors complained that the Party leaders had alienated themselves from the people since 1949 by claiming special privileges. Thus, whilst the ordinary Chinese wore – and still wear – lightweight clothing padded with cotton wool in winter, the party leaders had woollen uniforms; they also drove around in motor cars, and behaved as if they were a race apart and the sole source of light. A further complaint, one that was voiced by teachers at all levels, concerned the Party's refusal to accept criticism. Intellectuals who expressed opinions contrary to the views held by the top Party functionaries would, the teachers said, be classified as dangerous elements intent on usurping the power of the leadership. It was suggested that the difficulties and deficiencies of the Chinese educational system were the fault of the Party committees at the universities, whose members enjoyed absolute authority, but knew very little about education. The university teachers wanted university teaching and scholarship to be completely independent of politics. Accordingly, they called for a tripartite system of control, in which teaching and research would come under an academic council, university administration under a special executive body, and ideological training alone under the Party committee. But the university teachers were not the only educationalists to criticize the Party and demand a new educational system. Many of their colleagues in the primary and secondary schools also wanted to do away with the supervision by Party members and Party offices attached to their schools.

Bourgeois Views of the Writers

The views held by the Chinese writers were more or less in line with those advanced by the 'counter-revolutionary', Hu Feng. With the passage of time Hu's ideas had become more respectable, and by 1957 some of them were even adopted by the Party (although Hu still remained an enemy of the people). Thus, the 'king of culture', Chou Yang was able to say that 'white-washing and simplification' had deprived Chinese literary works of their verisimilitude so that they no longer appeared credible to the reader. The editors of literary magazines were also given a greater degree of freedom in the selection of articles and short stories for publication.

By and large, the writers – like the teachers – objected to the arbitrariness, dogmatism and privileged status of Party members. They attacked 'socialist realism' and, in the process, accused the Party of having disregarded the needs of the individual and the needs of culture. They also demanded the abolition of ideological education, insisting that the 'paradise' in which they were said to be living was a myth, and calling upon Chinese writers to depict life as they saw it, and to have the courage to expose the darker aspects of socialist society.[15] It was even suggested that writers did not need to be subjected to political education since their Marxist *Weltanschauung* developed organically, due to the creative character of their work. In 1956 Chinese writers began to reject the 'heroic types' beloved of the Party and to concentrate on 'individuality'. They even revived some of the concepts formulated by

Hu Feng – e.g., 'popular sociology' – and used them to expose the shortcomings of propagandistic literature. The opportunism of Party functionaries was another target for the writers. In 1957 they pointed out that after espousing the theory of a 'conflict-free society', the Party functionaries had roundly condemned this conception in the following year because the Soviet Union had come out against it. And they drew the moral for all to see: functionaries are never wrong, no matter how often they contradict themselves. By this time the writers had come out openly in support of Hu Feng's views, and in defending this position they compared Hu Feng with the French Jew, Dreyfus. Even Mao Tse-tung's dissertation on art and literature, which he composed in Jenan in 1942, was criticized on the grounds that it too was conservative and had long since lost its validity. Many writers also began to question whether Mao really had led such an ascetic life in Jenan, as has been claimed.

The writers responsible for these attacks, who had all been given ideological re-education but had remained 'incorrigible artists', consisted partly of old-timers from the Jenan era, and partly of young people who had grown up in the new society. Previously, every one of them had subjected the rightist elements in their ranks – especially Hu Feng – to violent criticism. But when the 'Hundred Flowers Campaign' was mounted they thought that, at long last, the time had come when they would be able to express their opinions openly and freely. This they did in discussions and public debates, in newspaper reports and articles. They also used short stories and allegories in order to illustrate the conflicts in Chinese society in general and the relationship between the artists and the leadership in particular. One of these short stories was entitled 'The New Arrival in the Organization Department'. It was the work of a 22-year-old writer and Party member;[16] and it made such a powerful impression on the Chinese public, because of its outspoken criticism of high-ranking Party functionaries, that it is, I think, worth while to reproduce its content here: The young hero, a former schoolmaster and a Party member, arrives in the department full of lofty Communist ideals. He soon realizes that the factory director is an egoist, who is interested only in his own professional and social status. Although the director constantly indulges in acts of criticism and self-criticism, he always relapses into his old bureaucratic ways. Our young hero reports this to his superiors, who refuse to listen, and insist that everything in the factory is in order. But the young man perseveres, and goes straight to the head of the department who tells him that it is not possible to accuse the director because he holds a very important position in the Party. In the end, however, the new arrival finds support, and an open letter appears in the *People's Daily*, in which the factory director is criticized. A mass campaign is launched against him, and it is proposed that he should be expelled from the Party, and dismissed from the factory. The whole district is organized, and a public meeting convened to discuss the case. At this meeting the young man suggests that since his superiors had tried to protect the director, they should also be criticized. But nobody pays any attention, nothing is done, and the new arrival is forced to recognize that high-ranking Party functionaries are never in the wrong.

The way in which the Chinese Communist Party sought to suppress conflicts between the intellectuals and the leadership was typical of the period of 'evil ghosts and demons' (another expression that was revived during the cultural revolution). The people were told that the intellectuals had not received sufficient ideological education. Campaigns were then launched against them, so that their education might be perfected by a process of criticism and self-criticism. At the same time, however, the Party conceded that in a socialist society intellectuals with bourgeois ideas might re-emerge at any time.[17]

3. Contradictions Between Cultural Development and the Requirements of Party Policy

For the Chinese Communist Party the intellectuals were a necessary irritation. The leadership needed them in order to build up the economy, and develop industry and culture; but it could never completely trust them because of their bourgeois origins and upbringing, and the non-proletarian attitudes which these had produced. When the intellectuals were urgently needed for a particular purpose – as in 1953 for the implementation of the first five year plan, and in 1956/57 for the intensification of the Party's programme of collectivization and socialization – a sort of ideological *détente* was established in order to gain their good will and induce a spirit of willing co-operation. But once the purpose had been achieved – as in 1953 – or the intellectuals threatened to exploit their new-found freedom – as in 1957 – the Party stepped in and re-imposed a firm ideological line. In 1958 the Party leaders decided that the time had come to replace the intellectuals by the masses. They rejected as a 'superstitious notion' the idea that knowledge was the prerogative of an intelligentsia insisting that as 'true proletarians' the workers and peasants could not only replace the intellectuals but even improve on their per-formance. In this attempt to substitute quantity for quality the Party leaders were intent on eliminating the 'private monopoly of knowledge', thus bringing culture into line with industry and agriculture, and making all three take a 'great leap forwards'. It was without much doubt this programme of rapid socialization that provoked antagonism towards the Party amongst the Chinese people at that time. In the cultural sphere the 'Great Leap Forwards' was strongly opposed by Ho Chi-fang, the last poet cum cultural functionary of the old Jenan school, who up till then had been a staunch supporter of the Party's cultural policy, and had always defended it against the advocates of a bourgeois ideology. Ho became the victim of a mass campaign, which was also meant to serve as a timely warning for his fellow intellectuals and bring them back to the Party's ideological fold. But the net result of the 'Great Leap Forwards' was to intensify the conflicts in Chinese society, raising them to such a pitch that they even penetrated the top echelons of the Party and led to the overthrow, in the cultural revolution, of the whole of the Party organization for propa-ganda and culture, and so split the leadership. For purposes of this study, however, I must restrict myself to the effects of this policy in specific intellectual spheres.

Conflicts over the Interpretation of Marxism

On March 1, 1961, *Red Flag*, the theoretical organ of the Chinese Communist Party, conceded that Marxism–Leninism was no substitute for scientific research, and that nothing could be achieved simply by reciting Marxist–Leninist theory. It also conceded that intellectuals could not be forced to adopt a proletarian attitude by administrative means, and suggested that the only circumstances in which they would ever do so was if they were convinced of the validity of such an attitude. This indicated a partial revision, at least, of the cultural policy pursued during the 'Great Leap Forwards', and justified the belief that there was an anti-Maoist faction within the leadership, which was then beginning to assert itself. The presence of ideological differences in the upper echelons of the Party was clearly demonstrated in 1964 and 1965 when a fierce philosophical dispute was conducted.

Feng Ting, a popular author who had done much to disseminate Marxist ideas, was criticized by the Party for his interpretation of this dispute. Ever since 1926, when he joined the Party, Feng had been acknowledged as an authority on Marxism, and had held several important posts in the field of propaganda and political education. From 1949 onwards he had been engaged primarily on Party work amongst Chinese industrialists. In addition to numerous articles, Feng published many books which invariably ran to several editions. These include: *The Common Truth* (10 editions of 390,000 copies), *The Communist Philosophy* (7 editions of 860,000 copies), and *The Historical Task of the Working Class* (3 editions of 400,000 copies). Almost 2 million copies of his books were printed in all. The principal charge brought against Feng was that he had propagated pacifist views. It is, in fact, perfectly true that he regarded the search for happiness as the major motivating factor underlying human behaviour: 'Happiness in everyday life means peace and no war, good food and beautiful clothes, a spacious and hygienic home, love and harmony between man and wife, parents and children. Without any doubt, we too are searching for happiness.' Feng spoke out against the 'glorification of the leader', he argued that conflicts should be resolved by peaceful means, and insisted that it was perfectly in order for a Communist to preserve his individuality and study his personal interests. After 1963, when Communist ideology was dominated by the concepts of the class war, the community spirit, and the spirit of self-sacrifice, such views were clearly unacceptable. Feng Ting's writings were particularly popular with the junior functionaries and the youth of China, who were naturally called upon to renounce their allegiance during the anti-Feng campaign.

At almost the same time the leadership mounted a campaign

against Yang Hsien-chen, a high-ranking Party member and a member of the Central Committee, who was rector of the Party Academy in Peking from 1955 to 1961. Although Yang did not have the popular appeal of Feng Ting, as rector – and one of the professors – of the top Party school he was in a position to shape the ideological attitudes of senior Party functionaries. Yang held that the positive forces present in all antithetical relationships were mutually attractive, and over a period of time must inevitably create a harmonious fusion despite the influence exerted by negative forces. He regarded this as the first principle of dialectics, and taught his pupils accordingly. Mao Tse-tung, on the other hand, considered that it was a secondary factor, and from 1962 onwards Mao urged the people to intensify the class war. Yan's view is closely allied to the Russian view that, provided there is a mutal desire for peace, socialism and capitalism can co-exist in a state of harmony; and it is possible to argue that Yang was influenced by Soviet theorists when he came to evolve his ideas. But, taking everything into consideration, this seems unlikely, for the concept of harmony is typically, and traditionally, Chinese. Yang's students traced his theory back to the Ming philosopher Fang Ming-chia, and even to the early Taoists Chuang-tse and Lao-tse.[18] In fact, the concept of harmony formed the nucleus of both Confucianism and Taoism. For the followers of Confucius harmony was the 'golden mean' whilst the Taoists held that all antitheses were eventually resolved when they were fused in the absolute. Both the search for happiness and the rejection of the class war were in line with Confucianist theory, which held that the utopian society would be brought about as a result of goodness, benevolence, self-perfection, and domestic bliss and piety. Thus, both Feng's and Yang's ideas undoubtedly constituted an extension of China's 'negative' cultural heritage, and so when Foreign Minister Chen Yi admitted to a student audience in September 1961 that his thinking had been influenced by both Confucius and Menzius, he was being perfectly truthful. Liu Shao-chi also propagated a Confucianist ethic – that of self-perfection – in his book *How to Become a Good Communist*, which was combated by the Party on a nation-wide scale. It is quite obvious from the severity with which the Maoists proceeded against Yang Hsien-chen that they were deeply perturbed by this continuation of China's negative cultural heritage: in the spring and summer of 1964 over 90 critical articles were published and countless meetings were organized at regional Party schools, universities and institutes in order to discredit Yang's doctrine of harmony.

China's Cultural Heritage and New Party Policy

In 1953 the Party called upon the intellectuals to carry out a critical re-appraisal of China's vast cultural heritage. In 1956/57 – during the period of relative *détente* on the ideological front – greater significance was attached to this project, and a number of serious enquiries were initiated. But in 1958 came the 'Great Leap Forwards', and the whole undertaking was abandoned. Instead of allowing the intellectuals to continue their re-appraisal of the past in modern terms, the Party tried to dispense with the intellectuals altogether, and replace them by proletarians with a genuine proletarian outlook. But the 'Great Leap Forwards' ran into difficulties, the economy was threatened, and the Party was obliged to make fresh overtures to the intellectuals. Once contact was re-established, the old project for the investigation of China's cultural heritage was revived. Writing on this subject in March 1959, the Peking *People's Daily* stated that it was not in keeping with Marxist theory to neglect the cultural achievements of 'our ancestors'. Shortly afterwards, the leader writer in *Red Flag* accused Party functionaries of having completely misunderstood the old slogan 'More of today, less of the old'. The Party's new policy, he said, was to examine the past in the interests of the present. The chairman of the Youth League also took the functionaries to task when he said that whereas the *Party* was clearly entitled to pronounce on politics, scholarship was the prerogative of scholars. However, this did not mean that the Party intended to give the intellectuals a free hand. The leadership was well aware that the ideological attitudes of the intellectuals were as suspect as ever. It knew that even young cultural workers from non-bourgeois backgrounds had become bourgeois intellectuals and right wing deviationists. Apart from the leftist students – who, according to Mao Tse-tung, constituted only a minority element – China's intellectuals were all classified as petits-bourgeois. But intellectuals were needed for the programme of socialist construction, and so they were recruited. At the same time, the Party tried to win them over to its own way of thinking.

Even when it relaxed its ideological grip, the Party still kept the intellectuals under surveillance, and it still laid down general guide-lines. Consequently, those engaged on research into China's cultural heritage were required to conduct their investigations within a Marxist framework. But many intellectuals sought to circumvent this requirement. Thus, one of the foremost historians in China argued that although the class war was undoubtedly the principal factor at work in historical development, it would not do to be too dogmatic in this respect since the peasants in the old China had not been opposed to the feudal system as such but only to particular estate owners and emperors. He also pointed out that the hostilities in pre-revolutionary China had often been due, not to the class war, but to wars between different nationalities. Having made these specific points, he ventured a general statement. Although ideology was important, it was not a substitute for historical source material.[19] He then went even further by pointing out that the criteria established by the 'foreigner' Hegel could not be applied to Chinese history since Hegel had had no knowledge of China. It goes without saying that, in this context, the names Marx, Engels and Lenin were synonymous with Hegel. In every possible way this historian and other Chinese intellectuals tried to show that historical determinism was not a suitable means of analysing Chinese culture.

The Chinese intellectuals also devised an ingenious stratagem that enabled them to revive their traditional culture within the new socialist society. This stratagem was very simple and very effective. All they had to do was to discover ideas advanced by classical writers which corresponded to theoretical tenets established by Marx and Lenin, for they were then able to identify philosophers who had lived 2,000 years before the communist era as genuine exponents of Marxism–Leninism. Thus, *I Ching* – a book on natural philosophy, prophecy and mysticism – was said to contain references to the law of op-posion (the process whereby quantitative growth is replaced at a given point by qualitative change), to Marxist epistemology (which holds that all knowledge is derived from experience), and even to the conception of the continuing revolution. Moreover, Confucious was supposed to have advocated the Marxist idea that experience leads to knowledge, and action to ideas. The scholars who engaged in this quest for parallels were not all older men. Many were young students of philosophy who had grown up under the People's Republic.[20] The leadership was well aware that this new development would produce ideological confusion. For if the people were encouraged to think in traditional terms, and were told that these were identical with Marxist theory, it was obvious that the revolution would soon lose all meaning for them; and given the natural proclivity of the Chinese to project their utopian visions into the past rather than the future, they would eventually come to concentrate on the old China to the exclusion of the new.

If this enquiry into China's cultural heritage had been conceived simply as a means of educating the intellectuals, its findings would have been largely academic and consequently relatively harmless. But since its principal objective was to open up this field of knowledge, thus raising the general cultural level of the population whilst at the same time eliminating one more esoteric stronghold, it was an important social and ideological undertaking and one that was fraught with considerable dangers. As it happens, the leadership was forced by the difficult socio-political situation in which it found itself, to conduct this re-appraisal of the past. Western culture had been condemned in the Chinese People's Republic ever since its inception, and it was not long before the Soviet Union was repudiated as a hotbed of revisionism (with the inevitable result that all Soviet aid to China was cut off from 1960 onwards). This left the Chinese people – who had been striving desperately to establish a modern, technologically based society – financially and culturally destitute or, as Mao Tse-tung put it in 1959, 'poor and blank'. After the rupture with the Soviet Union China was thrown back on her own resources, and – since it is impossible to create a new society in a complete vacuum – she was obliged to investigate her past. Hence the fresh overtures made to the Chinese intellectuals. In the course of this new development the study of literature, philosophy and history was encouraged amongst the whole of the Chinese population, and new editions of the classics were published. In setting up this campaign, which was promoted under the slogan 'Learn from the ancients in order to serve the moderns', the Party made due allowance for differences in intellectual ability between the different sections of the community. Consequently, the new editions of classical works published at that time were designed to meet the requirements of various groups. At least three publishing houses were instructed to produce books of this kind. One of these was the China Press and Book Company, which brought out a *Manual of Chinese Culture* in folio form in 1960. This anthology, which – according to the editor's preface – was intended for 'functionaries with senior secondary school education, secondary school teachers, students and lovers of the classics', reappeared as a series of individual bound volumes – about 10 in all – in 1962; and between May 1962 and August 1965 (i.e. three months before the outbreak of the cultural revolution) a further 9 editions of these printed volumes appeared, each edition consisting of 306,800 copies per volume. The China Press has bookshops in every major city, which means that distribution presented no problems. The Manual contained poems and prose excerpts by 'poets, historians, philosophers, politicians and scholars' from the last three thousand years of Chinese culture. A glance at the table of contents is instructive. For example, this lists a long poem celebrating the undying love felt by an emperor of the Tang dynasty for his dead concubine, and a number of other poems dealing with the themes of romantic love and personal happiness. The prose excerpts include chapters from Leo-Tse, the Taoist mystic Liä-tse, and Confucianist philosophers such as Hsüntse and Menzius. There are also historical excerpts with feudal titles such as 'Kan Lo Became Chancellor at Twelve Years of Age' and 'The Genealogy of Confucius', and mythological stories such as 'The First Woman Patches the Coat of Heaven' and 'The Warrior Shoots Down Nine Suns'. Clearly, the editor's intention was to provide the readers of this manual with adequate literary material so that they would be in a position to contribute to the development of a 'new popular socialist culture' and so help in the construction of socialism. But it is difficult to see how the cause of proletarian ideology could be furthered by filling the heads of 'functionaries with senior secondary school education, secondary school teachers and students' with such anti-proletarian ideas, which were calculated to strike a responsive chord in the Chinese mind.

The China Press and Book Company produced at least two more serial publications on classical literature, both for readers with a lower intellectual training. The first of these — *The Propagation of Classical Literature* – contained a selection of classical works rewritten in modern colloquial Chinese whilst the second – *The Basic Primer of Classical Literature* – provided an introduction to the different literary epochs and styles, and to the lives and works of many classical writers. All of the volumes in these series ran to several editions. In addition, the China Press published individual studies of aspects of classical literature and classical writers, and biographies of well-known historical characters, mostly warriors.[21] Complete works – such as *Water Margin* and *The Dream of the Red Chamber* – were also published, both by the China Press and by the two other publishing houses engaged in the reproduction of classical literature at that time: The Press for Popular Literature and The Authors' Press. These too ran to several editions. As a result of this campaign for the dissemination and popularization of classical literature, contemporary authors began to write in the classical idiom and to propagate traditional ideas. Many of them used classical settings in order to make thinly veiled attacks on the Party and the government.

Literature as Criticism of the Leadership

The way in which Mao Tse-tung and his policies were criticized by contemporary writers is well illustrated by two historical dramas which appeared in 1961. The first of these, *Hsieh Yao-Huan*, was written by Tien Han, a well-known dramatist who composed the text of the Chinese national anthem and is also a Party member. Hsieh Yao-Huan was lady-in-waiting to the Empress Wu, of the Tang dynasty. The action of the play takes place during the closing years of the empress's reign. A peasant revolt is about to break out over the action of a group of imperial ministers, who have expropriated lands given to the peasants under an earlier agrarian reform. Hsieh Yao-Huan takes the peasants' part. She reminds the empress that in the early part of her reign she had always protected the peasants' interests but that of recent years her regime has become so alienated from the masses that the country is on the brink of civil strife. She accuses the empress of having joined with her flatterers in persecuting those who dare to tell her the truth. Then, when the revolt finally breaks out, Hsieh begs the empress to give the peasants' fields back. At this point Hsieh is murdered by the flatterers. When her husband hears about her death, and about the circumstances leading up to it, he predicts to the empress that her regime will know no peace unless she returns the land to 'those who plough it' and drives the flatterers from her court. The political allusions in this play are not hard to find: the Chinese peasants were dissatisfied with the 'communization' programme which had resulted in their being dispossessed, and unless Mao was prepared to restore their lands to them, his regime would 'know no peace'. It is also pretty obvious that the heroine Hsieh Yao-Huan was meant to symbolize the forces of opposition to Mao's policy of rapid socialization, and perhaps even to personify the Minister of Defence, Peng Te-huai, who spoke out against the 'Great Leap Forwards' and severely censured the establishment of people's communes before being deposed at the end of 1959.

Wu Han's drama *Hai Jui is Relieved of his Post* is very similar. Hai Jui, a just official of the Ming dynasty, has jurisdiction over the town of Soochow. The peasants in the surrounding district complain to him that their fields have been confiscated by their local officials and that, despite this, the officials still insist that they must pay their taxes. Hai Jui orders his subordinates to return the confiscated fields, and sticks to his decision in the face of threats and attempts at bribery. Finally, the local officials, supported by the estate owners, complain to the emperor, who relieves Hai Jui of his post. In this drama, too, it is perfectly obvious that the author was using a historical setting in order to criticize modern conditions. He painted a picture of peasant distress arising out of dispossession – alias communization – and demanded that the government should return the lands that had been confiscated to those who ploughed them. Hai Jui clearly represents the deposed Minister of Defence Peng Te-huai, whilst the all-powerful emperor is unquestionably Mao Tse-tung. This becomes even more apparent if we consider the article published by Wu Han in 1959 which he called 'Hai Jui Reviles the Emperor'. In this article Hai Jui addresses the emperor as follows: 'In earlier years you did much good; but ... today all officials, both in the capital and in the provinces, know that you no longer act on the basis of reason but according to your own purely despotic and perverse whims. You think that you are always right, and you reject all criticism, but you make many mistakes ...' It should be noted in this connexion that all of Mao's critics, amongst both the youth and the intellectuals, believed that before the proclamation of the People's Republic, Mao and his party had been on the side of the people but that since then they had 'sat on the people'. A similar opinion was expressed by Ko Pei-chi, the reader in industrial economy at the Chinese People's University in Peking, in 1957: 'When the Communist Party came to the city in 1949 the inhabitants wined and dined its members ... Today the people prefer to keep their distance from the Communist Party, as if its members were gods or demons. As for the Party members, they behave like detectives, and keep the people under surveillance.'[22]

As chairman of the 'Association of Chinese Actors and Singers' Tien Han was responsible to the heads of the propaganda department of the Central Committee of the Party and rendered Chou Yang, the 'king of culture', every assistance in his efforts to root out bourgeois ideas and rightist deviationism in theatrical circles. And yet he spoke out against Maoist policy. So did many others in Chou Yang's clique, including Shao Chüan-lin – the secretary of the Party committee attached to the 'Association of Chinese Authors', who was Chou Yang's right hand man – and Keng Cho, the deputy chairman of the local branch of this association in the province of Hunan. (Incidentally, a deputy chairman who is a Party member is usually more powerful than a chairman who is not; although less well known, he is considered to be politically more reliable.) At the artists' conference held in August 1962 in Dairen (Manchuria) all three of these functionaries criticized the policy of rapid socialization embarked on by Mao in the 'Great Leap Forwards'. Kang argued that the principal source of conflict in Chinese society at that time was not the basic antithesis between capitalism and socialism, but the incompatibility of the ideological policies pursued by the leadership and the personal needs of the peasants. He accused the Party leaders of having betrayed their own ideals, and called upon them to abandon the 'Great Leap Forwards', and to concentrate instead on alleviating peasant distress. At the same time he urged Chinese writers to depict the abuses, the poverty and the misery that had resulted from this new policy.[23] When he rose to speak, Shao Chüan-lin outlined his theory of the average man. He argued that far from being the perfect, disciplined proletarian heroes portrayed by Chinese writers, the vast majority of workers and peasants were just ordinary people with no very definite views about politics, either one way or the other. In Shao's opinion, the principal conflict in Chinese society was the psychological conflict between good and evil in the individual, i.e. in the average man. Accordingly, he called upon Chinese writers to depict this 'painful process in the individual'. And so, according to Shao, ideological re-education is a 'painful process', in which – metaphorically speaking – the individual is immersed three times in pure water and three times in blood serum, and then boiled three times in salt water. Literary stories, Shao insisted, should be primarily artistic rather than political, and the reader should be able to identify with the – average – hero. Shao also impressed on the Chinese writers that they should not try to present ready-made solutions, but should simply state the problem, and leave the reader to work out his own solution. Although less obviously opposed to official Party policy than Kang's ideas, Shao's theory could have had a pernicious effect on Chinese socialist society. What guaranty was there that a reader who had purged himself of passion by identifying with the hero would not draw anti-Maoist conclusions from his experience?

The Chou Yang clique was not the only group to criticize Mao's policies at that time. A second group consisting of members of the Party Committee for the city of Peking, which included the author of *Hai Jui is Relieved of His Post*, also attacked the leadership in the same thinly veiled manner. The leaders of the Peking group were Wu Han (the deputy mayor of Peking), Teng To (formerly chief editor of the *RMRB* and, at that time, secretary of the Party Committee for Peking) and Liao Mo-sha (a member of the Committee). These were influential men, and they were able to publish regular articles in the Peking *Daily News*, the Peking *Evening News* and the magazine *Front*, in which they ridiculed Mao Tse-tung's policies. Teng To wrote a series of articles for the Peking *Evening News* under the title 'Evening Conversations in Yenshan', which subsequently appeared in book form, and in which he made covert attacks on the leadership by using historical settings. For example, in a satirical article entitled 'Study More, Criticize Less' he wrote the following passage about Wang Anshih, a statesman of the Sung dynasty who had introduced unrealistic agrarian reforms: 'True, he had new ideas; but lacked practical experience and detailed knowledge. He despised everybody, and criticized everybody unjustifiably. His chief weakness was his lack of humility.' Clearly, this was meant to be construed as a pen portrait of Mao Tse-tung. In a second article entitled 'Talking Nonsense' Teng pilloried those Party functionaries who rejected scientific research as a waste of time. He insisted that no scientific theory was immutable, and that provided they were well reasoned, new arguments must always be accepted. In this connexion he called upon the youth of the country to abandon dogma, and to learn to think for themselves. Here, too, it is quite apparent that what Teng was really advising young people to do was to abandon Marxist dogma. After all, Marxism–Leninism was also a scientific theory and, consequently, subject to change.

A further series of articles, which Teng published in conjunction with Wu Han and Liao Mo-sha and which appeared under the general title 'Reports from the Three Family Village', was even more critical. In one of these articles, a satirical piece entitled 'Special Treatment for Amnesia', this trio drew their readers' attention to the fact that amnesia sufferers are renowned for their inability to keep their promises, and then went on to suggest that such forgetfulness might well be symptomatic of a serious mental disorder. In another article entitled 'Boasting' they ridiculed Mao's axiom 'The east wind is our benefactor, the west wind our enemy', and suggested that the time had come to stop boasting. People should think more, they said, and talk less.

It is worth recalling at this point that those who opposed the Party's policy of rapid socialization in the 1960's were not bourgeois intellectuals with little or no political influence. On the contrary, they were high-ranking Party members. None the less, it was only because they enjoyed the protection of certain members of the Party leadership that they were able to criticize Mao's policies for years on end with apparent impunity. But the day of reckoning finally came for these critics, and their protectors, in the cultural revolution, when they were exposed as revisionists and thrown out of office.

CHAPTER III

WORKERS AND PEASANTS

Our country is a democratic people's dictatorship run by the working class in accordance with the terms of the alliance between the workers and the peasants.

MAO TSE-TUNG

1. Contradictions Among the Workers

It seems ironical that so little publicity should have been given to the most important class in Chinese Communist society, namely the workers, and regrettable that, as a result, no really systematic study of this section of the community has been undertaken. However, it would be wrong to assume that, because the workers have received relatively little attention from the Chinese press, there have been no conflicts between them and the Party leaders. In theory – as is clearly stated in the motto at the head of this chapter – the workers are the true leaders of the Chinese people's dictatorship. In practice they take their lead from the Party, which represents their interests and acts on their behalf. The first conflict between the workers and the Party leaders came shortly after 1949 during the discussions held to decide the future role of the trades unions. The crux of the argument was whether the unions should continue to represent the workers' interests or whether they should become an executive branch of the Party.[1] It was at about that time that the Party leaders first began to combat what they regarded as the malpractices of 'economism'. The fact that they found it necessary to act in this way is a clear indication that there was a continuing conflict between the workers and the leadership from the early 1950's onwards, for one of the basic tenets of economism is that the workers' economic interests should take precedence over the requirements of Party policy. For the Party, which had set its sights on the establishment of Communism at the earliest possible moment, the reverse was true. And so conflict was unavoidable.

Trades Unions and the Party

The conflicts between the workers and the leadership were also reflected in the relations between the trades unions and the Party. The essential function of a trade union organization is to protect the workers whom it represents from attempts on the part of their employers to suppress or exploit them. But in China there is only one employer, the state, and that is in the hands of the Party which not only represents the interests of the workers but also acts on their behalf. In 1957 a trade union functionary, who was also a Party member, described the difficult situation in which he found himself and which was presumably typical:

. . .

'As a Party member I naturally had to conform to Party discipline and carry out Party resolutions. But since I had been elected by the masses [the workers] to be their trade union functionary, I also had to implement their requests, especially those with majority backing. I had to familiarize myself with their situation, and study their problems. I also had to explain certain difficulties, which they had not understood, and ask them for their opinions on various matters. But the net result of my endeavours was a reprimand from the Party committee, which accused me of having organized the masses in order to undermine the leadership, and of having sown the seeds of discord between the masses and the leadership. I was told that I should discuss my problems with the leadership, because otherwise I would simply be providing them with a "tail". It was pointed out to me that I was to carry out the resolutions promulgated by the leadership at all times, irrespective of whether I thought they were right or wrong, and that in the case of unpopular measures I was to convince the masses that they were perfectly in order.'[2]

Clearly, the workers did not always approve of Party policy. But that did not stop it from being put into effect.

Productivity and Individualism

'Discord' between the workers and the leadership was caused by many different factors. One of these was the near impossibility of reconciling the need for high productivity with the need for adequate safety measures. In order to raise productivity the Party tried to inculcate a competitive spirit, it awarded special prizes, and provided special ideological training. It also encouraged all Chinese workers to 'make a gift' to the state of so many working hours each week; in other words, to do unpaid overtime. Some would come to work an hour or two before their shift was due to start, others would stay on in the evenings. No doubt there were those who did this willingly, out of a spirit of genuine enthusiasm. But if we consider the extent to which the Chinese workers were exposed to bourgeois influences, it seems likely that a majority will have taken exception to this system. Certainly, this appears to have been the case where the younger workers were concerned. They were often told that they should emulate their older colleagues, and try to acquire some of their zeal.[3] To display enthusiasm for one's work is to display a genuinely 'proletarian' attitude. And because the workers failed to do this, the Party tried to inculcate a sense of enthusiasm by administrative means. Accordingly, it abolished piece-rate working, which by 1957 had become more or less standard procedure throughout Chinese industry, and replaced it by a new system based on a flat rate for the job with bonus payments for special merit. This merit was calculated largely in terms of the ideological attitudes displayed by the workers, due allowance being made for the enthusiasm which they brought to their work. On the basis of these assessments the workers were placed in three categories, and those in the lowest category received no bonus payments. Thus, enthusiasm was institutionalized.

I have already referred to the fact that higher productivity could not easily be reconciled with the need to ensure safe working conditions. It also militated against industrial health. Many accidents occurred, and there was a high incidence of illness. There were many reasons for this, but two stand out: 1. the drive for higher productivity or, alternatively, the Party's insistence on enthusiasm, which led to an increase in both the tempo of the work and the length of the shifts, thus undermining health and inducing accidents; 2. the low standard of industrial training, which also resulted in numerous accidents, due to the fact that the workers lacked the necessary skill to operate complex machines. A further factor was the conscious disregard of industrial safety precautions by the functionaries, especially during the 'Great Leap Forwards' when they often exhorted the workers to greater efforts with statements such as:

'Don't talk to me of safety during the "Great Leap Forwards".'[4] Although the Chinese Communist Party has long since realized that its production programme is being seriously prejudiced by industrial accidents and illness, the underlying conflicts which are the cause of these problems have yet to be resolved. There are still no fixed working hours, and working conditions have not been rationalized.

Proletarian Consciousness and Individualism

Like all the other classes in Chinese society, the proletariat was criticized for subscribing to bourgeois ideas. After accusing the workers of adopting a self-centred attitude, the Party insisted that they must regard the interests of the state and of the community as if they were their own, and must give their 'unreserved allegiance' to the Chinese Communist Party. They were also told that they must do what the Party required of them, and go wherever the Party sent them. In order to ensure that the Chinese proletariat adopted suitably proletarian attitudes the Party set up small production units consisting of anything between 10 and 100 persons. The members of each unit lived and worked together, and were watched over by functionaries and Party members, who were specially allocated by the Party and 'ate, worked and lived' with the members of the unit. The advantage of such communal organizations is obvious: whenever problems arose the functionaries and Party members were always available to resolve them in strict accordance with Party policy, thus inculcating correct proletarian attitudes. Party members had to study in detail the mental attitudes, not only of the members of their unit, but also of their relatives, so as to be able to intervene at a moment's notice and correct ideological errors on the spot.[5] The members of these units were also organized into a militia in order to strengthen 'the political awareness, the solidarity, the work discipline and the work output' of other workers and employees. In each of these units lists were posted at the end of the working day which provided certain basic information about the members: whether they had attended work, what their output had been, and how economical they had been in their use of materials. In the evening these figures were discussed by the whole unit and each individual worker was either praised or criticized. All the members of these units were told that they must fulfil seven basic requirements in order to become good proletarians: 1. possess firm proletarian convictions, 2. fulfil their production quota, 3. always present themselves for work, 4. observe work discipline, 5. work as a team, 6. acquire technological skills, 7. keep themselves clean and do gymnastic exercises.[6] Over and above this, they had to obey the supreme commandment: to study the thoughts of Mao Tse-tung.

The organization of workers in production and militia units was an intelligent measure, devised by the Party in order to undermine their individualism by removing them from the traditional pattern of family life. It also enabled the functionaries and Party members to keep a much closer watch on work performance and ideological attitudes, and to detect, and try to rectify, unproletarian ideas before they became ingrained. This they were able to do, not only for the workers, but for their relatives as well, since they were also required to study their ideological attitudes in order to counteract harmful family influences. But although this scheme was well conceived there is little to suggest that the workers who joined these production units acquired a genuinely proletarian outlook. There were two principal difficulties. In the first place, it seems questionable whether mental attitudes can be 'purged' in the manner envisaged by Mao, who thought that a man's brain could be washed as easily as his body; and in the second place, there is good reason to think that the Party members and functionaries responsible for inculcating correct proletarian attitudes in these workers were themselves ideologically suspect. Time and again the Chinese press reported that the industrial workers were bringing too little enthusiasm to their work, that there was too much malingering, and that those who did set to work with a will were accused by their colleagues of being career-minded.[7] Not, one would have thought, a glowing testimonial for the production units! Incidentally, the functionaries attached to these units tended to cultivate only the ideologically progressive members, avoiding those with reactionary views lest they should be accused of associating with malcontents and forming dissident cliques in order to oppose the Party. And so, despite the Party's persistent attempts, over a period of many years, to inculcate pure proletarian ideas in the minds of the workers, many of the members of this all-important class were still preoccupied with their own self-interests when the cultural revolution was mounted in November 1965.

2. Contradictions Among the Peasants

With the progressive implementation of the Party's programme for the collectivization of agriculture, conflicts between the peasants and the leadership became more pronounced and more bitter. We have already seen that the class war in the countryside was called off for the duration of the Sino-Japanese war in the interests of national unity. But when the policy of agrarian reform was reintroduced in May 1946 a new class war – which was always violent and occasionally bitter – was waged against the estate owners and big farmers, who at that time were said to account for 10 per cent of the rural population. Their lands, draught animals and equipment were confiscated by the army and redistributed amongst the peasants, and they themselves were declared enemies of the people. Discriminatory action was taken against their children, and even their grand-children, who were regarded as persons of suspect loyalty and, in many cases, as potential enemies because they had been exposed to bourgeois and feudal influences during their child-hood.

Collectivization and the Functionaries

The need to prosecute the class war was not the only reason for introducing the agrarian reform. This reform was also designed to serve an economic purpose, for Chinese agriculture was expected to provide both the food needed for the industrial workers and the capital needed for industrial expansion. After the introduction of the agrarian reform the peasants were urged to increase their production so as to improve their own living conditions and give a much-needed boost to the national economy. At that time they were allowed to rent or buy land, employ agricultural labourers, lend money on interest and engage in normal capitalist business practices because 'a kulak economy is more productive than a peasant economy.'[8] According to *Xuexi*, a theoretical Party organ, this permissive attitude had an immediate effect, not only on the peasants, but also on the rural functionaries. Many of them believed that with the defeat of the Japanese imperialists and Chiang Kai-shek, and the implementation of the agrarian reform, the revolution had already been brought to a successful conclusion (as was in fact stated by the Minister for Agriculture in the middle of 1951). Consequently, they assumed that the time had come to enjoy the fruits of the revolution, that they could relax their endeavours on behalf of the nation and devote their energies to the accumulation of personal wealth. This sort of attitude was particularly prevalent in the old 'liberated areas' in the north and north-east of China, where the local functionaries were said to be behaving like kulaks of the old school, employing labourers to work on their fields and lending money at exorbitant rates. An enquiry into the affairs of six Party branch offices in the province of Shansi in northern China revealed that 39 out of a total of 141 Party members had engaged in capitalist practices of this kind.[9] A second enquiry into the affairs of a further 185 Party branch offices in the same province found that 49 of these had a good record, and another 88 a satisfactory record, but that the remaining 48 had either relapsed into capitalist practices, or had come very near to doing so.[10] It would seem from the information available to us that between 10 and 14 per cent of the Party members investigated at that time were expelled from the Party,[11] and that disciplinary action was taken against many more. Apparently, those who were expelled and forced to relinquish their Party posts were not altogether displeased. That, certainly, is the implication of the following statement by one of these ex-functionaries, who was obviously speaking for his colleagues as well as himself: 'If we don't do our work well, we are criticized by our superiors. If we adopt the wrong kind of attitude when we come to implement Party resolutions, the masses complain. If we neglect our fields, our wives grumble at us. So, it's better not to be a functionary.'[12] In point of fact, it is hardly surprising that so many of the Party functionaries in the rural areas should have subscribed to bourgeois or feudal ideas. Many of them were perfectly happy with the way things were in the countryside at that time, and their political and ideological knowledge appears to have been almost non-existent. In the course of a survey carried out in 1951[13] in four Chinese villages 109 Party members were asked if they knew: (a) the ultimate objective of the Chinese Communist Party, and (b) the different phases that would have to be passed through before that objective was achieved. The answers were surprising. Everybody knew that the ultimate aim of the Communist Party was something called 'Communism', but nobody knew anything at all about the intermediate stages leading up to Communism. Of those interviewed about a third had joined the Party during the Sino-Japanese war and the other two thirds during the revolution mounted against the Kuomintang. In their report the functionaries who carried out this survey assumed that, in view of their almost total ignorance of ideological matters, these Party members could never have studied Marxism–Leninism or the thoughts of Mao Tse-tung. This casts an interesting light on the Party membership in rural areas. So too does the observation that, of the 109 people interviewed, 37 were illiterate, and a further 35 almost illiterate.

After the completely incorrigible functionaries had been eliminated from the Party those who remained were given political education. In carrying out this large scale ideological operation the Party was fortunate in that it was able to tape the patriotic feelings aroused at that time by China's involvement in the Korean war. Thanks to the anti-American campaign, which was then in full swing, the Party was able to point out that if the Americans won the war, the Kuomintang would return to China and sweep away the new agrarian reforms, and that if the Party functionaries relaxed their vigilance, the estate owners and kulaks would try to regain their property and seize power in the villages in order to facilitate the return of the Kuomintang. Thus, the concept of the class war acquired real meaning. As a result of this education campaign the Party was able to step up its programme for the collectivization of agriculture. Unfortunately, the Party functionaries were overzealous in their support. In the case of the high level Party committees this excess of zeal led to a spate of officialism whilst at village level the functionaries became authoritarian. The senior functionaries were completely out of touch with their colleagues in the small district committees, and so had no idea of just how primitive working conditions were in the countryside. As a result, they issued directives and made demands which were completely nonsensical in terms of local conditions. For the most part, the senior functionaries wanted to see immediate material progress; they did not concern themselves with how this was to be achieved, they disregarded the reports sent in from the villages describing local conditions, and simply sat in their offices issuing orders and bringing pressure to bear on the local functionaries to ensure that their orders were executed without delay. The bureaucratic attitude adopted by the men at the top encouraged authoritarianism amongst the men on the spot, who had the thankless task of implementing their directives. This caused great distress for the peasants, and was also counter-productive in terms of work output. In one district in northern China, for example, 70,000 wells had to be sunk, and the people's militia was mobilized to maintain work discipline amongst the peasants. The pressure brought to bear on these peasants was so great that some of them committed suicide;[14] and when the 70,000 wells had been completed, it was found that 40,000 of them were useless. In another case, local functionaries forced the peasants to uproot young saplings in order to test a new strain of seed. The orders to do so had been issued by one of the high level committees.

According to official Party policy, the peasants were to be allowed to decide for themselves whether to join the collective system or not, and the transition to collective farming was to proceed in stages. In actual fact, the local functionaries in the countryside forced the peasants to form 'Groups for Mutual Assistance', and, in some cases, to join cooperatives. In the process they used threats and meted out arbitrary punishment. Numerous peasants were accused of having failed to support Chairman Mao, of being right wing deviationists and even counter-revolutionaries.[15] They were disdained and insulted, made to pay fines, or denied the right to irrigate their land. The rural functionaries also submitted false returns. In one district in northern China 2,400 'Groups for Mutual Assistance' were recorded although only 400 had actually been formed.[16] Another group of local functionaries was instructed to persuade the peasants in their village to form such groups, and within a few days they reported to their superiors that 90 per cent of the peasants had done so. Their superiors thought this sounded rather improbable; but instead of trying to discover what the real figure was, they simply knocked 40 per cent off, and then sent the return on to their own superiors.[17] On occasions, the local functionaries even forced people who had nothing to do with farming to join the 'Groups for Mutual Assistance', which were, of course, intended only for peasants. The methods used by the local functionaries undoubtedly caused conflicts and, in some cases, open hostility between the peasants and the leadership. Things eventually reached such a pitch that An Tzu-wen, who was then Assistant Director in the Organization Department of the Central Committee, was obliged to make the following statement: 'In the lower Party and government organizations authoritarianism and alienation from the masses have become dominant ... Authoritarian methods are also quite common in the organizations for agricultural production and national health, whose functionaries come into direct contact with the masses. As a result of these methods, the masses have suffered enormously in their fight against drought and disease, in the use of improved strains of seed, and in their attempts to obtain loans. In certain parts, where the village, area and district functionaries have transgressed against Party discipline and against the law, suppressed criticism, and protected counter-revolutionaries, the situation is even more intolerable ... These manifestations threaten the interests of the people, distort Party policy, and undermine the relationship between the Party and the masses.'[18]

Although the Party mounted a campaign in 1953 against 'officialism, authoritarianism and transgressions against discipline and the law', it was still unable to eliminate all the malpractices of its functionaries. The fact of the matter was that, to some extent, officialism and authoritarianism were a natural consequence of Party policy. They were also one of the reasons why collectivization was pushed through by the end of 1956 despite the fact that Mao Tse-tung had said in the middle of 1955 that the peasants would not be expected to join cooperatives – let alone collective farms, which were to be established at a later stage – until 1960. Incidentally, when Mao made this statement he prefaced it with a criticism of the excessive caution and anxiety evinced in respect of collectivization by his colleagues, which unleashed a wave of self-criticism amongst Party members, both in Peking and in the provinces. By June 1955 – one month before Mao's speech – only 14·2 per cent of peasant holdings had been incorporated into cooperatives, but by December of the same year this figure had risen to 59·3 per cent, and a further 4 per cent had been incorporated into collective farms. By June 1956 – 11 months after Mao's speech

– the number of peasant holdings incorporated into collective farms had risen to 63·2 per cent whilst the figure for cooperatives had dropped to 28·7 per cent.[19] Many of the cooperatives were no sooner established than they were taken over to form part of new collective farms. This process is well illustrated by the development in the province of Kwangtung. There, only 7 per cent of peasant holdings had been incorporated into cooperatives by September 1955, but by November this figure had risen to 40 per cent, and by January 1956 to 80·7 per cent. Moreover, by March 1956 44·3 per cent of peasant holdings had joined together to form collective farms, and by November 1956 this figure had risen to 88·9 per cent. This rapid transformation took place despite Mao's insistence that work must proceed systematically and his warning against left-wing adventurism which, he said, would alienate the peasants and create conflicts between them and the Party. It was surely no accident that the leadership decided to launch the 'Hundred Flowers Campaign', in which the working methods of the Party functionaries responsible to the provincial Party Committees were criticized, in 1956.

Collectivization and the 'Middle Peasants'

In the speech which he delivered in July 1955 Mao Tse-tung stated that between 60 and 70 per cent of the rural population were in favour of the collectivization of agriculture. He also stated that the estate owners and kulaks, who had been branded as outcasts in 1942, accounted for 10 per cent of the rural population. In point of fact, this estimate appears to have been too high, for in a survey of 192,760 rural holdings distributed over 22 Chinese provinces it was established that only 6 per cent of the rural population were members of this class. But even if we were to accept Mao's figure of 10 per cent, this would still leave a further 20 to 30 per cent who were opposed to collectivization. Who were they? Apparently, the more affluent members of the rural middle class, i.e. the wealthier farmers. This is the clear implication of the directives issued to the Party functionaries at the time, who were told that they must look for support to the 'peasants and small farmers'. According to the above-mentioned survey, 21·1 per cent of the rural population were classified as farmers, nearly half of whom had been peasants prior to the agrarian reform. Of course, the wealthier members of the rural population had been branded as outcasts by the Party, and were therefore potential class enemies.

The wealthier farmers had a great deal to lose from collectivization. During the cooperative stage they had to hand over their fields, draught animals and all large agricultural implements – ploughs, etc. – to their local cooperative, which paid them a hire charge. Their situation became even worse when the collective farms were set up, for the payment of hire charges was discontinued, and all they received for the use of their tools was a depreciation allowance; they then had to live from their wages, which were often short, for as outcasts they could be cheated with impunity. For the wealthier farmers collectivization meant the loss of a secure income, and arbitrary treatment at the hands of the local Party functionaries. To a lesser extent, the poorer members of the rural middle class also stood to lose by collectivization. As small farmers, it is true, they would have been the first to go to the wall under a capitalist economy. But, then, capitalism would also have held out the prospect of financial advancement. And, in any case, they had better fields, better draught animals and better tools than the peasants, and were loath to give them up. It is hardly surprising, therefore, that Mao Tse-tung should have instructed the local Party functionaries to mobilize support amongst the politically reliable members of the rural community before concerning themselves with the others. These 'others' were, of course, the small farmers, both old and new, who accounted for 20·5 and 18·4 per cent of the rural population respectively. Ideally, the Party would have preferred to disregard the small farmers. However, it had no choice in the matter, for unless it could win them over it would have had only minority support for its collectivization programme, since the 'reliable members of the alliance of the working class' accounted for only 32·6 per cent of the rural population.[20] Even so, the situation in the country-side was precarious, for about 30 per cent of all country dwellers were politically unreliable and potential class enemies, 38·9 per cent were relatively unreliable, and – as we have just seen – only 32·6 per cent were reliable.

By the end of 1953 only 0·2 per cent of China's agricultural holdings had been incorporated into cooperatives. By June 1955 this figure had risen to 14·2 per cent, and by June 1956 no less than 91·9 per cent of Chinese holdings had been collectivized, of which 63·2 per cent had joined collective farms.[21] Since it had been laid down by the Party that collectivization was to be purely voluntary, it would seem from these statistics that it had been a great success and had met with an enthusiastic response from the peasants and farmers. But there is a second set of statistics which tells a very different story and shows that, far from displaying the 'community spirit' called for by the leadership, the peasants had been extremely 'egotistic'. From 101,718,000 in July 1954 China's pig stock dropped to 87,920,000 in July 1955, and 84,400,000 in July 1956.[22] Although no comprehensive statistics were ever published, it is quite apparent from the reports which appeared in the provincial press that her stock of draught animals was also drastically reduced during this period. Pigs and draught animals were quite indispensable. Without draught animals – buffalo and horses – men would have to pull the ploughs, and without pigs the Chinese would have lost their principal source, not only of fresh meat, but also of manure. Why then did the stocks of these animals decline so drastically during the collectivization programme? The answer to this question, which was furnished by the Minister for Agriculture Liao Lu-yen back in February 1955, is perfectly simple. When the local functionaries told the peasants that their animals would be taken from them and placed in cooperatives or collective farms, the peasants preferred to slaughter them rather than give them up. Nor was this the only sign of non-cooperation. Due largely to the ham-fisted and authoritarian way in which the functionaries tried to force the collectivization issue, the peasants also neglected their fields: no manure was spread, very few crops were sown, and those that were sown were not properly cultivated. In March 1955 the *People's Daily* described the situation as extremely serious, and not long afterwards the collectivization programme was suspended, and the peasants were allowed to opt out of the agricultural cooperatives. This respite – which the Party referred to as a period of 'consolidation' – lasted until July 1955, when Mao Tse-tung ordered a resumption. New rules were then drawn up for the cooperatives which made some allowance for the peasants' 'egoism'. Thus, the peasants were permitted to retain a piece of land for private cultivation, and they were also permitted to keep their draught animals on condition that they hired them out to the cooperatives for an appropriate charge. But these new regulations made very little difference. As a general rule, the land allocated for private cultivation was only half what had been promised; it was also of very poor quality, and was situated a long way from the peasants' homes. Moreover, in some districts the peasants were given no land at all whilst in others they were allowed to use it only during the growing season. Certain cooperatives even established set hours for private cultivation, and anybody who worked on his land outside of those hours was fined. As for the other aspects of collectivization, they went on as if there had never been a respite. Fruit trees, animals and agricultural implements were either confiscated or bought for a purely nominal price. Meanwhile, the pig stocks – the barometer of public opinion in the countryside – continued to decline until they reached an all-time low in July 1956: 84,400,000.[23] The economic situation became so grave, and food supplies were in such short supply that the Minister for Agriculture and the Party secretaries in the provinces criticized themselves as one man for the inadequacy of their planning and their failure to understand the needs of the countryside. It was then decided to make further concessions to the 'egoism' of the peasants. Free markets were allowed, and the amount of land allocated for private cultivation was doubled. Only then did the pig stocks begin to increase until by the end of 1956 they regained their pre-1954 level.

But with the increased allocation of private land, the peasants became too independent of the collective farms. On average, 20 per cent of the peasants' income at that time came from the sale of pork, pig manure, vegetables, and – in some cases – milk in the free markets.[24] In the more fertile areas the proportion was as much as 50 to 60 per cent. The peasants preferred to work on their own land, and earn a bit of extra money by doing odd jobs, because it was far more profitable than ploughing fields for the collective farms. During this second period of relaxation they were quite contented with their lot, as is quite evident from the increase in pig production: by the end of 1957

China had 145,895,000 pigs. But during the same period corn production in China increased by only 1 per cent,[25] which was highly unsatisfactory since Chinese agriculture had to supply the needs of the industrial workers and provide capital for the expansion of industry, and since the birth rate in the People's Republic was going up by between 2 and 3 per cent per annum. In an attempt to redress this imbalance without alienating the peasants, the Party decided on a two-pronged attack. On the one hand, it abolished the free markets whilst, on the other hand, it decentralized the collective farms and made the old cooperatives, which had continued to operate within the collective system as subsidiary units, the new basic units of Chinese agriculture. As such, they acquired the property rights previously vested in the collectives. It was hoped that this new policy would make agricultural planning a more rational process, and would enable the Party to evolve a more equitable wage structure. Clearly, the first measure was designed to curb the peasants' natural 'egoism' by preventing them from selling their products in a free market. The second, which was a compensatory measure, was meant to channel that egoism into the collective system, for it was felt that if they were able to earn more by working within the system, they would gradually lose all interest in private enterprise. At the same time, a socialist educational campaign was carried out in the countryside to persuade the peasants to abandon their old self-centred attitudes and acquire a community spirit. The peasants' yen for private enterprise was further undermined when the Party organized them into work groups to dig irrigation canals and collect manure, which kept them fully occupied and left them no time to work on their private holdings. And yet in February 1958 the *People's Daily* was obliged to report that a large part of the peasants' income still came from private sources. Eventually, when 'communization' was introduced in the autumn of 1958, the peasants lost their private holdings, and their animals again came under collective ownership. At long last, the Party leaders hoped to eradicate peasant egoism. But, once again, they had miscalculated the strength of peasant feeling, and in February 1959 they were obliged to direct their functionaries to return the pigs.

The existence of people's communes was first reported in the Chinese press on August 18, 1958. By the end of August, 30 per cent, and by the end of September 98·2 per cent,[26] of all peasant holdings had been 'communized'. This was represented as the outcome of a spontaneous popular movement, which had been inspired in the first place by the strong socialist attitudes of the peasants. But from what we know of the 'collectivization' programme it seems reasonable to assume that this spontaneous movement may also have owed something to the authoritarianism of the local functionaries. Private holdings, animals, orchards and odd trees were all transferred to the communes. The communist principle of rendering 'to each according to his needs' was also put into practice in so far as everybody was given a fixed ration of food in the communal canteens irrespective of how well, or whether, he had worked. On the other hand, some overzealous functionaries even 'communized' the peasants' clothing, quilts, cooking utensils and savings. However, in December 1958 the Party began to retreat from this extreme position when it abolished the free meals system on the grounds that it had made the peasants work-shy; at the same time the peasants were given back their savings, their cooking utensils and personal belongings, and also a few fruit trees and small animals. Over and above this, they were guaranteed 8 hours sleep a day, but were told that they would have to pursue political studies – ideological re-education – for two hours each day.[27] This ideological campaign was accompanied by a parallel campaign to purge the authoritarian attitudes of local Party members and functionaries. Once again, peasant egoism had won the day.

After pointing out in December 1958 that the introduction of communization did not mean that henceforth all goods would be held in common but that, on the contrary, the principle of collective ownership would still form the basis of the Chinese economy, the Central Committee of the Party retreated still further from the concept of people's communes at the famous Lu-Shan Conference in 1959. On that occasion it decreed that the ownership of the principal assets of Chinese agriculture was to be vested in the production units (the former collectives) and that these would also be responsible for general planning. About twelve months later, however, this planning responsibility passed to the production companies (the former cooperatives). Shortly afterwards, free markets were re-established, and the system of private holdings was reintroduced. Subsequently, this trend towards 'de-communization' grew even more pronounced, for in 1962 it became apparent that in many rural areas responsibility for planning, production and wages had passed to the work groups (formerly the Groups for Mutual Assistance) and that these were once again apportioning work quotas and distributing parcels of land to individual peasants.[28]

But despite the allowances made for their egoism by the Party's repeated retreats from communization, the peasants were still unhappy. They objected to the Party's bureaucratic methods, which led to the formulation of plans that took no account of local conditions, and to the authoritarian attitude of the functionaries, who implemented those plans without regard for their interests. The result was unsatisfactory all round, for not only were the peasants prevented from getting on with their work, which provided them with their best source of income, but the communal work, for which they were mobilized by the Party, also suffered. Although it is perfectly true, as one provincial newspaper pointed out, that the peasants made a brave sight when they were marching across the countryside to some new communal project, the quality of their work and, in some cases, even their work output left much to be desired. The mobilization of peasant labour for water conservation projects was particularly resented. In northern China alone 70 million peasants were recruited for the excavation of irrigation canals in 1959.[29] The result of their labours was not an unqualified success, for the water fed to the fields was drawn from deep wells, and in many districts it turned the land alkaline. This happened in several different parts of the country – the north, the north-east, the north-west and the province of Kiangsu. In all, something like 10 to 20 per cent of China's arable land was affected.[30] Another aspect of agricultural policy to which the peasants took exception was the Party's insistence on deep ploughing and close sowing, for these impaired the fertility of the soil and so had the effect of reducing rather than increasing the size of the harvest. This effect was reinforced by the Party's disregard for the seasons. The local functionaries were told to increase the number of harvests to two in the north and three in the south, and they carried out their orders to the letter without stopping to consider the consequences. The net result of their unswerving allegiance was that the peasants had to work much harder, and to no real purpose. Commenting on this state of affairs, the *People's Daily* told the functionaries that they should consider the ways of nature before even attempting to implement Party directives, and that they should also consult the peasants, who had a great deal to offer in the way of practical advice. As a result of the misguided policy directives issued by the Party, the conflicts between the peasants and the local functionaries grew still more intense. So too did the conflicts between the functionaries and the Party Committees. The functionaries were in an invidious position. If they failed to carry out directives, they were accused of right wing opportunism; if they carried them out, they were accused of left wing adventurism.

Even after the collectivization policy had been in operation for a number of years the peasants had not acquired a collective outlook. Many of them were still bothered by the idea that the crops they produced in the communes belonged to 'everybody', and they far preferred to work on their private holdings, because then the crops belonged to 'them alone'. The peasants also failed to take proper care of the tools they used in the communes so that in no time at all they were either lost or rendered useless. Many of their own tools, on the other hand, had been in use for generations. The 'collective indolence' of the Chinese peasants was so pronounced that on several occasions senior Party functionaries, accompanied by militia units, had to be despatched to the countryside to supervise their work, especially during the harvest. In the province of Shantung the regular army spent 'five million man-days' in the villages 'working' with the masses. Many production companies were supervised by troops throughout the entire year. These army units also organized political courses for the local functionaries,[31] whose reliability appears to have become suspect in the mid 1960's.

Like most Party members, the local functionaries came from peasant stock and consequently shared the ambivalent attitudes of the peasants who, although capable of revolutionary activism, also revealed a propensity for the accumulation of property, i.e. for capitalism. In 1962 a local newspaper reported a case in which 16 out of the 18 functionaries attached to one of the people's communes had spent so much time working for themselves, and had neglected the work of the commune to such an extent, that more than 50 per cent of the production units had also failed to make any contribution. By 1964 the situation in the communes had become so critical that the Party was obliged to launch a special educational campaign to stress the need for socialist attitudes. At the same time it set up 'associations of peasants and smallholders' in all parts of China to supervise the functionaries. Judging by the following statement, which was addressed by one of these peasants to his local functionaries, the members of these associations appear to have relished their task: 'If you are unjust, we will criticize you. If you do not accept our criticisms, we will have you relieved of your posts.'[32] The *People's Daily* explained why the Party had found it necessary to have the functionaries supervised in this way: '. . . the functionaries must accept supervision from their brothers, the peasants and small-holders, so as to ensure that the revolution can be carried to a successful conclusion, and always keeps its [red] colour.'[33] In actual fact, this decision was illogical, for the functionaries had themselves been entrusted with the organization of the new educational campaign, which was designed to inculcate socialist attitudes in the masses, and were also responsible for the supervision of agricultural production. And now they were to be supervised by the peasants and small-holders. This ambiguous situation could only aggravate the conflicts which already existed between these two groups, especially in view of the fact that the peasants were not exactly renowned for their industry. Speaking on Shansi radio in June 1964 a commentator said: 'You must rely on the peasants if you want to stage a successful revolution, but you must rely on the small farmers if you want a successful production programme.'[34] However, although this commentator's assessment of the peasant's work potential was probably pretty accurate, it is doubtful whether they were as revolutionary as he claimed, for we have already seen that in their attitude to property they were decidedly conservative. But this move to set up representatives of the masses as judges of Party conduct triggered conflicts, not only between those directly concerned, namely the peasants and local functionaries, but also in the higher echelons of the Party. For the high level committees were sharply divided over the question of whether the masses should be allowed to criticize Party functionaries. The opposition view was stated in succinct terms by a Chinese newspaper in December 1964: 'If the masses criticize the functionaries, the functionaries will no longer be able to control them. It is perfectly in order for the high level Party committees to criticize the functionaries. But if the masses do so, we will have chaos.'[35] The situation in the countryside was extremely dangerous. There was a general conflict amongst the rural population involving enemies of the people, unreliable elements, peasants and local functionaries, and there was also a specific conflict between the peasants and the local functionaries over the question of peasant supervision. To make matters worse, both the peasants and the functionaries were guilty of unproletarian attitudes and actions. Finally, there were conflicts between the central and the local Party committees, which aggravated matters still further. The only way in which these conflicts could be resolved was by mounting an ideological revolution that would give all of these dissident groups a common purpose. This was one of the objects of the cultural revolution.

The Peasants and Folk Tradition

'Some people have very strange notions. If the harvest is good, they thank heaven for sending them the rain and the wind. But if the harvest is bad, they blame the people's commune.'

This statement appeared in an article in the *People's Daily* in 1959. The author of the article went on to explain that the reason why superstition was able to survive in a socialist society was that, after existing for thousands of years, it was deeply ingrained in people's minds, and China's agricultural production was not yet good enough to convince the peasants that their daily ration of rice was not a gift from heaven. But superstition really was widespread in China at the time when the people's communes were being set up, especially amongst the peasants. According to an article in *Red Flag* it seems that whenever graves had to be removed to a new cemetery because the site of the original cemetery was needed as agricultural land, the peasants, although outwardly compliant, would seethe inwardly because the 'lucky' spot chosen for their ancestors' last resting place had been desecrated. Apparently, they also asked their ancestors to forgive them, pointing out that it was not they, but the functionaries, who were responsible.

The Chinese newspapers made a special point of explaining 'supernatural manifestations'. 'Ghostly lights', their readers were told, had nothing to do with ghosts but were due to the presence of phosphorescent substances. Thus, if an image of the Buddha was seen to glow, it was not a miracle but a physiological phenomenon. Similarly, earthquakes were not caused by bulls or dragons living in the bowels of the earth, and were not an omen of the coming harvest. Moreover, if a person was struck by lightning, it was not a divine judgement executed by the god of thunder. These, and many more, explanations of popular superstitions appeared in the Chinese press in the late 1950's and early 1960's.

A number of strange occupations and cult practices also managed to survive in the People's Republic. For example, we find soothsayers, geomancers and witches (women who received visitations from spirits, demons and gods). People still continued to build temples to their gods, and to their ancestors,[36] and – in accordance with the age-old custom of deifying persons of exemplary virtue – they continued to pray to famous historical personalities such as Kuan Yü. In 1964 children were still not allowed to leave the house, and no guests were received on the 'day of the spirits', which fell on the 14th day of the 7th month according to the lunar calendar. People also burnt paper money to placate the spirits, and set out food for wandering ghosts. In many places the peasants in the production units stayed away from work, treating the day of the spirits as a holy-day.[37] In 1965 it transpired that this holy-day was being actively supported by the socialist economy. It seems that certain co-operative stores were selling paper money, paper houses and paper horses for the sacrificial ceremonies, and incense sticks to burn at the altars erected by the people to their gods and ancestors, and that these cult objects had been manufactured in people's communes. It also transpired that the Party had omitted to draw 'the class line in respect of the dead', for people were found to be mourning the death of capitalist parents and grandparents, and some were even tending the graves of class enemies.[38] It soon became apparent that the ideological revolution would have to transform, not only the reactionary mental attitudes of the Chinese peasants, but their reactionary 'souls' as well. This was also one of the objects of the cultural revolution.

CHAPTER IV

THE PARTY

The Chinese Communist Party is the dominant nucleus of the whole of the Chinese nation. Without such a nucleus the cause of socialism could not triumph.

. . .

A number of anti-revolutionary revisionists, who will try to seize power when the time is ripe, have wormed their way . . . into the Party.

MAO TSE-TUNG

We have seen in the preceding chapters that a general conflict gradually developed between the Party leaders and their subordinates. Apart from a few rare cases – for example, when Mao Tse-tung criticized his colleagues in the Central Committee for being unwilling to proceed with the collectivization of agriculture with the necessary despatch – Party policy had always been 'correct', although it had sometimes been misunderstood or wrongly applied by the Party functionaries. Whenever this had happened, the senior functionaries had been accused of officialism, and the junior functionaries of authoritarianism. Of course, their position was impossible. If they implemented Party policy – which always proceeded by 'leaps and bounds' – the masses were discontented, whereas if they sympathized with the masses, they were looked upon as *intriguants*, and accused of trying to incite popular unrest. This applied especially to the agricultural sphere, in which the majority of Party functionaries were employed. Clearly the leadership could not afford to be as unpopular as this, and it would seem that a further reason why Mao decided to mount the cultural revolution was the need to channel the resentment felt by the functionaries away from the leadership in general and towards the small group within the leadership whose members were treading the 'capitalist path'. At the same time, a full 5 per cent of all Party members, who had been accused of revisionist tendencies, were delivered up to the vengeance of the people, partly in order to resolve – but only temporarily – the conflict between the masses and the Party, and partly to provide a warning for others. Mao appears to have foreseen the need for such a warning early on, for back in 1959 he drew attention to the unsatisfactory state of rural attitudes. Only 30 per cent of the peasants, he said, supported the communization programme, an equal number were opposed to it whilst the remainder would take their lead from whichever group gained the ascendancy.[1] And we have already seen that, with the passage of time, it was the 'de-communization' group that became dominant.

1. The Conflicts Between Mao Tse-tung and the Cultural and Educational Functionaries

The cultural functionaries played a major part in inner-Party conflicts. As a general rule, they were the first to enter the lists when the leadership mounted a campaign, obediently criticizing the victim even when – as in the case of Hu Feng – they obviously shared his views. But after each campaign the cultural functionaries returned to the attack, advocating and disseminating the heretical ideas which they themselves had helped to expose, until the leadership was obliged to mount yet another campaign. Typical examples of such follow-up campaigns – which were often conducted by Mao Tse-tung in person – were those mounted against the makers of the film *Wu Hsün Chuan* and the interpreter of the novel *The Dream of the Red Chamber*. But Mao was not always able to impose his will. For example, the film *The Secret History of the Ching Palace*, which portrayed the events of the Boxer Rising at the turn of the century, was repudiated by the Party leadership on the grounds that it revealed treasonable and capitulationary attitudes, and Mao called upon the cultural functionaries to criticize and condemn it. They, however, refused to comply with his directive, and it was not until the cultural revolution was launched that this film – and the functionaries' dereliction – were publicly criticized. Mao's cultural ideas – which, incidentally, he has never systematically formulated – met with the fiercest opposition from within the Party in the period between the 'Great Leap Forwards' and the cultural revolution. During that time the cultural functionaries published innumerable novels, short stories, satires, allegories and essays, in which they made veiled attacks on Mao Tse-tung and his policy. They also published studies of the Chinese classics, which were then appearing in vast editions. Thus, the *Dream of the Red Chamber* was reinterpreted in accordance with the bourgeois critical criteria condemned by the leadership in the campaign against Yü Ping-po. Historical dramas were published and produced, and old operas from the repertory of the Peking Opera, in which feudal ideas were disseminated, were revived. Characters such as the just officials Hai Jui and Pao Kung, who had defended the common people against oppression on the part of the authorities, were particularly popular with these functionaries, who used every medium of communication, including radio and the cinema, in order to spread their bourgeois and feudal conceptions, and so undermine Mao's socialist ideology. As a result, Mao Tse-tung was forced to recognize, at the end of 1963, that class problems existed in all branches of the arts, and that these were dominated by the 'dead', i.e. by the bourgeois and feudal ideas of earlier generations. Six months later he pilloried the cultural associations within the Party, accusing[2] them of having opposed Party policy in their magazines, and of having failed to do justice to the Party's programme of socialist reconstruction. Mao complained that, of recent years, these associations had become more and more revisionist in their outlook and suggested that if they did not mend their ways, they would soon be indistinguishable from the Petöfi clubs (i.e. the groups of intellectuals who led the Hungarian Rising in 1956). But, of course, the Party's cultural associations were responsible to the local Party Committees; and these were responsible in their turn to the Propaganda Department of the Central Committee, which was under the direct control of Chou Yang who consciously sought to sabotage Mao's cultural ideas.

According to the revelations made in the course of the cultural revolution, Chou Yang was guilty of many 'crimes' in his relationship to Mao Tse-tung. It was he who authorized the filming of Wu Hsün Chuan's life, and subsequently he did his utmost to stifle criticism of this film. Even after Mao's own criticism had appeared in the *People's Daily* Chou still tried to stem the rising tide of condemnation by instructing his 'lackeys' to proceed *cautiously*, with the result that Mao had to form a special committee before he was able to launch his investigation of the case of *Wu Hsün Chuan*.[3] Later, after the film had been subjected to general criticism, Chou claimed that a number of the statements made about it were arbitrary. He argued, like Hu Feng, that the supreme principle of art was truth, and insisted that artists must be free to chose their own subject matter because the process of artistic creation was essentially a personal struggle between the artist and life. Chou praised the chivalry of Don Quixote, which he regarded as the highest form of morality and the *only one* to which the Chinese people should be encouraged to aspire. During the 'Hundred Flowers campaign' Chou condemned the dogmatic cultural policy pursued by the Party, which, he said, had resulted in the production of superficial and purely propagandistic literature. Essentially, Chou wanted to see the Chinese artists freed from political controls.

As early as the spring of 1959 – before the Lu-Shan conference – Chou had begun to propagate the 'Hai Jui spirit' by having Hai Jui operas performed, and by encouraging the Chinese writers to produce Hai Jui dramas. In a speech delivered to the cultural functionaries of the People's Liberation Army he poured scorn on the much vaunted 'Great Leap Forwards', which he described as an attempt to 'beautify an ugly face'. The paeans of praise expended on this campaign, he said, were about as euphonious as songs sung by old women. Chou was also opposed to the publication of the so-called primitive poetry composed by peasants and workers. As for the real poets, for them he wanted to open up a 'broad path of artistic creation' along the lines advocated by Hu Feng. Chou considered that literature should serve, not only the peasants and workers, but the whole nation (which for him included the banished classes of the national- and petits-bourgeois). Even after Mao Tse-tung had proclaimed the class war, Chou continued to press for the investigation of China's cultural heritage. He was, of course, also ultimately responsible for the revival of classical literature and opera, the re-emergence in modern works of traditional ideas, and the new wave of anti-Maoist publications. But Chou's greatest 'crime' was almost certainly his determined attempt to undermine the Mao cult. Amongst other things, he insisted that Communist China had not produced a single major work of scholarship, thus effectively repudiating the claims made for Mao's adaptation of Marxism–Leninism, which was supposed to be the 'greatest work of scholarship' of modern times. Chou Yang also took exception to the adulation of Mao Tse-tung in contemporary literature and drama, in radio and television. Moreover, he sought to invalidate Mao's conception of 'metaphysical materialism' by pointing out that although politics were the very soul of all social enterprises, for this very reason they could not possibly possess material properties. In every possible way Chou tried to block the rays of the 'red sun', i.e. Mao Tse-tung, and during the cultural revolution he was accused by the Maoists of having behaved 'as if the gifts of heaven really came from him'.

2. Contradictions Within the Top Party Leadership

The conflicts within the leadership were due to two principal factors: 1. rivalry in terms of the personality cult; 2. opposition to Mao's un-Marxist view that before progress could be made in a quantitative sense, a qualitative change would have to be brought about (by setting up people's communes and introducing the 'Great Leap Forwards').

The Personality Cult

We have already encountered an example of such rivalry in the previous section. Chou Yang's opposition to Mao was essentially a matter of rivalry, for it stemmed from his personal objection to what he regarded as Mao's vain glory. But although, as the undisputed king of Chinese culture prior to the cultural revolution, Chou controlled a very important section of the ideological superstructure, he was never a really serious contender for Mao's crown because he was not a top-ranking Party member. Where Marshal Chu Te was concerned things might have been very different. If Chu Te had not led his troops to Chingkanshan at the beginning of the revolution, if he had failed to afford Mao Tse-tung wholehearted military and political support, it is by no means certain that the revolution would have succeeded. Until 1956 Chu was commander in chief of the Red Army, and led the Chinese forces against both the Japanese and the Kuomintang. At one time he was better known than Mao himself, and the people referred to the two men, not as Mao and Chu, but as Chu-Mao.[4] Thanks to his military victories Chu was a popular hero, and was especially popular with the army. If anybody could have disputed Mao's military reputation, it was Chu Te. In 1941 he was acclaimed as the 'father and creator of the Red Army' and the 'steadfast helmsman in the revolutionary storm',[5] titles which have since been transferred to Mao Tse-tung. Various victories won by the revolutionary army, which are now attributed to Mao's military genius, were in fact due to Chu Te. But none of this was as damaging for Mao's image as the fact that the celebrated Chinese guerilla strategy, which is now firmly attributed to him, was actually formulated by Chu Te: 'When the enemy advances, we retreat; when he remains stationary, we harass him; when he is tired, we attack him; when he retreats, we pursue him.'[6] As it happens, Chu Te – who was born in 1886 – did not pose a real threat to Mao. But if he had wished, he could certainly have undermined the popular image of Mao as the great military genius – an image that has been taken at its face value by the world at large, which is strangely addicted to the hero cult – although it is unlikely that he could ever have deposed him.

The one man who might conceivably have done so was Liu Shao-chi, the 'Chinese Khrushchev', who was the second most powerful man in the Party prior to the cultural revolution. In 1962 Liu published an amended version of his article *How to Become a Good Communist* both in *Red Flag* and in the form of a pamphlet, which was reproduced and circulated *en masse* (a fact duly noted by the Red Guards in the cultural revolution, who accused Liu of trying to compete with Mao Tse-tung as an ideologist). But although this pamphlet exerted considerable influence on the members and candidate members of the Party – who naturally wanted to be good Communists – it did not seriously dispute Mao's position as leader. However, a film which appeared shortly afterwards under the title *The Earth is Burning*[7] did dispute his position. This film was concerned with the Party's activities amongst the workers at the An-Yuen coalmine in the year 1921, and it showed how a 'messianic' Liu was sent out to the mine to organize a strike. There was not a single reference to Mao in the whole film, although in actual fact he too had been involved in this incident. When Liu first appears, the dark clouds in the sky are suddenly transfixed by countless shafts of light which cast a bright glow on the earth, and when he enrols a group of workers as Party members, the rosy hues of the dawn are seen in the east. This was significant, for both of these forms of symbolism were normally reserved for Mao Tse-tung. In this film Liu was represented as the 'sun' and the 'leader', and in the final scene he is shown standing on a rostrum receiving the acclamation of the crowd, who call out to him: 'May he live for ten thousand years, may he live for ten thousand times ten thousand years'. This acclamation was, of course, reserved for the emperor in the old, and for Mao Tse-tung in the new, China. But, then, the whole purpose of the film was to show that although Mao Tse-tung may have been the peasants' leader, Liu Sho-chi was the workers' leader; and since the Chinese Communist Party was the representative of the workers, and China was supposed to be governed by a dictatorship of the proletariat, it naturally followed that the workers' leader was the rightful 'sun'. It is quite obvious that Liu exerted considerable influence on Party members at that time, and was held in high esteem by them. This is demonstrated by an incident, which was reported in February 1966. During the cultural revolution the *People's Daily* and the New China News Agency called upon all Party functionaries to emulate the late District Secretary Chiao, who had devoted his life to the service of the Party, and in their articles both of these organs attached special importance to the fact that this model functionary had constantly studied, not only Mao's writings, but also Liu's pamphlet *How to Become a Good Communist*. These exhortations elicited an immediate response, and for weeks on end the press was inundated with letters from district secretaries throughout China, who solemnly undertook to model themselves on Chiao.

But Liu Shao-chi did not appear to be the sort of man who would be particularly interested in self-glorification, and it seems unlikely that he was actually trying to outdo Mao in terms of the personality cult with a view to usurping the leadership. What was probably happening at that time was that the 'capitalist faction' within the leadership was trying to build him up as the workers' leader so that when the peasants' leader Mao eventually died, he would emerge as the natural successor, and could then quietly abandon Mao's policy of qualitative change, as manifested in the 'Great Leap Forwards', and revert to the old policy of quantitative growth. It was not for nothing that Mao sought to create a vast army of young revolutionaries; he really did have good reason to fear the restoration of capitalism or, to put it in another way, the abolition of Maoism. There is firm evidence that the projected 'de-Maoisation' of the Chinese Communist Party was something more than an idle fancy, for as early as 1956 the Minister of Defence Peng Te-huai (who was deposed for trying to sabotage the 'Great Leap Forwards') stated that it was a waste of time erecting statues to Mao since they would all have to be taken away again at a later date. And in the same year Liu Shao-chi and the General Secretary of the Central Committee Teng Hsiao-ping, acting on Peng Te-huai's advice, deleted the 'thoughts of Mao Tse-tung' from the Party statutes, although up till then they had formed their principal basis. This, of course, could not have happened without the consent of many other high-ranking Party members. Finally, it should be noted that, as late as 1967, Lin Pao – Mao's heir apparent – was still concerned with the 'problems' that might arise when Mao reached his 'hundredth year'.[8]

The Dispute over Priorities

In the second half of the 1960's the Chinese cultural functionaries tried to convince the world at large that the revisionists exposed in the course of the cultural revolution had been opposing Mao's policies and sabotaging his directives ever since the 1920's. But this could not possibly have been the case since Mao Tse-tung did not become leader of the Party until 1935. What is quite certain, however, is that the Party leadership had been divided over a number of fundamental issues ever since the proclamation of the People's Republic in 1949. Mao Tse-tung and the Chinese revisionists were at loggerheads over the question of whether the Party should concentrate on industrialization or socialization during the transitional period leading up to the establishment of a Communist society. Liu Shao-chi, the 'Chinese Khrushchev', took the orthodox Marxist line, according to which the industrial revolution must be completed before socialism can be introduced. He argued that a full programme of industrialization should be carried out, with the aid of the national bourgeoisie, and insisted that the country would not be ready for socialization until industrial production was running at a high level. For agriculture he recommended a free enterprise system. Liu considered that the peasants were naturally conservative and egoistic, and he proposed, therefore, that they should be encouraged to 'enrich themselves' during the transitional period because, if they did, then the state would also benefit. Only when Chinese industry was in a position to mechanize 50 per cent of agriculture, he suggested, would it be advisable to go over to a collective system. Up to 1954 Liu's ideas were shared by many of his colleagues in the top echelons of the Party. It was only in 1955 that Mao Tse-tung was able to assert his own – contrary – view; but by then he felt strong enough to criticize his opponents in the Party leadership for their timidity, and to compare them with women whose feet had been bound since birth. Prior to 1955 the revisionists are said to have dissolved over 20,000 agricultural cooperatives.

Although these basic conflicts within the leadership had always posed a potential threat to Party unity, it was not until Mao Tse-tung initiated the 'Great Leap Forwards' that this threat was made good. The first indication that the differences between the opposing factions could no longer be bridged was given by Marshal Peng Te-huai, who began to agitate against Mao even before the famous Lu Shan conference. In the group discussions which were convened to work out an agenda for the conference the Marshal maintained that the decision to establish people's communes was premature and that those who had taken it must have been suffering from a 'brainstorm'. Without even bothering to develop the collective farms to their full potential, he said, this group of high-ranking Party members had begun to experiment with people's communes, and in doing so had not only failed to make the necessary distinction between what was politically desirable and what was economically possible, but had also abused Mao Tse-tung's personal prestige. Finally, Peng warned his colleagues against indulging in personal recriminations, insisting that everybody was at fault, including Chairman Mao. In other words, Peng Te-huai was accusing Mao Tse-tung and his followers of having confused economics with politics, thus succumbing to the hot-headed and infantile attitudes of left-wing adventurism. He clearly considered that they were primarily responsible for the negative outcome of their venture, although he also blamed the remaining members of the leadership for not having prevented them from indulging in this act of folly. In an open letter addressed to Mao Tse-tung and dated July 14, 1959 Peng Te-huai returned to this subject, accusing the party of having persisted with its bourgeois adventurism in 1959 despite the disastrous experience of 1958 when 'communization' had been rushed through in under 3 months with the result that 30 million yuan had been literally poured down the drain, and the labours of the 90 million people who had erected improvised blast furnaces in school playgrounds, people's communes and sometimes even in courtyards had been completely wasted. In their enthusiasm, Peng said, the functionaries had confused fantasy with reality, announcing production figures which had no foundation in fact, and generally behaving as if the era of plenty had already dawned. In conclusion, Peng pointed out that the Party had alienated itself from the people and provoked dissatisfaction at all levels of society through the simplistic belief – one held by many Party members – that practical difficulties would automatically resolve themselves provided the Party's general political and ideological line was faithfully adhered to.

However, the criticism of Mao's policy at that time was not a one man crusade. Others were involved besides Peng Te-huai, for when he was deposed the whole of the army general staff and eight provincial Party secretaries were relieved of their posts, and – with the single exception of Lin Piao – the newly appointed members of the general staff were exposed as right wing deviationists in the course of the cultural revolution. But there were also indications that many other high-ranking Party members were dissatisfied with Mao's policy of rapid socialization in the period preceding the Lu Shan conference. For example, Po Yi-po, a candidate member of the Politburo, had collected incriminating evidence with which to oppose this policy, although he refrained from presenting it to the conference because by then proceedings had already been initiated against Peng Te-huai. Liu Shao-chi actually spoke out in Peng's defence during the campaign mounted against him. At that time the Party was threatened by internal strife which, as Mao Tse-tung pointed out in 1959, might easily have destroyed it. After 1959 the opposition to Mao's policies within the leadership grew stronger. In 1961 Liu claimed that 70 per cent of China's economic difficulties had been caused by the 'Great Leap Forwards', and warned that the peasants, the workers and the functionaries were all discontented. In the following year he argued that the responsibility for agricultural production should revert to the individual peasant families and that the peasants should be given more freedom. Chen Yün – a member of the Standing Committee of the Politburo and, as such, a top

Party member – also expressed anti-Maoist views in a speech which he delivered in 1961. He went even further than Liu, insisting that the Party should restore to the individual peasants, not only the responsibility for agricultural production, but also the ownership of the land. In addition, Chen criticized the Party's headquarters for attributing the disastrous effects of its own misguided policy to faulty administration at local level with the result that the village and district functionaries had become alienated from both the leadership and the rural population. At a conference held in 1962 Chen stated categorically that the production of food and textiles had declined to such an extent that it no longer met the needs of the population. According to Chen, millions of mou (1 mou = 670 square metres) of arable land had become barren, agricultural implements had been ruined through neglect, and it had proved impossible to raise pig production because of the shortage of pig feed. Chen also claimed that the Chinese economy was threatened by inflation because, due to the decline in industrial output, the peasants were buying no industrial products, so that instead of going into production, their money was flowing into the villages. Teng Hsiao-ping – the General Secretary of the Central Committee and a member of the Standing Committee of the Politburo – also attacked the 'Great Leap Forwards'. He spoke in favour of peasant 'individualism', and on occasions even tried to arrange the agenda for sessions of the Central Committee on his own initiative, thus by-passing Mao Tse-tung. Looking back on these events, it is quite clear that the Party's successive retreats from communization, and the various concessions which it made to the peasants, would never have been entertained but for the pressure brought to bear by the opposition forces within the leadership.

But it was not only the agricultural and industrial implications of the 'Great Leap Forwards' which incited opposition. Educational and cultural policy had also had to make a prodigious leap, and it too came in for criticism. The principal objective of Mao's educational policy during this period was to ensure that educational institutes of all kinds acquired their own factories and farms, and all factories and people's communes were provided with their own educational institutes. But between 1960 and 1962 this policy was gradually abandoned, and the schools and universities were allowed to revert to their original system, and to dispose of their industrial installations and farms. At the same time, a large number of schools which had failed to reach a certain educational standard were closed down. Most of these were new foundations set up by the communes, and it would seem from the available statistics that in 1962 the total number of schools attached to people's communes sank from 22,175 (with 2,300,000 pupils) to 3,715 (with 266,000 pupils). For those schools which remained open, and also for the universities, new regulations were introduced (60 for the universities, 50 for the secondary schools, and 40 for the primary schools) in order to standardize educational procedures and raise the general level of educational achievement. And so, once again, academic ability took precedence over ideological reliability; the talented pupils and students were encouraged, and the backward ones weeded out. As a result of this policy change children from bourgeois homes, who enjoyed the advantage of having been brought up in a cultured atmosphere, found it easier to gain university places. Between 1960 and 1962 many of the demands made by the teachers during the 'Hundred Flowers Campaign' were fulfilled. Thus, the Party Committees attached to the schools and universities became largely supervisory bodies; they were responsible for the implementation and administration of the new non-Maoist educational policy, but they were no longer entitled to determine either the curriculum or the teaching methods. This responsibility passed to the teachers themselves who, incidentally, were referred to during this period as 'working intellectuals serving the cause of socialism'.

In the spring of 1964 Mao Tse-tung tried to regain the initiative in the educational sphere by launching a large-scale building programme to provide new schools and universities at which the pupils and students would spend half of each day in their class-rooms and the other half performing manual work and acquiring practical knowledge. The real purpose of these new-style educational institutes was to inculcate proletarian attitudes and train a large body of young people prepared to renounce their selfish interests and become true adherents of socialism. But Liu Shao-chi contrived to thwart Mao's plans, doubtless with the knowledge of the competent departments of the Central Committee. Acting in collaboration with the Ministries of Education, University Education, Agriculture and Health, he convened five separate national conferences in order to establish and propagate his own educational theory, which allowed for the coexistence of two distinct educational systems: one based on normal schools, the other on the new 'work-schools' devised by Mao Tse-tung. At the same time, Liu insisted that, in both systems, the one quality that must be encouraged at all costs was diligence, which should take precedence over proletarian education. Thus, according to Liu, the heart and soul of education was, not politics, but knowledge, both theoretical and practical. Clearly, young people educated along such lines would never become true adherents of socialism in the sense envisaged by Mao. On the contrary, they would be highly skilled technocrats who would seek to develop the country in accordance with purely objective criteria which would necessarily preclude sudden bursts of socialization. And in Mao's view that was simply a recipe for revisionism.

Maoism and 'Liuism'

I have already analysed some of the differences between Mao Tse-tung and Liu Shao-chi in the preceding section. We have seen that where Liu stressed the importance of knowledge in education, Mao was more concerned with the development of a revolutionary attitude, and that, as far as industry and agriculture were concerned, Liu favoured steady growth whilst Mao chose to proceed by a series of sudden bursts. Liu persisted in his opposition even after Mao had mounted his counterattack on the 'revisionists', which culminated in the cultural revolution. At the end of 1963 Liu Shao-chi's wife went to live in one of the people's communes in order to improve its working methods and make it a more efficient organization than Mao's own model commune. Her commune received a special subsidy so that it could invest in mechanization and modern equipment, thus increasing production and improving the peasants' working conditions. The whole object of this exercise was to provide tangible proof that Liu's agricultural policy – which was based on the need for mechanization and better working conditions – was the right policy for China. But Liu was not given time to prove his point, for Mao Tse-tung cut his experiment short by launching the cultural revolution.

In addition to education, industry and agriculture Liu also

dealt with a wide range of other subjects, which he analysed in considerable detail. Thus, 'Liuism' – which provided the general guide lines of 'revisionist' policy and exerted considerable influence in the country at large – was a comprehensive and broadly-based doctrine. Of all the 'poisonous plants' cultivated by Liu Shao-chi, by far the most objectionable from the Maoist point of view was his pamphlet *How to Become a Good Communist*. This pamphlet was written in 1939, and in 1942 was one of the documents used by the party as a yardstick for mapping out its reform programme and, more particularly, for testing the quality of its cadres. By 1962 20 million copies of Liu's article had been printed. This compares very favourably with the figure for *The Selected Works of Mao Tse-tung*, which was only 11 million in 1966. In the revised edition of 1962 Liu accused Mao of having set himself up as the Chinese equivalent of Marx and Engels, of behaving towards his Party as if he were a Lenin or a Stalin, and of shamelessly demanding that Party members should treat him as their 'leader' and make a public display of their loyalty and enthusiasm. He also pilloried the 'left wing opportunists' – Mao and his followers – for having branded a group of military men, including the Minister of Defence Marshal Peng Te-huai, and a number of Party secretaries as 'right wing opportunists' in 1959:

'It is perfectly clear that the "left wing" opportunists adopted a misguided attitude to the question of conflicts within the Party. In the opinion of these people – who appear to have been quite mad – concord within the Party could serve no useful purpose, not even if it was based on perfect agreement over fundamental principles. And so, even when there were no basic differences between Party members, they wantonly set out in search of adversaries, branded a number of their colleagues as "opportunists", and set them up as "clay pigeons" so that they could be shot down in an inner-Party conflict. By staging a bogus conflict, and shooting down these clay pigeons, they thought they were initiating a transcendental process that would enable the Party to continue its development, and contribute to the victory of the proletariat in its revolutionary struggle. They thought that . . . the only way of showing themselves to be true "Bolshevists" was by starting an inner-Party conflict.'[9]

It is not surprising that Liu should have censured the left wing opportunists for having disrupted, and perhaps even destroyed, the unity of the Party, for he believed that synthesis was the true basis of dialectics. (Mao, of course, thought of dialectics in terms of conflict.) The many un-Maoist ideas advanced by Liu – e.g. conceptions such as the 'compliant tool', the 'concurrence between personal and communal interests', 'class concord' and the 'Party of the whole people' – all ultimately derived from this synthetist philosophy. Liu's conception of the 'compliant tool' is based on the view that allegiance to Party discipline is the most important of all communist principles. This view, which presupposes that every individual will obey his superiors and respect the will of the majority, is of course completely in line with the doctrine of 'democratic centralism', and would normally have met with Mao Tse-tung's approval. In fact, this was incorporated into the 'Little Red Book', which was conceived as a means of mass education. But after the introduction of the 'Great Leap Forwards' the revisionists at Party headquarters appear to have been in the majority, which meant that Mao and his followers were unable to endorse the idea of majority rule. Consequently, they argued that it was incumbent on the individual to obey his superiors only if their directives were *correct*, and in support of their thesis they pointed to the fact that Lenin had refused to become the 'prisoner of the majority', and had not hesitated to 'oppose everybody'. This argument was extremely convenient, for it justified Mao's opposition both at home and abroad, i.e. to the majority view within his own Party and to the Soviet view within the international communist camp.

A further difference between Liu and Mao is to be found in their respective attitudes to the individual. For Mao personal and communal interests are antithetical. He considers that the proletarian revolutionary must banish all thought of personal advantage and subordinate himself completely to the interests of the community. By contrast, Liu considered – like Hu Feng – that the interests of the community were simply the sum total of the interests of all the individuals in that community and that, consequently, the one could not exist without the other. From this it followed that if the Party studied the interests of the individual, then this too would be of benefit to the community.

Considered in these terms, the 'interests of the community' ceases to be a purely abstract conception. Incidentally, this synthetist theory of Liu's helps to explain the policies which he advocated in the 1960's. Reformulated in concrete terms, it means that in his work the individual has to put aside his personal interests and concentrate on the common good. However, it does not follow from this that he is to deny himself entirely. For if he serves the community, then as a member of the community he too will benefit. Moreover, the community will take note of his achievements and his unselfishness, and will reward him by appointing him to important posts. Thus, personal and communal interests enter into a reciprocating relationship which is – quite literally – of benefit to one and all. The psychological conflict identified by the Maoists becomes superfluous so that nobody has to be boiled 'three times in pure water, three times in salt water, and three times in blood serum'. But as far as the Maoists were concerned, Liu's theory was simply a sophisticated form of egoism which had to be destroyed.

This theory of Liu's raised the question of inter-class relationships. In other words, which classes were to be regarded as part of the community, and which were to be excluded? After the collectivization of agriculture and the socialization of industry had been completed in 1957 Liu Shao-chi considered that the basic conflicts between the different classes had been resolved. He argued that the estate owners and capitalists had been eliminated *as a class* and that, consequently, enemies of the people no longer existed on any significant scale. The former capitalists, he said, had become 'new-style' capitalists, and it was possible, therefore, to resolve any conflicts which arose between them and the workers in a peaceful manner. But although Mao Tse-tung also stated in 1957 that the conflicts between the capitalists and the workers were largely 'internal', i.e. local affairs which posed no threat to the national leadership, he was still not prepared to accept the capitalists as equal members of society. On the contrary, he insisted that they must first be criticized and re-educated. It was Liu who promised the capitalists that if they would teach the functionaries all they knew, he would arrange for them to be reclassified as leftists at the end of two years. Liu expounded his conciliatory theory of the class war in at least six provinces with the result that, in those provinces, capitalists were frequently employed as factory directors, business managers, etc. In Shanghai alone 15,000 senior positions of this kind were given to capitalists, who will almost certainly have infected a large number of Party functionaries with unrevolutionary 'economist' ideas.

But the influence exerted by Liu's conception of a conflict-free society was not restricted to industry and trade. It also had a considerable impact on the mass media, due primarily to three speeches which Liu delivered before an audience of journalists in 1956.[10] In these speeches he criticized the Chinese newspapers for their subjective and biased coverage of both foreign and home affairs, insisting that they should tell the 'truth', not only about western imperialism, but also about Chinese socialist society. Liu then called for the liberalization of the press, whereupon Teng To, the chief editor of the Peking *People's Daily*, Wu Leng-Hsi, the director of the New China News Agency, and Mai Yi, the director of the Department for Radio Administration, tried to reorganize the mass media – which up till then had been instruments of proletarian, i.e. Party, propaganda – and turn them into a 'communal weapon' that would procure a voice for the whole of society. In the anti-rightist campaign of 1957 the only news publication to be exposed was the Shanghai *Wenhui Bao*, and this happened only because Mao Tse-tung himself had written a leading article for the Peking *People's Daily*, in which he called upon the people to criticize this publication. In 1961 Liu again sought to promote the liberalization of the news media, on this occasion by instructing the *People's Daily* that it should not confine itself to reporting the 'present struggle' but should also comment on other aspects of Chinese society which had nothing to do with the 'present struggle'. Shortly afterwards, the *People's Daily* started a column in which it criticized Party policy and proposed ways of improving it. Subsequently, the radio stations also joined the fray by broadcasting historical stories and other 'information programmes', and many local newspapers followed suit by starting 'information columns' in which they indirectly ridiculed or criticized Mao's policies. In 1964, the conflict conducted in the mass media between the Maoists and the Liuists was greatly intensified, and became much more open. At that time Liu recommended that the media should not pay undue attention to the 'thoughts of Mao Tse-tung' on the grounds that this might be dangerous. And so the newspapers

cut Maoist propaganda back to a minimum, and continued to
do so right up to the cultural revolution.

Revolutionary Fervour and Officialism

It would not be true to say that the dissension within the leadership was directly responsible for undermining the Party's
revolutionary fervour and initiating the never-ending growth of
officialism. What is true, however, is that Liuism was undoubtedly conducive to bureaucratic methods. Revolutionary
fervour and officialism are mutually exclusive. Before 1949,
when the People's Liberation Army was still fighting the
Kuomintang, revolutionary fervour had been the order of the
day. But once the People's Republic had been established, an
administrative infrastructure had to be created in order to
govern the country; and this meant that officialism was bound
to follow, if only because China is such a vast territory. It is,
of course, no accident that for thousands of years successive
Chinese administrations have been famous for their bureaucratic procedures.

And so, once it had come to power, the Chinese Communist
Party was obliged to install a bureaucratic administration in
order to govern the country and implement the directives
issued by the leadership. The fact that the Party retained the
services of so many former Kuomintang officials is proof enough
that the new administrative system really was bureaucratic,
although if further proof is needed, it is to be found in the fact
that the leadership was obliged to mount a nationwide campaign (the 'Anti-Three Evils' movement) shortly after the
proclamation of the People's Republic in order to counter the
excessive bureaucracy of its functionaries. A bureaucracy presupposes a strict hierarchy, and it is this hierarchy which determines both the status and the salaries of its members. By 1957
the hierarchical principle was so firmly established in the Chinese
administration that ritualistic symbols had been evolved in
order to give visible expression to differences of status. Thus,
the functionaries in the higher grades sat in armchairs and had
large calendars, the functionaries in the middle grades sat on
wicker chairs and had medium-sized calendars, and those in the
lowest grades sat on wooden chairs and had small calendars.
There were at least 24 different grades in the rural administra-

tive service, and the functionaries in those grades received widely differing salaries. For example, grade 6 functionaries were paid ten times as much as their colleagues in grade 24. It goes without saying that, far from engendering revolutionary fervour, a system of this kind, in which status, power and salary all depended on promotion, was calculated to attract career-minded young men. And since Party members stood a far better chance of promotion, it was inevitable that a large number of those careerists should have wormed their way into the Party. The fact that the vast majority of Party members joined *after* the liberation was no accident. Functionaries intent on promotion had to be very careful to behave in a politically acceptable manner at all times. When they first joined the state service they had to submit a *curriculum vitae*, in which they were required to state their own class origin and that of their relatives and friends, and give a brief account of their ideological development. Clearly, these things were important. But they were not the only consideration. For once a year every functionary had to examine his mental attitudes, his statements and his actions, and submit a written assessment of his behaviour to his colleagues and superiors. They then discussed and criticized his self-assessment before placing it, together with their comments, in his personal file. And these annual reports were a further factor in determining career prospects. But it was also very important for a functionary who was seeking promotion to gain the approval of his immediate superior, for his application could not go forwards unless it was recommended by this superior. However, he could not afford to indulge in overt acts of flattery, since this would offend his colleagues, who would only have to wait for the next anti-rightist compaign in order to accuse him of trying to further his career by means of sycophancy. Consequently, the only safe way for a young functionary to set about obtaining promotion was by sharing the views held by his superior and implementing his directives promptly and efficiently.

This kind of attitude was prompted in the first instance by the bureaucratic structure of the Chinese administration. But it was reinforced by the conceptions of Liu Shao-chi, who actively encouraged the state and Party functionaries to seek promotion, and who once drew a revealing parallel between joining the Communist Party and passing the government service entry examination in imperial China. It was not that Liu did not expect the individual functionary to serve the Party. He did. But he also offered him the prospect of material rewards. If he put his personal interests aside and worked selflessly for the Party, he would find that his personal interests would also receive their due. This – as we have already seen – was the crux of Liu's theory. But what this meant in practical terms was that every functionary had to support his superiors willy nilly, and in the first half of the 1960's the majority of high and middle grade functionaries were non-Maoists who wanted to consolidate China's economic position, and so were opposed to revolutionary tactics. This was why Mao's supporters attacked what they called the 'independent kingdoms' within the Party during the cultural revolution. For if the non-Maoist functionaries who held senior positions in the Party received the unswerving allegiance of their subordinates, their departments would no longer be subject to Mao's authority. They would indeed be independent kingdoms.

But there was another side to Chinese bureaucracy which militated against Liu Shao-chi. The fact of the matter was that the administrative system created considerable discontent, especially amongst the younger Party members, who held the lowest posts. A few years after the proclamation of the People's Republic the chances of promotion were quite good because the former Kuomintang officials were weeded out and their posts were given to new and politically more reliable people. But, almost invariably, the senior posts went to the members of the old guard, who received preferential treatment on account of their long years of service. This caused bad blood between these older men, who had first hand experience of the revolutionary process, and their younger colleagues, whose strength lay in their educational qualifications. Not unnaturally, the senior functionaries took good care to safeguard their positions, and used their authority to prevent the younger functionaries from penetrating the higher echelons of the administration. These younger men were in much the same position as the less talented secondary school pupils, who were denied further education under the terms of Liu's educational policy and so lost their chance of a decent career; and, like them, they were discontented with their lot. A further consideration which militated against the younger functionaries was the fact that the children and relatives of long serving Party members (all Party members were placed in one of four categories depending on their length of service) [11] were more likely to be selected for promotion, partly because their political background was impeccable, and partly because the leadership wanted to remain on good terms with the senior functionaries to whom they were related. The net result of this state of affairs was that, when he came to launch the cultural revolution, Mao Tse-tung was able to call on the services of a vast army of discontented pupils, students, Party members and functionaries.

PART II

Contradictions in Chinese Society
during the Cultural Revolution

CHAPTER V
THE YOUNG REBELS

'In the final analysis, all Marxist truths can be reduced to a single proposition: Rebellion is justified . . . In accordance with this basic principle the people rise, offer resistance, fight, and construct a socialist system.'

MAO TSE-TUNG

The proletarian cultural revolution was officially launched in November 1965 when Yao Wen-yüan, who is said to have acted at the instigation of Mao Tse-tung, attacked Wu Han, the deputy mayor of Peking and the author of the highly successful historical drama *Hai Jui is Relieved of his Post*. Yao criticized Wu Han for urging the people to learn from the 'just' official Hai Jui, and for propagating the idea that the land should be restored to the peasants. This was the first of a series of attacks on Wu Han, which subsequently developed into a general campaign against various publicists and academicians who shared his views. For a while it was not clear to the outside observer what the real object of this campaign was. But all doubts were removed when, on May 8, 1966, the army newspaper accused the editors of the Peking *Daily News*, the Peking *Evening News* and the magazine *Front* of propagating revisionist ideas and trying to bring about the restoration of capitalism. All three of these publications were organs of the Party Committee for the city of Peking, whose members included Wu Han and his 'accomplices' Teng To and Liao Mo-sha, the trio responsible for the celebrated series 'Notes from the Three-Family Village'. Up till then these 'renegades' had enjoyed the protection of Peng Chen, the No 5 in the Party hierarchy and secretary of the Peking Party Committee. It came as no surprise, therefore, when the *RMRB* reported at the beginning of June, 1966, that the whole of the Peking Party Committee had been stripped of its powers and 'reorganized'. This was the first phase of the cultural revolution.

But, of course, it was not the last. The cultural revolution was not mounted simply in order to depose Peng Chen, and bring the Peking Party Committee into line. It was a far more ambitious undertaking than that. What Mao was aiming at was a total purge of the Party superstructure. This was already apparent during the initial campaign against the members of the Peking Party Committee who were criticized, not for specific actions, but for their un-Maoist attitudes. Such attitudes were widespread in the spheres of education and the arts, both of which featured prominently in the cultural revolution. Thus, at the beginning of June 1966, the regional propaganda departments, the newspapers and the Party Committees attached to the Chinese universities, technical colleges and secondary schools were also engulfed by the great wave of purges. At the same time, the teaching staff were stripped of their authority, leaving the pupils and students free to indulge in political activities. Many of them, especially those who felt hard done by, joined the revolution. The most active of all were the secondary school pupils with acceptable proletarian backgrounds who either expected to be, or had already been, refused university places because they lacked the necessary academic qualifications. It was no accident that the second phase of the cultural revolution was dominated by the youth of China.

1. The Role of the Communist Youth League

It is common knowledge that Chinese youth was represented in the cultural revolution by newly-formed organizations such as the Red Guards. On the face of it, this seems surprising, for one would have expected the Communist Youth League to have played a dominant role. The truth of the matter is that the League leaders offered their services, only to have them rejected by the Maoists because, like the Party itself, the League had been infiltrated by non-Maoist elements. It will be remembered that in the course of the cultural revolution the Party functionaries were accused of 'waving the red flag in order to oppose it'. So too were the League functionaries. As far as the League was concerned, certainly, there was some substance in this charge, for in the two years preceding the cultural revolution it was much easier for dissident elements to join the League, due partly to the relaxation of the entry regulations, and partly to a change of policy with regard to selection. In 1964 it was decided that new applicants needed only one recommendation from a League member where previously they had needed two, and in 1965 the League announced that in future it proposed to recruit a much larger number of children from bourgeois homes because it considered that by the time they were old enough to join the League these children would have shaken off their childhood influences. Just one month before the start of the cultural revolution this announcement was repeated. And it appears to have achieved its object, for in 1965 no less than 8·5 million young people joined the Communist Youth League. In certain parts of the country, it is true, the 1965 intake was still predominantly proletarian. Thus, in the provinces of Szechuan, Liaonin and Kansu, and in the city of Shanghai 80 per cent of the new recruits were said to come from worker or peasant families. But in other provinces the percentage of working class recruits was much lower, for at the beginning of 1966 the League pointed with pride to the fact that many members had been recruited from the ranks of the old capitalist class. These members, it was claimed, had adopted a new ideological attitude, and were determined to carry the revolution to a successful conclusion.

This was one of the reasons why the Maoist leadership mistrusted the Communist Youth League. But there were other reasons as well. For example, after adopting the 'thoughts of Mao Tse-tung' as the ideological basis of its new statutes at the League's annual conference in 1964, the League leaders did not call upon the assembled delegates to endorse them by public acclamation, although they adopted this procedure in respect of the Party's general policy of socialist development (which embraced the 'Great Leap Forwards', the provision of people's communes, and the new programme of scientific experimentation). Moreover, although the League's first secretary, Hu Yao-pan, called upon the membership to learn from China's military leaders, when he came to enumerate those heroes, he omitted to mention Lei Feng, who had been identified by Mao Tse-tung as the ideal hero. Hu also endorsed the revisionist educational policy formulated by Liu Shao-chi, insisting that pupils and students must be given adequate leisure time in which to relax, and must also be allowed to discuss non-political subjects with one another. In 1965 the Central Committee of the Communist Youth League was forced to convene a plenary session in order to pass a resolution authorizing the mobilization of its members so as to boost agricultural production. This flatly contradicted Liu's educational policy, which was then in force, and for the next six months the League leaders contrived to suppress the resolution. Moreover, when the resolution was finally published at the end of this period, the leaders were at pains to point out that the League had always contributed to the production programme. They conceded that mistakes had been made in the past but only in relatively unimportant matters, and they insisted that the League's general policy had always been correct. Clearly, the conflict between the Youth League and the Maoist leadership was not a trivial one. If it had been the League would not have put up such a stout defence. But there was a second incident in 1965 which is even more revealing. In August of that year the propaganda department of the Communist Youth League decided to explain the implications of its statutes in a series of 11 articles in the magazine *Chinese Youth*. But only eight of these articles were published, the last of the eight appearing in November 1965, which also brought the first overt moves in the cultural revolution. The reason why the remaining three articles failed to appear was not revealed until June 1966, when it transpired that, following the 'reorganization' of the Party Committee in Peking, the Peking Committee of the Youth League had also been overthrown. Its chief crime was its adamant refusal to implement any new directives which contravened its own statutes. Consequently, it was not prepared to recommend to its members that they should 'study and apply the works of Mao Tse-tung as a matter of vital concern', which at that time was tantamount to high treason.

In 1966 the Youth League made a sudden change of course, and from then onwards gave its wholehearted support to the new Maoist measures. It refused to accept any more members from non-proletarian homes, and did its utmost to encourage the study and implementation of the thoughts of Chairman Mao. It reaffirmed its loyalty to the Party, endorsed the Party's directive to suspend the enrolment of new university students for a period of six months, and acclaimed the secondary school pupils who were playing an active part in the cultural revolution. But it was all in vain. When the Red Guards took to the streets in August 1966, the Communist Youth League and its two national organs – the newspaper *China's Youth* and the Magazine *Chinese Youth* – disappeared from the scene.

2. The Origin and Development of the Red Guards

We have already seen that various new youth organizations were formed during the cultural revolution in China. Of these the most active by far was the organization of the Red Guards, whose revolutionary deeds brought them international renown and ensured them the full backing of Mao Tse-tung and the army, thus enabling them to dominate the political and social scene in the second half of 1966. The founder members of this organization are believed to have been secondary school pupils, whose parents were either workers, peasants or smallholders, revolutionary functionaries or soldiers. Precisely when the organization was founded has yet to be established, but it is generally thought that pupils at the secondary school affiliated to the Chinghua University in Peking formed the first cell.[1] It is also thought that in June or July of 1966 there were still no more than a few dozen Red Guards, which would be consistent with the – highly plausible – view that large scale juvenile participation in the cultural revolution came about as a direct result of the publication in the Peking *People's Daily* on June 18, 1966, of the resolution passed by the Central Committe[2] and ratified by the Council of State, which stipulated that all university entrance examinations should be postponed for a period of six months to ensure that 'the revolutionary fervour of the leftist students does not cool off'. The Central Committee also decided that in future far less significance would be attached to end of term reports, and that the new educational system would be determined by the mass line of the Party, which meant that it would be concerned with the inculcation of proletarian attitudes. This gave new heart to the leftist pupils and students, for it assured them of the support of the Central Committee the most powerful body in the Party. It also served as a signal to those whose sympathies were not with the left, to swim with the stream of the cultural revolution if they were not to be swept away by it.

The leftist members of the younger generation, i.e. those with proletarian class affiliations, felt that they had been cheated under the old 'bourgeois' educational system. In theory, they were the leaders of the people's dictatorship, but in practice they had been effectively prevented from assuming their dominant position by the emphasis placed on examinations and end of term reports. Because they had tended to lag behind their bourgeois contemporaries in terms of academic achievement, the proletarian pupils at Chinese secondary schools had been systematically excluded from the institutes of higher education. Instead of going to university, they were almost invariably directed into industry or agriculture as 'educated workers and peasants'. Such young people had every reason to support the cultural revolution. They had nothing to lose and a great deal to gain.

The principal theatre of the class war over the future development of education was Peking. This is hardly surprising, for it was there that the first moves in the cultural revolution were made. The central figure in this initial phase was Peng Chen, who was protecting the authors of the 'Three Family Village' and was a real thorn in the flesh of the Maoist leadership. Peng Chen had considerable power, for not only was he Mayor of Peking and First Secretary of the Peking Party Committee, he was also a member of the Politburo and of the Secretariat of the Central Committee. Most important of all, however, he was head of the five man group set up by the Central Committee to implement the cultural revolution. He was, therefore, ideally placed to sabotage this enterprise, and sought to do so by reducing it to an 'academic discussion' with his 'February theses of the five man group for the [implementation of the] cultural revolution'.[2] Peng also supported the slogan 'All are Equal in the Face of Truth', and by doing so effectively denied the Maoist contention that 'proletarian' truth takes precedence over all other truths. By these means he sought to protect his bourgeois associates from leftist criticism. But in May 1966 the Central Committee announced that Peng's 'February theses' – which, it was said, he had formulated without the knowledge of the other members of the five man group – were inimical to the proletariat and, consequently, invalid. Peng was the first high-ranking functionary to be deposed. After his elimination the five man group was reorganized, and further measures were planned against the numerous 'anti-socialist, capitalist agents' in the 'Central Committee, the different Party and government headquarters departments, the provinces, the towns and the autonomous areas'.[3] This new development naturally encouraged the leftist pupils and students in Peking to seek to implement the cultural revolution in their schools and universities even more rigorously, and to press for the abolition of school reports and examinations, which were the cornerstone of the existing educational system. It was no accident that the cultural revolution should have found its principal outlet in the educational sphere following the Central Committee's repudiation of Peng Chen in May 1966.[4] Within a matter of weeks a crisis point was reached, and in early June Liu Shao-chi was obliged to send work groups to numerous schools and universities to take control of the local revolutionary movements, and so render them harmless. The activities of one such group, which went to the Chinghua University in Peking, have been widely reported. It seems that for a period of two months – from the beginning of June to the beginning of August 1966 – the leftish students at this university continued to attack their revisionist functionaries until they were finally forced to yield by Liu's work group, which then rehabilitated the functionaries and placed them back in the saddle. Thus, by the time the work group left the Chinghua University, both the provisional committee set up to control the cultural revolution and the provisional headquarters of the Red Guards were in the hands of the revisionists. But although this undoubtedly constituted a serious setback for the young rebels, they continued to fight back.

The Central Committee's resolution postponing all university entrance examinations was preceded by considerable agitation on the part of proletarian secondary school leavers whose career prospects had been prejudiced by the workings of the non-Maoist educational system. In the hope of improving their prospects, a number of these pupils wrote letters to the Central Committee and to Chairman Mao, in which they expressed their indignation over the existing educational system and proposed an alternative. These rebels rejected the revisionist tenet which stipulated that both the educational and the employment opportunities offered to secondary school pupils should be determined by merit. They also insisted that school reports should no longer play any part in deciding which pupils were to be accepted for university training. Instead, they wanted all secondary school leavers to go straight from school into industry, agriculture or the army, so that they could be 'hardened and educated in the tempests of the three revolutionary movements [the class war, the battle for production, and the campaign for scientific development]'. Subsequently, they wanted the party to 'select the best of its splendid proletarian sons and daughters . . . and send them to university'.[5] Meanwhile, until such a system could be introduced these rebellious pupils demanded that all university places should be reserved for secondary school leavers with *firm proletarian views* who had played an active part in the cultural revolution. But the bourgeois children also wanted to go to university, and faced with the postponement of the entrance examinations and the probable introduction of new selection procedures for university applicants, many of them decided that the time had come to join the ranks of the activists and help promote the cultural revolution. This undoubtedly contributed to the rapid growth of the Red Guards. As early as June, 1966, the Red Guards at the secondary school attached to the Chinghua University formulated the slogan: 'Rebellion is the kernel of Mao Tse-tung's doctrine!' They complained that ever since the proclamation of the People's Republic, revisionism had been the dominant force in China's schools, and they attacked all those revisionists who, having first actively opposed the young leftist rebels, had now started a whispering campaign against the Red Guards, accusing them of prejudice, arrogance and brutality. The Red Guards in Peking also anonunced their intention of suppressing 'rightist rebellion' without mercy. From then onwards they became much more active, and soon acquired considerable prestige. It is said that on July 29, 1966, Mao Tse-tung gave his blessing to a conference convened by different groups of Red Guards and that at the beginning of August representatives of these groups were invited to sit in on a plenary session of the Central Committee, at which the general guide-lines for the future conduct of the cultural revolution were laid down. But the 'heroic' Red Guards had their really great moment when they appeared in their tens of thousands at a mass meeting on August 18. Their representatives were invited on to the rostrum to review the march past side by side with the Party leaders, and were allowed to hold speeches in which they undertook to implement the cultural revolution with a will of iron. But the most significant aspect of this mass meeting was that Mao Tse-tung accepted the offer of a red armband, thus becoming Supreme Commander of the Red Guards.[6] From then onwards these young rebels thought of themselves as Mao's soldiers and, as they themselves said, with such a commander they had 'nothing to fear'. Immediately after this mass meeting the Red Guards stepped up their revolutionary activities. From August 20 onwards they walked the streets of Peking *en masse*, distributing leaflets, posting wall newspapers, and holding meetings at which their members made public speeches. They gave streets, schools and shops new revolutionary names, and made it their business to rid the nation of unseemly hair styles (men's shoulder length cuts, women's permanent waves, 'beehives', etc). They also took exception to blue jeans and tightfitting trousers, various Hong-kong fashions, and indecent photographs and magazines.[7] The 'iron brooms' wielded by the Red Guards were forced into every dark corner of Chinese society and swept away everything that was remotely connected with the past. In the schools and universities the Red Guards took the bourgeois pupils and students, teachers and professors, firmly to task; they seized high-ranking Party Members, dressed them up as clowns, and forced them to parade through the city and make public confession of their crimes; they destroyed old works of art, and ransacked private dwellings in search of old books, foreign currency, gold and silver, and weapons; and they had clashes – many of them bloody – with Party functionaries, workers, peasants, and other groups of young people. By and large, however, the discipline of the Red Guards was remarkably good, for in the whole of this vast movement, in which millions of people were involved, there were no really serious large scale disturbances. Moreover, the Red Guards performed countless good deeds, helping the workers and peasants, and giving support to the old and infirm.

The mass meeting of August 18, 1966, was not the first occasion on which the young people of China had demonstrated their *wanderlust*. Two days before, another mass meeting had taken place in Peking, and had been attended by pupils and students from all parts of the country. This sudden urge to travel was a turning point in the cultural revolution. From then onwards the Red Guards became known, not only for their rebellious spirit, but also for their mobility, which enabled them to exploit their rebelliousness to the full. At that time all young people were allowed to use public transport free of charge, and were also entitled to free food and board wherever they went. As a result, millions of pupils and students flocked to Peking or travelled the country, rebelling against the authorities and discussing their revolutionary experiences. They went into the factories and people's communes to eliminate malpractices, and in doing so greatly disrupted production. They attacked Party members in positions of authority quite indiscriminately, i.e. without first trying to assess them by reference to the four categories established by the leadership (good – fairly good – seriously at fault – secretly revisionist).[8] In short, they went much further than Mao and his followers had intended, partly because they were fired with enthusiasm for the revolutionary cause, and partly because power had gone to their heads. Although Mao Tse-tung had specifically stipulated that the Red Guards were to join forces with the left in order to win over the centre and so isolate the extreme right, this crucial tactical directive was ignored. Indeed, it was almost as if the left was intent on alienating the centre and driving it into the arms of the extreme right, thus strengthening this 5 per cent minority instead of paving the way for its elimination. Further difficulties were posed by the *wanderlust* evinced by Chinese youth, for this placed a heavy strain on the railways, which were China's principal means of transportation. According to a Red Guard who fled the country after the cultural revolution, the travel concessions granted to youth organizations in the months of August and September alone swallowed up 20 per cent of the annual transport budget. For all these reasons it became necessary to restrict the revolutionary activities of Chinese youth, and as a first step in this direction the leadership sought to bring the Red Guard units under centralized control, for at that time the individual units in the various towns operated quite independently of one another. In February 1967 an example was set in Peking, where the leaders of the three major factions within the Red Guards set up a 'Congress of Red Guards at Universities and Technical Colleges', which was followed shortly afterwards by a 'Congress of Red Guards at Secondary Schools'. But these alliances could not be effective whilst the Red Guards in individual units, many of which owed no allegiance to any of the three major factions, continued to feud amongst themselves. The plain fact was that the Red Guards in different, and sometimes even in the same, schools were hopelessly divided. Meanwhile, the Party leaders tried to get the pupils and students to return to their schools or universities, and sent out army work groups to help resolve their differences and build up a system of alliances. At the same time, they made a tactical change in their conduct of the cultural revolution, and began calling upon the pupils and students to purge their own 'souls' of bourgeois attitudes in the hope that this would put an end to their feuds.

3. Contradictions and Conflicts

The first Red Guards were the children of junior functionaries,[9] who had seized on the cultural revolution as a heaven-sent opportunity of eliminating their rivals, the 'fine young gentlemen' from bourgeois homes who had been favoured by the revisionist educational system and so had obtained all the best academic and professional positions. In theory, the ultra-leftist pupils and students conceded the possibility of children from former bourgeois homes rejecting their parents' ideological views and joining the proletariat. In practice, however, this possibility was denied to them, for the ultra-leftists maintained that these bourgeois children lacked the ideological training that was needed if they were to adopt a genuinely proletarian outlook. But once the Red Guard movement had fired the imagination of Chinese youth – following the mass meeting of August 18, 1966 – the young bourgeois also wanted to join in. Many, who had been refused membership of their local units, banded together to form their own independent units. Thus, the stage was set for conflict. By September 1966 violent disputes were being waged over the question of class affiliations between the so-called 'five red' or proletarian Red Guards (the children of workers, peasants, revolutionary soldiers, martyrs and functionaries) and the 'five black' or bourgeois Red Guards (the children of estate owners, kulaks, anti-revolutionaries, bad elements and rightists). The proletarians forbade the bourgeois to come to Peking on a 'tour of inspection', and called for an enquiry into the class affiliations of all Red Guards so that those in the 'black' categories could be thrown out of the organization. Meanwhile, they asked that these bourgeois Red Guards should be made to pay for their own journeys, accommodation and food, and should be banished from Peking. But the bourgeois units came to Peking. It was imperative for them that they should do so, because by taking an active part in the cultural revolution they would be able to demonstrate their ideological fitness, and so obtain their school leaving certificates. The fact that both the further education and the future employment of these young people depended on their participation in the cultural revolution casts an interesting light on the 'opportunist' outlook of both the bourgeois and the proletarian Red Guards. The proletarians were prepared to go to any lengths to keep the bourgeois out of the new movement, which would have effectively eliminated them as professional rivals, whilst the bourgeois, for their part, were prepared to engage in revolutionary activities of the most extreme kind in order to safeguard their university and career prospects. The conflict between these two opposing factions was so bitter that in the Shanghai sports organization alone no less than five Red Guards corps were attacked and subsequently disbanded.

But quite apart from these inter-class conflicts, there was also considerable animosity between the different units of the proletarian Red Guards. Back in August 1966 an article in a wall newspaper drew attention to the indifference of many young proletarians, who had failed to play an active part in the cultural revolution and were simply waiting for everything to be done for them. Some young proletarians openly admitted that they had no intention of participating. And as the revolution gathered momentum the conflicts within the proletarian faction became more pronounced. By October 1966 five cardinal sins had been identified: (1) people were not prepared to do anything which might prejudice their future careers; (2) people were loath to be the first to join the revolution because they feared the latecomers would get better positions; (3) people tried to avoid criticizing bourgeois functionaries lest this should undermine party solidarity and cause the person concerned to lose face; (4) people were loath to act for fear of committing errors and laying themselves open to criticism; (5) people did not understand the tactics that were being employed in the cultural revolution, and some did not even understand its aims.

It was not long before the 'theory of descent' advanced by the original Red Guards was rejected by the leadership as a reactionary doctrine. This meant, in effect, that the young ultra-leftist revolutionaries had lost their battle against the bourgeois pupils and students, although at that particular juncture – January 1967 – they had not yet been identified by the leadership as the authors of this theory. Commenting on this development, the *People's Daily* and the *Red Flag* pointed out that after rightly opposing the discrimination practised against the 'five red' categories of the Red Guards, a small group of 'biased' and 'naïve' ultra-leftists had then gone to the other extreme. It was also suggested in these publications that both the ultra-leftists (who had evolved this theory) and the pupils and students in the 'five red' categories (who had been misled by it) had not been properly educated and needed 'gentle' correction. Subsequently, the ultra-leftist 'theory of family descent' was exploited by the bourgeois reactionaries in an attempt to sow discord in their opponents' ranks. Then, in March 1967, Chou En-lai publicly identified the young ultra-leftist revolutionaries as the authors and propagators of this false theory and called upon the Red Guards to oppose and criticize them.

The Red Guards were the pioneers of the cultural revolution and, as such, the precursors of the cultural revolutionaries proper. But once they had exposed the anti-Maoist elements at Party headquarters and in the various Party departments in 1966, they had fulfilled their political role. However, they remained as ardent as ever, especially the leftists, and it became apparent that their revolutionary fervour would pose a problem. After the Party leaders identified by Mao Tse-tung as enemies of the people had been deposed, a number of the Red Guards turned their attention to the Committee for the Cultural Revolution attached to the Central Committee,[10] in which Chiang Ching, Mao Tse-tung's wife, was the senior Party representative. With this, the revolutionary fervour of Chinese youth became introverted, and the members of the Red Guard movement were exhorted by the leadership to carry out a 'campaign for the rectification of working methods' in their own ranks. This preoccupation with internal matters which set in following the elimination of the class enemy, i.e. the bourgeois revisionists, led to the emergence of numerous conflicts in the movement at the beginning of 1967. The situation was greatly aggravated by the lack of discipline and absence of any sense of solidarity. In many units things were so bad that the members were rendered incapable of concerted action. But if anarchy was the greatest problem facing the Red Guards at that time, the second greatest was undoubtedly a need for personal recognition. Many Red Guards were quite prepared to attack the 'revolutionary Party leaders' if by doing so they would be acclaimed as heroes. This motivation also made itself felt at a group level, and quickly led to a situation in which different units of the Red Guards engaged in bitter rivalry and branded one another as anti-revolutionaries. Faced with this clique mentality, the Party leadership decided to launch a new campaign to eliminate personal egoism in the ranks of the Red Guards.[11]

The founding of the Red Guard movement was a spontaneous act on the part of a small group of secondary school pupils in Peking, although it soon received the backing of the Party leadership.[12] During its later stages, naturally, the Red Guard movement was not spontaneous. Over 11 million provincial Red Guards visited Peking, whilst those living in the capital were sent on nationwide tours to drum up support for the revolutionary cause. All this entailed a great deal of planning, for these young people had to be provided with free travel, free food and free accommodation. Special reception centres were set up in all major towns, and sometimes in smaller towns and villages as well. In Peking alone it took over 100,000 people – soldiers, officers, government and Party functionaries – to administer this vast project. Originally, it was decided that every student and every secondary school pupil in the whole of China should be given the opportunity of visiting Peking, and although this programme was suspended in November 1966 to enable the Party leadership to make an interim evaluation of the campaign during the winter months, it was always intended that the project would be resumed in the following April and carried on throughout the summer of 1967. An undertaking to this effect was given in November, and repeated in December, 1966. But in the following year this undertaking was quietly forgotten, which would suggest that the leadership's interim assessment of the campaign had proved negative, or that it no longer served any useful political purpose. Probably both factors carried weight with the Maoist leaders, for although they must have been perturbed by the disruption of the rail freight services and the considerable cost of housing and feeding such vast numbers, they would doubtless have reconciled themselves to these burdens if the exercise had still seemed worthwhile. As it was, their rebelliousness made them undesirable allies. In November 1966 the party leaders announced that the secondary schools and universities would remain closed until after the summer holidays in the following year. But early in 1967 they changed their minds and instructed all secondary school pupils and students to return to their classrooms as from March 20, 1967. Clearly, this constituted an attempt to check the excesses of the leftist Red Guards, many of whom had even dared to attack the Committee of the Cultural Revolution set up by the Central Committee, and criticize the Maoist leaders. If they had been allowed to continue to roam the country and visit Peking at will, they would probably have tried to depose the entire Party leadership. They were safer in their classrooms, where the Party functionaries could keep them under surveillance, and steps could be taken to re-educate them.

Red Guard units had already run into trouble with the Maoist leadership back in 1966. About ten days after the first mass meeting in Peking they had been told to take note of the 16 points enumerated by the Central Committee in its resolution of August 8, 1966 concerning the implementation of the cultural revolution. Above all, they were told that in their dealings with the bourgeois revisionists they must use reasoned arguments and not brute force. This directive was published in all parts of China and transmitted on repeated occasions by the provincial radio stations. And at the second mass meeting on August 31, 1966, Lin Piao, Mao's right hand man, also impressed on the Red Guards that they must unite with the great mass of the people in order to 'defeat a handful of bourgeois rightist elements'. In doing so, he said, they must fight 'with arguments rather than force', even when they were dealing with 'people in positions of power who had followed the capitalist path, or with estate owners, kulaks, counter-revolutionaries, and bad or rightist elements'. Lin's words were echoed by Chou En-lai, when he urged the Red Guards to emulate the methods employed by the People's Liberation Army, using persuasion instead of coercion and so winning over the forces of the centre. Chou then went on to make a highly significant remark: 'Irrespective of the sphere or the institution in which the cultural revolution is implemented it can only be really effective if it is conducted by the masses.'[13] In other words, the Red Guard units were not to interfere, either in one another's affairs, or in the affairs of other Party organs. Instead of trying to monopolize the cultural revolution, they were to concern themselves with the ideological attitudes of their fellow pupils or students and concentrate on the detection and exposure of revisionists in their own ranks. This view was adopted as the official Party line, and ten days later Chou dealt with this question in greater detail. On this second occasion he pointed out that the cultural revolution had the power to galvanize production, for by revolutionizing people's attitudes it would enable them to produce more quickly, more efficiently and more economically. And since it was imperative that production should be maintained, Chou forbade the Red Guards to enter factories, commercial concerns, people's communes and official departments in the various districts. In all these different spheres, he said, the cultural revolution had to be pursued in a systematic manner. Consequently, the Red Guards would be expected to demonstrate their solidarity with the workers and peasants by allowing them to carry out their own revolution without interference. Chou even suggested that the Red Guards should go to the villages to help with the autumn harvest, so that by working in a disciplined and orderly manner they might acquire some of the genuine revolutionary zeal and diligence of the peasants. These admonitions are readily understandable if we consider the background of violence against which they were made. In August 1966 many Red Guards were killed by members of the civilian population, who had taken exception to their revolutionary acts. In September the incidence of violence increased. In Chingtao, for example, 40,000 workers were mobilized in order to oppose the itinerant Red Guards units, and pitched battles were conducted between units from Peking and the local populace.[14] Similar battles were fought in virtually every major city, mostly between Red Guards from Peking and local workers, peasants and functionaries.

Another reason why the leadership tried to check the coercive practices of the Red Guards was that it could not afford to allow the great mass of the population, which adopted a central position politically, to become alienated from the Party. And so, in mid-November, 1966, the Red Guards were forbidden to arrest or try people on their own initiative. Such acts were condemned as illegal, and a contravention of Party discipline. Early in 1967 the Guards were forbidden to search houses, confiscate private property, lock people out of their homes, beat them, force them to kneel on the ground, or parade them through the streets wearing clowns' hats and carrying placards. These new directives appear to have been disregarded – which is hardly surprising since up to October 1966 such practices were still being commended as 'revolutionary' acts – and in June 1967 they were reissued. On this second occasion they were endorsed by all the important Party and government departments, and were enforced by units of the Red Army, which arrested offenders and handed them over to the courts for prosecution.[15] By 1967 discipline, not rebellion, was the order of the day.

For the Maoist leadership the unauthorized attacks on Maoist Party organizations and the constant disputes between different units of the Red Guards, and between the Red Guards and other youth organizations, were a reminder that the young people of China still subscribed to bourgeois ideas. But these were not the only manifestations of bourgeois attitudes. For example, many young people seemed to think that the sole purpose of the cultural revolution was to depose the revisionist members of the leadership; and so they overlooked the need to change their own attitudes and to generate a political-ideological education of the masses, although this was in fact the ultimate objective of the revolutionary movement. The Party leadership was well aware of this, and it rightly assumed that young people of this kind, who had observed the letter but not the spirit of the cultural revolution, would one day relapse into revisionism. That day was not long in coming, for by the beginning of 1967 many of China's young rebels no longer believed in the 'spiritual power of the thoughts of Mao Tse-tung'; they argued that no project could be carried to a successful conclusion unless the necessary tools were provided, a view which was repudiated by the leadership on the grounds that it made no allowance for the 'initiative and creativity of the masses' and reduced them to mere robots. It was not long before many of these revolutionary rebels began to demand motor cycles, bicycles, telephones, good food and other consumer articles. They looked upon themselves as veteran revolutionaries, repudiated all latecomers as opportunists, and blocked their attempts to join the revolutionary organizations. By doing so, they isolated themselves from the people. This was a serious situation for the leadership, for by the beginning of 1967 the genuine revolutionaries, i.e. those who had really taken the revolution to heart, were in a minority.[16] Something had to be done to reform these veterans, who were well on the way to becoming out and out revisionists.

The leadership tried to resolve this problem by setting up Red Guard congresses and reopening the schools and universities. Both of these undertakings were difficult, and both met with initial setbacks. I have already drawn attention to the Peking congress, which was recommended as a model to the Red Guards in the provincial towns and districts. Peking was the obvious starting point for this new campaign, for in February 1967, when this congress was established, the Red Guard units in the capital were far and away the most rebellious. But although 120 Red Guard units attached to 58 schools and universities promised to unite, it would seem that the system of congresses evolved by the leadership failed to achieve the broadly based unity that was so badly needed. This may have been due, to some extent, to the strategy adopted by the Party in the course of 1967. Amongst other things, the Red Guards were encouraged to work in factories. As a result, many of them who were more interested in earning money than promoting the Maoist cause, left the Red Guard movement and took no further part in the cultural revolution.[17] In many cases these schoolboy and student workers earned more than the regular factory hands, who were extremely resentful of the fact. And so one section of the Red Guards was corrupted. Another section was openly rebellious; its members became embroiled in street battles both with the workers and with one another, and disregarded the ban on Red Guard travel imposed by the Party in April 1967.[18] Quite apart from the threat to life and limb, and the destruction of property, which they entailed, the battles conducted by opposing Red Guard units sometimes had serious political implications. The incident which took place in Wuhan is a case in point. In June 1967 there were two Red Guard organizations in Wuhan, which had been feuding with one another for several months. One of these – the 'Million Fighters' – occupied the Yangtse Bridge, the biggest bridge in China, on June 17. The rival organization, which was bent on dislodging the 'Million Fighters', asked the local army commander to intervene. But he refused to do so, arguing that the 'Million Fighters' had the support, not only of the people of Wuhan who had been misled by the revisionists, but also of bourgeois elements in the army, and that consequently it would be unwise to try to move them. It was perfectly true that in Wuhan, as elsewhere, the revolutionaries were in the minority. But in Wuhan they appear to have been extremely enterprising, for they went over the head of the local army commander and appealed to Peking for help. As a result, two Party representatives appeared in Wuhan in mid-July with instructions from Chou En-lai for the local army commander, who was told that he must withdraw support for the 'Million Fighters' forthwith. This did not suit the commander's purposes at all, and he promptly arrested the representatives, accusing them of having falsified their instructions. Two days later Wuhan was besieged by ships of the Chinese navy, and loyal troops stationed in the vicinity were ordered to march for Wuhan and take control of the town.[19] On the third day the Party representatives were released, and shortly afterwards were fêted at a mass meeting arranged by Lin Pao to celebrate the Party's victory. Meanwhile, loyal troops patrolled the streets of Wuhan; for it was important to demonstrate the local victory to the masses so as to gain their support in the drive against right wing deviationism in the army;[20] and it was also important to impress on the Red Guards the need to patch up their differences and unite under the Maoist banner.

We have already seen that the attempt to bring about a reconciliation between the opposing factions within the Red Guard movement was accompanied by a move to get the pupils and students to return to their classrooms. This, too, was initiated in February 1967, when the Party leadership announced that a revolutionary movement which tried to dispense with formal education was misguided and that consequently all pupils and students must re-enrol at their schools and universities, so as to implement the cultural revolution in these institutes and gain control of them for the Party.[21] With so many young rebels roaming the countryside or else sitting idly at home,[22] the cultural revolution of Chinese youth had lost its momentum.[23] The initial reaction to the 'back to school' directive was distinctly cool. At one secondary school in Shanghai, which had provided tuition for 2,000 pupils prior to the cultural revolution, only a few dozen presented themselves for re-enrolment. Moreover, there was a complete dearth of the wall newspapers which had come to symbolize the revolutionary fervour of the Red Guards in 1966. Faced with this lack of response, the leadership decided to experiment by placing a number of schools under military command. Accordingly, units were seconded from the Red Army and sent to these schools, where they provided military and political training for the pupils. One school in Shanghai, which had 1,800 pupils, was allocated 300 soldiers, which meant that each soldier was responsible for six pupils. This ratio was more or less standard in all the schools chosen for this experiment. The pupils were organized in military units (from platoons to battalions), they took part in military exercises, and they studied the writings of Mao Tse-tung. They were also subject to army discipline. The experiment was successful in so far as it quickly enabled the leadership to call a temporary halt to the conflicts between rival units of the Red Guards, between the Red Guards and other youth organizations, and between the pupils and teachers, in the schools concerned. Encouraged by this initial success, Mao Tse-tung issued a new directive at the beginning of March 1967, in which he called upon the army to expand its educational role by providing military and political training for more and more groups in universities, secondary schools and the senior sections of primary schools, and to assist with the reopening of the schools and their reorganization in accordance with the 'triple alliance'[24] so as to ensure that they fulfilled the tripartite requirement of 'endeavour, criticism and reform'.

We are told in one of the first reports issued by the army department responsible for educational matters that a military unit was attached to the 89th secondary school in Peking – the vast majority of whose pupils came from working-class backgrounds – in March 1967. Prior to this, various unsuccessful attempts had been made to persuade the pupils and teachers at this school to unite for the sake of Party solidarity. Instead of joining forces in order to oppose the 'reactionary capitalist line', they had become embroiled in 'civil wars'; bitter feuds had been fought – day in, day out – both by different factions amongst the pupils and teachers, and also between the pupils and the teachers. But when the soldiers arrived and began to apply their Maoist method, they soon disposed of this internecine strife. First, they made the pupils and teachers study the writings of Mao Tse-tung in order to impress on them that they were all serving the same cause. Once this unanimity of purpose had been established, they launched a 'bitterness campaign', in which everybody was called upon to criticize the oppressive measures of the old society and of the revisionist leaders, and to bear witness to the happiness conferred by the new society. This 'opened the eyes' of the teachers and pupils, and taught them to concentrate their feelings of animosity on a 'handful of powerful men in the Party' and their lackeys. The soldiers then proceeded to extirpate the desire for personal recognition, ultra-democratic activities and all forms of egoism. This helped to pacify a number of the teachers, who had seriously considered giving up their profession because they had been afraid that their pupils would either physically assault them or else accuse them of political misdemeanours. It also reconciled the pupils, many of whom had not been on talking terms with one another; and, above all, it cured their *wanderlust*. By now the pupils were ready to unite under a common banner. But here too the soldiers proceeded methodically, giving successive classes a systematic education until, just two months after their arrival at the school, they were able to reorganize the Red Guards, creating a homogeneous structure, in which all the old rival units were fully integrated. At that point a revolutionary committee based on the triple alliance, was set up. The pupils were then called upon to refute the theoretical premises of the revisionist line, and to denounce the revisionists for relying on bourgeois 'specialists'.[25] The revolutionary pupils and teachers – the three categories of revolutionary, non-revolutionary and counter-revolutionary pupils and teachers were still maintained in 1967 – were divided into 97 study groups. These different groups were then required to study the same prescribed texts, all of which were taken from the writings of Mao Tse-tung, and at the end of the week each individual in each group had to submit a written report outlining what he had learned from the 'thoughts of Chairman Mao'.[26] These reports were then read by the other members of his group.

One would have thought that at this stage the schools would have been able to dispense with the services of their military mentors. But it is quite apparent from the case of the Jenan Secondary School in Tientsin that this was not so. The Jenan school enjoyed a considerable reputation in China. It was Mao Tse-tung's model school, and it was there that Mao first tested · his system of 'soldiers in the schools'. We know that in Jenan the soldiers had to help the revolutionary committee to 'steel itself' and 'establish its authority', for there were many who continued to oppose the committee, even though it enjoyed the support of the military. Moreover, the members of the revolutionary committee in Jenan gradually developed 'a tendency to sit in their office and issue orders, and also to waste a great deal of time in conference'. Like the educational functionaries whom they had replaced, they became bureaucratic, and started to alienate themselves from the masses. When this happened, the soldiers reminded the committee members that they too must learn from the army, and they sent them into the classrooms to maintain contact with the pupils and staff, thus ensuring that the school was run on a personal basis. Moreover, it was the soldiers who explained the abuses of the old educational system to the pupils.[27] Under army management a clean sweep was made of anti-Maoist groups, and a new political department was set up. The different school grades and classes were reorganized in the form of companies and platoons, and a political instructor was allocated to each company. The political commissar attached to the army unit took it upon himself to help the chairman and members of the revolutionary committee with all political work. The remaining members of the unit helped the teachers with the political and ideological work among the pupils. In addition, a corpus of regulations was established by the army unit to cover the political work of the school. In fact, the unit did its utmost to ensure that the school could learn from the example of the People's Liberation Army. Like the army, the model school in Jenan was to be transformed into 'a red school for the teachings of Mao Tse-tung'.[28]

Military work units were sent out to the Chinese universities, and secondary and primary schools, at the beginning of 1967. Although they were treated with far more respect than the working groups sent out by the 'revisionist' municipal Party committees in 1966 (which were quite unable to assert themselves in the face of pupil opposition), they also had their difficulties. Because of the sheer size of the undertaking, the army was forced to employ a considerable number of soldiers with inadequate political understanding. In many units the soldiers had only a vague idea of what was expected of them, and had to be told by their superiors what to do in the schools and how to do it. Many lost interest; once the revolutionary committees had been set up, they saw no point in staying on, and asked to be posted back to the army. But even the units with qualified personnel were by no means entirely successful. The unit sent to Jenan, Mao's model school, is a good example. In May 1967 it seemed as if the army's work in Jenan had been completed. But before the summer was out, there were serious disturbances. The ultra-left pupils began to rebel against the revolutionary committee, which would have been overthrown if the army had not intervened. In November the pupils rebelled again. On that occasion they rejected the policy of re-establishing formal education so that the cultural revolution could be implemented in the schools, arguing that this was simply an attempt to reintroduce the old bourgeois educational system, and they demanded the restoration of the freedoms which they had enjoyed in 1966. One group of pupils took particular exception to the March directive authorizing the establishment of army units in Chinese schools, and they gave vent to their feelings by visiting the neighbouring primary schools and telling the senior pupils, who would be transferring to Jenan in 1968, about the restrictions which would be imposed on their liberty. As a result, the army was obliged to send soldiers into the primary schools to counter these rumours.[29] Thus, ultra democratic attitudes survived even in Mao's model school.

Despite the presence of military units in Chinese schools, there was growing unrest amongst the pupils, which reached its climax in the summer of 1967. One reason for this was undoubtedly the political immaturity of the solders. Many of them were completely out of their depth; they simply did not know how to cope with the different youth organizations, and could never feel certain that they had backed the right group. At one secondary school in Peking a large number of pupils, mostly from working class and peasant homes, refused to recognize the revolutionary committee and realigned themselves in new groups, which also attracted recruits from other schools in the capital. For two months these groups did their utmost to overthrow the revolutionary committee and prevent the implementation of the cultural revolution in this school. Their assault was so violent that even those teachers and pupils who had remained loyal to the army unit thought it advisable for the soldiers to withdraw. In the event, the soldiers stood their ground, and eventually succeeded in reimposing their authority.[30] But this was the sort of anarchic situation with which the army had to contend and which prompted the Party leadership to issue a further directive in October 1967, calling on all pupils and students to return to their classrooms forthwith in order to implement the cultural revolution in the schools and universities. According to the original timetable, this revolution should have been completed in the primary schools by February, in the secondary schools by March 1, and in the universities by March 20, 1967. There was, therefore, an obvious need to remind the youth of its responsibilities. But there was an important difference between the two directives. In October much greater significance was attached to the eradication of personal egoism and its replacement by a sense of dedication to the socialist cause, which was to be acquired by identifying wholeheartedly with the teachings of Mao Tse-tung.

On the second anniversary of the first mass meeting in Peking the Red Guards in particular, and Chinese youth in general, were told that far from despising the workers and peasants, they should try to learn from them, just as they should try to learn from the soldiers of the People's Liberation Army. They were also told that they must study the teachings of Mao Tse-tung at all times, and loyally support the cultural revolution. But the youth, and especially those of the ultra-left, had a different interpretation of the cultural revolution. In January 1967 the army command ordered all army cadets, who were then roaming the countryside, to return to their academies at once. Very few did so, and in February special measures were taken to enforce compliance: the reception and information centres set up to facilitate Red Guard travel in the previous year were closed down; and the cadets and students were told that unless they reported to their academies within twelve days, they would have to pay for their own fares and incidental expenses. But this second directive was also disregarded with the result that a third had to be issued. This appeared in April 1967, and was signed by no less a person than Lin Piao. Even the Red Army – which was the backbone of the cultural revolution – was being openly defied by its most junior recruits, although a general directive had been issued by the Party in March 1967 prohibiting unauthorized travel for all young people, and calling upon Party functionaries, political commissars attached to the army, and the leaders of the mass organizations, to explain the reasons for this new policy to the youth. If anything, the situation deteriorated following this general prohibition. More and more groups of pupils set off on journeys around the country, and in April 1967 the Party leadership, the Council of Ministers, the army leadership and the Committee for the Cultural Revolution were obliged to issue a joint decree forbidding unauthorized travel.

But it was not only the pupils, students and army cadets who caused difficulties for the Maoist leaders. The young people who had been sent to work on the land, both before and during the cultural revolution, were also a problem. They welcomed the prevailing yen for travel as a heaven-sent opportunity of returning to the towns. Many of them gave false names and addresses at the reception centres, and then proceeded to stage street battles, damage state property, carry out house searches, and apprehend opponents; but above all, they tried to establish themselves as permanent residents in the towns.

Despite the repeated directives issued by the authorities in the course of 1967, ultra-left youths were still travelling around the country in 1968. But they did not travel for the fun of it. They were not bent on pleasure but on the implementation of the cultural revolution in its original form. Wherever they went, they joined forces with the indigenous ultra-leftists and tried to overthrow the local revolutionary committees, i.e. the newly-formed organs of the executive, which were based on the triple alliance.[31] Their programme was precisely formulated by the five Chinese symbols: *ta-tsa-ching-chao-chua* (*ta* represents the overthrow of one's enemies, *tsa* the destruction of property, *ching* the confiscation of property, *chao* disputes between rival groups, and *chua* the arrest of individuals from hostile groups). These young people were not brawling hoodlums but genuine revolutionaries. Long before 1968, it is true, they had been branded by the leadership as counter-revolutionaries. But they did not see themselves in this light. On the contrary, they blamed the leadership for changing course, and adhered rigidly to the 1966 version of the cultural revolution. In its original form the revolution had presupposed the elimination of the whole bureaucratic apparatus in both the Party and the army.[32] But although many of the revisionist and bureaucratic leaders were criticized in 1966, only a relatively small number of them were overthrown, and in the course of 1967 they were able to reassert their authority by means of the local revolutionary committees, which were essentially bureaucratic institutions. Inevitably, this led to a protracted conflict between the 'conservatives' and the 'revolutionaries'; and since the conservatives had the backing of the leadership and the army, the revolutionaries declared their intention of inciting armed rebellion.[33]

The pupils and students who obeyed the Party directive to return to their classrooms posed as big a problem in 1968 as their itinerant colleagues. They believed that the principal conflict was between the masses and the revolutionary committees which were regarded as organs of a new bourgeois authority and consequently as instruments of oppression. Faced with such massive distrust, Mao Tse-tung decided on a new course of action: 'If the proletarian revolution is to be successfully implemented in the educational sphere, the working class must take control, the great mass of the workers must play an active part and, by collaborating with the soldiers of the Liberation Army and with the activist pupils, students, teachers and school workers who are determined to carry the proletarian revolution to a successful conclusion in the educational sphere, establish the new revolutionary triple alliance. Workers' propaganda groups must remain in the schools for a considerable period, they must take part in all school activities involving the tripartite ideological process of "endeavour, criticism and reform", and they must have absolute control of school administration. In the villages the schools must be administered by the workers' reliable allies, namely the peasants and smallholders.' Clearly, the workers' propaganda groups were not sent to the schools to replace the army units but to reinforce them. They went into the schools and universities in order to 're-educate the Red Guards and the revolutionary teachers and students'; and it was hoped that where the soldiers had failed on their own, they would succeed with the aid of the workers.[34] The first workers' group was sent to the Chinghua University, which had acquired a reputation for its Red Guard activities, towards the end of July 1967. Until then the military unit attached to this university had been unable to halt the feud waged by the two rival Red Guard units, which had continued to fight amongst themselves even after they had been officially amalgamated. But together the soldiers and workers quickly pacified these rival factions. Having done so, they divided their combined force into a hundred small working groups, whose members attended all university classes and work sessions, and lived with the students and teachers. Like the military unit, the workers' propaganda group also held regular ideological study groups, only by this time there was much more for them to combat. By the midsummer of 1967 the Maoist leadership had called upon its supporters to combat egoism (and all related 'isms), revisionism, counter-revolutionary or bourgeois educationalism, reactionary 'polycentrism' (the rejection – in theory or practice – of the existing Party and administrative organizations as revisionist, dictatorial or oppressive structures and their replacement by new and independent organizations), and the incitement of hostility to the Party amongst the masses. In its propaganda sessions the workers' group was primarily concerned with impressing on the students the need for 'everyone to practice more self-criticism'.

The 'Workers Propaganda Group for the Dissemination of the Teachings of Mao Tse-tung' – the official title of this new organization – met with the same initial success as the military unit which it had come to reinforce. And so the leadership decided to form more of these groups, one for each Chinese university, and one for each of the primary and secondary schools in which the pupils were still rebelling against the new Maoist line. The workers' groups were to remain in these institutes indefinitely and take control of all university and all (urban) secondary and primary education. The youth were no longer being encouraged to rebel. They were now expected to learn from the workers and soldiers how to become proletarian intellectuals.

4. The New Educational System

China's future depends on her youth, and the quality of her youth depends on the education provided for them. Consequently, if we wish to assess how the contradictions among the youth are likely to develop in the future, we must start by considering the type of education provided at the present time. Prior to the cultural revolution Chinese education was essentially bourgeois, and the vast majority of young people who attended the Chinese schools and universities during that period not unnaturally acquired a bourgeois outlook. Even today most of the Red Guards, and most of the revolutionary pupils and students in China, fall into this category. They have to be re-educated, not by the old bourgeois teachers, but by the workers, peasants and soldiers. What is now required are not merely specialists but educated workers with a socialist outlook. The general guide-lines for present-day Chinese education are to be found in the following statement by Mao Tse-tung: 'They [the pupils and students] are concerned primarily with their studies, but they must learn other things as well, i.e. apart from pursuing their studies, they must acquire some knowledge of industry, agriculture and military matters, and they must learn to criticize the bourgeoisie. The length of school and university courses must be reduced, and the whole educational system must be revolutionized. The present state of affairs, which allows bourgeois intellectuals to control our schools, may on no account be allowed to continue.' We must now consider the way in which this policy is being applied.

Basically, both primary and secondary schools and universities in urban areas are to be administered by local factory managements, whilst those in rural areas are to come under the jurisdiction of local production companies or brigades. Unfortunately, very little has been published about either the structure of the rural primary schools or the details of their curricula. We know that the teachers are paid in the same way as the peasants, i.e. on a points system, and that for the most part the pupils spend their time either studying the writings of Mao Tse-tung, learning about the class war and acquiring a basic knowledge of arithmetic or else working on the land. What is also quite certain is that the old bourgeois intellectuals are no longer allowed to play a major part in the running of these schools. Some of them have been exposed as counter-revolutionaries, and some have been dismissed as part of a general economy drive; by and large, the number of old style bourgeois teachers at any given school has been limited to four or five.[35] To make good the shortage caused by these dismissals, and also to ensure acceptable ideological standards, a new type of teacher has been enrolled: the 'educated peasant'.

The educated peasants, it will be remembered, were the secondary school pupils and university graduates who were sent to work on the land. They are now being recruited as teachers, provided they have completed a minimum of two years in productive work and – as is usually the case – have politically acceptable class affiliations. In addition, older peasants give lessons on the class war (i.e. to talk about the bad old days); general agriculture; workers demonstrate agricultural machines; bookkeepers give lessons in simple arithmetic; peasant 'medical orderlies' teach first aid; and militia units hold drill sessions. Under the old educational system the more fortunate pupils in rural areas attended school for a nine year period, spending six years at primary and three years at junior secondary school. In the majority of cases, this nine year course has now been replaced by a seven year course which combines both primary and junior secondary tuition, and is available to all pupils. Children who have not yet reached school age are also allowed to attend these new style schools if they wish to do so. This arrangement serves a triple purpose; it dispenses with the need for nursery education, it enables these young children to acclimatize themselves over a period of time, and it frees the older children of the necessity of looking after younger brothers and sisters. School fees, examinations and rigid age limits for school attendance have been abolished. During the peak agricultural periods the pupils work on the land, and they also cultivate the fields allocated to their schools. This relates class-room teaching to agricultural production, and enables the schools to cover at least part of their expenses. Under this new system approximately 95 per cent of all country children are able to attend school. This compares very favourably with the old system, where the percentage was much lower. In one production company prior to the cultural revolution there were more than 30 partially or completely illiterate young people out of a total population of 54 families (peasants and small-holders).

Instead of saying 'Good morning' to their teachers, the pupils now start the day by greeting each other with: 'We wish Chairman Mao a long life.'[36] They then spend the first hour reading quotations from Mao's works. Once a week the pupils meet in general assembly to discuss what they have learned from the 'study and creative adaptation of the "thoughts of Chairman Mao"'. Other assemblies are held, almost daily, in order to combat egoism and condemn revisionism. Since examinations and reports are thought to be bourgeois (because they tended to engender careerist attitudes in the past), pupils are assessed on their ability to study and adapt the thoughts of Chairman Mao.[37] The end object of this revolutionary system is to produce physically healthy, morally just, and professionally competent primary school-leavers, and the methods employed to this end are manual work, the study and adaptation of the 'thoughts of Chairman Mao', and the acquisition of agricultural or technical skills.

But although this seven year combined primary and junior secondary school course is the standard educational system for rural areas, there are also a number of agricultural secondary schools. However, these are run in much the same way and are based on the same criteria as the seven year schools. Thus, the courses are short and highly concentrated, and tuition is linked with agricultural production (to enable the pupils to put their book knowledge into practice). In these secondary schools the teaching staff is also made up of peasants, members of military units, demobilized soldiers and 'educated peasants'. At the outset of their school careers the pupils are given a presentation copy of the writings of Mao Tse-tung, which they all study together with his latest 'directives'. The secondary school pupils also learn about the class war, and are taught to combat egoism, whilst in their arithmetic courses they carry out land surveys and calculate the cubic contents of piles of dung or grain silos. In addition, they pursue a limited course of study in the natural sciences based on the agricultural needs of their particular district. No other subjects are taught. Indeed, it is regarded as a sign of revisionism for any pupil to want to know more than is strictly necessary for his practical needs. The pupils receive military training in accordance with the principles evolved by the People's Liberation Army, i.e. the 'Three Primaries'[38] and the 'Three-and-Eight Working Method'.[39] As far as agricultural production is concerned, the pupils are required to work in their local collectives for a minimum of 90 days per year in order to qualify for their annual allowance of corn; and they also have to cultivate the fields allocated to their schools.

The urban secondary schools in present day China are much bigger than those in the rural areas and consequently their organization is somewhat different. They are, in fact, run by committees composed of representatives of the 'revolutionary pupils and teachers' and the leaders of the military units and workers' propaganda groups; and these committees are answerable to the revolutionary committees established in the neighbouring factories which, it will be remembered, have jurisdiction over the urban schools. Like the university students, these secondary school pupils are organized in platoons, companies and battalions, and each battalion has its own political instructor. Military training is given not only in accordance with the principles of the 'Four Primaries' and the 'Three-and-Eight Working Method', but also on the basis of the 'Four-Good-Companies'[40] and the 'Five-Good-Fighters'.[41] Naturally, the urban secondary school pupils are also expected to study the thoughts of Mao Tse-tung, condemn revisionism, pursue the class war and combat their own egoism.

The principal aim of urban secondary education is to train the pupils for the particular type of industrial work carried on in the factory to which their school is attached. In addition, the pupils are given military training by the troops from the local garrison, and are taught agriculture in the neighbouring people's commune. The school week embraces 24 educational sessions: 12 of these are devoted to the thoughts of Mao Tse-tung, 4 to the basic structure of industry and the particular type of industrial work carried on in the local factory, 4 to revolutionary literature and art, 2 to military training, and the remaining 2 to a number of incidental subjects. These 24 sessions occupy two whole days, and four half days, out of the six day working week. The remaining four half days are spent in the factory. This is the curriculum for first year students. In their second year, when they live in a people's commune, the pupils spend four sessions studying agricultural theory and practice instead of the structure of industry and local industrial practice, and they also spend their four working half days in the fields instead of the factory. Otherwise, the curriculum remains unchanged. Each year the pupils study one principal subject – the thoughts of Mao Tse-tung – and three subsidiary subjects. Mathematics, physics and chemistry are all taught as part of the four weekly sessions on industrial or agricultural theory and practice; other matters dealt with in these sessions include the study of documents, manual work, the use of industrial and agricultural machines, and the irrigation and fertilization of land. Secondary school pupils are admitted upon completion of a four year primary course, and they study for a further four years before leaving school altogether. The vast majority then become educated peasants, the remainder educated workers.

The theoretical advantages of the new system are considerable. Since all students study the thoughts of Mao Tse-tung as their principal subject and are supposed to model their actions on those thoughts, they should gradually come to identify with them and regard them as their 'soul', i.e. their *alter ego*; the lessons on the class war should encourage them to hate their class enemies and combat their own egoism; their close contact with units of the People's Liberation Army enables them to tackle each new task set by the Party as if it were a military operation, executing it thoroughly and conscientiously, even at the risk of their own lives; and since these pupils are being taught by workers, peasants and soldiers, they should come to respect these proletarian groups (instead of looking down on them) and so acquire a sense of solidarity with all members of the working class. Such as the theoretical advantages of the Maoist system.

But the practical advantages of this system are not to be despised either. The fact that all school-leavers go straight into agriculture or industry is raising the cultural level of the worker and peasant classes very considerably. It is also raising standards of workmanship and improving ideological attitudes amongst the proletariat, for these new recruits are both technically and politically well educated, and able to provide instruction and guidance for their older colleagues, whose own training had been far less satisfactory. Moreover, since these new school-leavers have received an all-round education they are able to work in whatever capacity is most needed: as political or industrial workers, as peasants or soldiers. Furthermore, the new style schools are virtually self-supporting. Consequently, it will soon be possible for the Party to provide universal education so that within the forseeable future illiteracy will no longer be a problem, and the whole of the Chinese population will consist of educated workers and peasants. And once educational and cultural equality has been established, the Communist era should not be too far removed.

But, of course, all these theoretical and practical advantages are still opposed by that old enemy of Maoist ideology: egoism. We have already seen that at the very outset of the cultural revolution many young people were dubious about the out-come of this new development. They saw no advantage in receiving a decent education if they were going to end up as peasants and be paid on a points system. Why waste time going to school, they thought, when they could be out in the fields totting up points for themselves. Others objected to school because it involved more manual work than study, and many of these unwilling schoolboys translated their thoughts into deeds, either by playing truant or by leaving school entirely. In some cases as much as one sixth of the total pupil body left prema-turely. So far, all the information released about recalcitrant pupils has concerned young people with right wing sympathies. Consequently, we have no means of telling, at present, how the leftist pupils have reacted to the new educational system. But this will be revealed when the next spate of conflicts breaks out in Chinese society. And these conflicts must come, for although there may be temporary lulls in the permanent revolution, it is an ongoing process that naturally produces its own opposition. The revisionist and bourgeois elements in Chinese society have not all been eradicated, and egoism still survives.

The implementation of the new educational system was a relatively easy matter at the primary and secondary school levels. Since the curriculum consisted of the teachings of Mao Tse-tung, and the practical aspects of industry and agriculture, the workers were quite capable of taking over as instructors. Consequently, most recalcitrant teachers and pupils could be removed and set to work on the land, where they could be effectively re-educated under the supervision of peasants and smallholders. The services of the 'revolutionary' teachers have been retained. After working for a probationary period in factories and people's communes, they are now being employed as auxiliaries in the new schools, where they discuss the theoreti-cal aspects of the natural sciences with the pupils.

The reorganization of the technical colleges has not posed any major difficulties either. To begin with, the technical incom-petence of the bourgeois 'specialists' was exposed. For example, the workers' propaganda group attached to the Institute for the Construction of Agricultural Machines in the province of Shantung took the students and lecturers out to a commune, where the lecturers were asked to service tractors, a practical task which proved too much for them but which the students were able to master after receiving demonstrations from the local peasants and workers. And if the peasants and workers could teach the students to service tractors, they could also teach the rest of their technologically based curriculum.

Things are very different, however, where the universities are concerned. It is not so easy to attach a university to a factory, or even to a group of factories, since only a small part of the university curriculum is applied in industrial processes. The situation is aggravated by the fact that the university students are older and consequently were exposed to the influences of a bourgeois educational system over a much longer period of time, with the result that they tend to look down on the workers. At the Chinghua University in Peking the students and lecturers joined forces on several occasions in an attempt to rid themselves of their workers' propaganda group, the first and most powerful of all the groups sent out by the leadership to implement the new educational policy. This attempt proved unsuccessful, for the workers' group received effective support from the personnel of the 61 factories in Peking. As a result, it was able to form hundreds[42] of subsidiary groups, which conducted a 'hard and meticulous politico-ideological campaign' amongst the students and lecturers. In 1966 the youth of China forced the workers to read excerpts from the writings of Mao Tse-tung; in 1967 the workers returned the compliment. At the same time the workers required the students and lecturers at the Chinghua University to perform onerous manual tasks, such as wading through cold rivers in order to dredge the bottom, or working on marshland. Resistance was quite useless, for the members of the workers' group had the backing of Mao Tse-tung, who rewarded them with a gift of mangoes and by receiving them in person, a distinction acclaimed by the Maoists and the Chinese press with great enthusiasm. But despite their unremitting zeal, the workers' propaganda groups have failed to gain the support of the students and lecturers. This has been due in no small measure to the indifference or animosity with which many of the workers in these groups have approached their university charges, thus provoking opposition and jeopardizing any chance of genuine collaboration. Consequently, the workers attached to the universities have been told by the leadership that they must improve their own political attitudes by studying the teachings of Mao Tse-tung, since they cannot hope to influence the students unless they abjure their false feelings of superiority and strengthen their proletarian ideals.

Thus, the members of the workers' propaganda groups failed in their attempt to implement the cultural revolution in the Chinese universities; and when university education was finally revolutionized, the initial impetus came, not from these special groups, but from the workers in a Shanghai factory,[43] whose educational philosophy is summed up in the slogan: 'The more books people read, the more stupid they become.' These factory hands wanted to see experienced workers appointed as university lecturers, and a number of university courses transferred from the class room to the shop floor. They also insisted that the majority of university places should go to workers with the right kind of family background,[44] and further stipulated that all *politically and ideologically* acceptable primary and secondary school-leavers who had completed between two and five years' manual work should be recommended for a university course. After graduating, these students were to be employed in the factories or people's communes as ordinary workers until they were granted 'certificates of competence' by the workers or peasants. A percentage of those who received such certificates would then be employed as technicians (but would still be expected to perform a certain amount of manual work), whilst the rest would continue as ordinary workers or peasants. The exact number redeployed would depend on the requirements of the production programme at any particular time. These were the principal ideas advanced by the Shanghai factory workers for the reorganization of university education. In fact they are much more than ideas, for they have received the backing of Mao Tse-tung, and are therefore binding on all Chinese universities and technical colleges. In July 1968 Mao said: 'It is also necessary to ensure that the universities continue to function; and here I am referring to the university colleges of science and technology. But we must reduce the length of university courses; we must carry out a revolution in the educational sphere, giving priority to the requirements of our proletarian policy and pursuing the course set out by the toolmakers of Shanghai by training members of the work force as technicians. In future, workers and peasants with practical experience should be selected for university training, and after studying for a few years they should be sent back to work in a practical capacity in industrial or agricultural production.' The duration of the new university courses has not yet been announced, although it seems likely that it will be between one and three years, depending on the type of course being pursued and the politico-ideological condition of the students.

The selection procedure for students remains problematical. The Shanghai toolmakers demanded that the students should come from the ranks of the workers. This was adopted by Mao, and it would certainly seem that, as far as scientific and technological studies are concerned, the workers are to be given priority. True, Mao went on to state that 'workers *and* peasants with practical experience should be selected for university training'. But what he had in mind for the peasants were the agricultural colleges, which will gradually be transferred to the countryside. It seems likely that the peasants will resent their exclusion from the scientific and technological sphere, and that this resentment will increase, rather than decrease, when their colleges are removed from the towns. But this is not the only source of possible conflict. The leadership proposes to send vast numbers of pupils and students to work on the land, many of whom will not be content with their lot. Moreover, the better positions are more likely to be offered to these 'educated peasants', which may cause resentment amongst the indigenous peasant class. This happened prior to the cultural revolution, and there is no reason to think that it will not happen again. Already a number of young people who were sent to work on the land as ordinary peasants during the cultural revolution have been promoted, and are now employed as teachers. Such discrimination between educated and indigenous peasants is bound to lead to conflict, as is the parallel discrimination practised against ordinary industrial workers in favour of those selected for university training. But there is a further difficulty which should not be overlooked. Chinese education is based on the needs of the factories and people's communes in the immediate vicinity of individual schools or groups of schools. Consequently, it is designed to produce educated peasants and workers, technicians and employees with varying degrees of specialist knowledge. But it makes no provision for really top grade scientists capable of mastering and teaching complex scientific disciplines. Where and how are they to be trained in future? At the end of November 1968 eleven Shanghai workers were put through a crash course lasting twenty days in which they were required to study the teachings of Mao Tse-tung and the implications of the class war, criticize Liu Shao-chi, and take part in the tripartite ideological process of 'endeavour, criticism and reform', whilst at the same time acquiring a working knowledge of surgery and internal diseases.[45] Will the leadership try to train top grade scientists by putting workers with good ideological credentials through a three week course? Or will it send them to university for three years? Or will it authorize postgraduate work at Chinese universities, thus encouraging a recrudescence of the élitism which developed following the 'Great Leap Forwards'? Clearly, the revolution is still continuing. So too are opposition and conflict.

CHAPTER VI
WORKER AND PEASANT REBELS

Pay attention to affairs of state.

MAO TSE-TUNG

The original object of the cultural revolution was to enable the young people living in the towns and cities of China to undermine the all-pervading influence of the old bourgeois culture and the overthrow the revisionist heads of cultural and educational institutes and government or Party departments. The workers and peasants were also expected to participate in this process, but what really mattered, as far as they were concerned, was that they should adopt a revolutionary attitude to their work, thus improving both the quality and the quantity of their output. With the radicalization of the cultural revolution in the summer of 1966 Red Guard units and other revolutionary groups were formed in a number of factories and industrial plants, but were dissolved shortly afterwards on orders from the Party leadership. For as the *People's Daily* of September 15, 1966, pointed out, the workers and peasants could not simply down tools and take a holiday, like the pupils and students. Nor could they travel to other parts of the country to discuss their experiences with other revolutionaries. The peasants were even instructed to refrain entirely from revolutionary activities during the autumn harvest. This was also explained by the *People's Daily*, which insisted that both the workers and the peasants should channel their 'revolutionary fervour' into their work, thus ensuring 'bigger, faster, better and more economical production'. And the youth were forbidden to engage in revolutionary activities in the factories, industrial plants and people's communes for fear of disrupting production. But despite the restraint called for by the leadership, the workers and peasants soon became involved in the militant side of the cultural revolution, as exemplified by the activities of the Red Guards. This was due partly to the contradictory nature of the directives issued by the Maoist leadership. For the working masses were told that they must write wall newspapers, hold public discussions and help to expose the revisionist 'demons' in the Party; and they were also encouraged to take violent revolutionary action without regard for the consequences. At the same time, however, they were required to restrict their revolutionary activities to their leisure hours and to report punctually for work each morning. This was asking too much, for in 1966 the revolutionary Red Guards were the heroes of the hour, and everybody wanted to emulate them. And so by August 1966 the first 'revolutionary left groups of the proletariat' were founded and immediately joined in the rebellion. They interfered in the pupils' cultural revolution, and bloody battles were soon being waged on the streets between these two rival factions. Subsequently, the revisionist 'demons' also took a hand, organizing the worker and peasant masses and inciting them to acts of violence against both the worker and peasant revolutionaries and, more particularly, the Red Guards.

It soon became apparent that the workers and peasants were finding it impossible to reconcile the need to maintain production with the need to promote the cultural revolution. Consequently, they tended to divide into two camps, one of which concentrated on production, the other on the revolution. This tendency was reinforced in September 1966 when a directive was issued by the Maoist leadership calling for the establishment of two separate leadership groups in all factories, mines, industrial concerns, building firms and people's communes, one of which would assume responsibility for production, the other for the implementation of the cultural revolution. At this juncture, priority was given to the production programme. Revolutionaries who disrupted production were quickly suppressed, and branded as counter-revolutionaries and saboteurs. But at the beginning of December 1966 things took a new turn. Far from being forbidden to enter the factories and communes, the young revolutionaries were encouraged to do so in order to learn from the workers and peasants, and ally themselves with them. For by then the leadership had decided[1] that the superstructure could not be successfully purged unless the cultural revolution was implemented within the infrastructure, i.e. in the factories and people's communes. Accordingly, those workers who had chosen to concentrate on the production programme were said to have been misled by 'demons' within the Party, and consequently fell from favour. From then onwards priority was given to the revolution. But the peasants and workers had been seriously influenced — both organizationally and ideologically –

by capitalism, revisionism and even feudalism.[2] And so when the revolutionary workers and peasants were given their head, production was disrupted even more seriously than it had been before.

1. The Leftist Workers and Peasants

Even before the so-called January revolution of 1967 conditions in Chinese industry and agriculture were pretty chaotic. The influx of young people into the industrial and agricultural units had triggered fresh conflicts between the revolutionary workers and peasants on the one hand and the revolutionary pupils on the other. The pupils, who liked to think of themselves as pioneers, were determined to implement the cultural revolution in the factories and communes. This was resented by the workers and peasants, who wanted to carry out their own revolution, and led to numerous conflicts, which were frequently aggravated by the fact that in some factories and communes the pupils were earning more than the permanent workers. But there were also conflicts between the workers and peasants themselves, especially after they had joined together in revolutionary groups. Every one of these groups was divided in practically every respect, and on the rare occasions when the members of one group achieved unanimity on a particular issue, their view was rarely supported by any of the other groups. The result was constant bickering, which erupted on frequent occasions into open conflict. Damage was caused to property, people were injured, and in a number of factories and communes production was brought to a standstill. At this point groups of workers and peasants simply downed tools and set off on long journeys to discuss their revolutionary experiences with their opposite numbers in other towns and districts, or else travelled to Peking to lodge complaints with the Party leadership or present pay demands. In the closing months of 1966 the revolutionary workers and peasants began to assume a dominant role, which eventually provoked the January revolution of 1967.

This January revolution constituted an attempt to eradicate the wave of economism which was sweeping the country and which had prompted a large section of the work force to demand better pay and conditions.[3] These workers and peasants had forgotten that the bourgeois system of incentives was an unacceptable way of increasing production in socialist China, and that only through the 'thoughts of Mao Tse-tung' would man's thinking be revolutionized so that they would increase production of their own free will. The people who had misconstrued the cultural revolution as an exercise in economism were employed in many different branches of industry and agriculture. They had organized themselves in revolutionary groups — such as the 'Workers' Purple Guards' – and they embarked on a series of strikes in support of their demands. They took possession of houses owned either by the state or by former capitalists, and requisitioned other articles of state property. They also engaged in fierce battles with their opponents, they forced the local functionaries to increase their wages and hand over money from welfare and other funds, and insisted, before setting off to tour the country or visit Peking, that their expenses be paid in advance. As a result of the strikes factories were closed down, ships were unable to load or unload their cargoes, road traffic was brought to a halt, and railway services were seriously disrupted. But when the workers in the water and electricity works, and the urban transportation systems, threatened to join the strike, the time had come for counter-action.

The revolutionary peasants in the rural areas, who had also succumbed to the temptations of the economist creed, travelled into the towns to press their demands for better conditions. They objected to the new economic plan, which called for the overfulfilment of the old quotas, and demanded the restoration of free markets. They also seized communal funds, equipment and corn stocks, and distributed them amongst themselves. And like their urban counterparts, they became embroiled in violent incidents.

The 'ill wind of economism' swept the whole of China. There were strikes even in Peking. It was the Red Guards who had to step into the breach and provide temporary services wherever possible. Nor had all the revolutionary peasants and workers become victims of economism. Some groups were well aware that this doctrine threatened to divert the cultural revolution from what was then regarded as its principal objective, namely the ousting of those in power.[4] The first reaction to economism – which came to be known as the January revolution – was launched in Shanghai. On January 4, 1967 the 'Headquarters of the Revolutionary Workers' in Shanghai, acting in collaboration with 11 Red Guard units from Shanghai and elsewhere, composed an open letter to the local population, which was published in the *Wen Hui Bao* on the following day. This open letter explained to the itinerant and striking workers the intrigues of those in power who were intent on sabotaging the cultural revolution. The workers were then urged to return to their posts without further delay. It should be noted in this connexion that the 'Headquarters of the Revolutionary Workers' in Shanghai was a headquarters in name only. In fact, theirs was just an ordinary group like any other. Five days later an 'urgent command' was issued on behalf of 32 revolutionary groups, one of which was this headquarters group. Of these 32 groups 13 were youth organizations, about half of which were based outside of Shanghai. Of the 19 workers' groups about one third were composite groups, i.e. their members came from a variety of professions. Such composite groups were later proscribed by the leadership. It is therefore readily apparent that the workers' groups involved in the January revolution were extremely heterogeneous, which is hardly surprising since many of them were formed in great haste. In the long term this was bound to lead to conflicts of interest and internal power struggles. Initially, however, these groups were at one in their determination to bring the cultural revolution back on to the right path. Shanghai was to be a model for the whole of China.

On February 5, 1967 China's first commune, after the model of the Paris Commune, was set up in Shanghai with the approval of 'our beloved and great leader Mao Tse-tung' and with the support of the army and the executive committee of the Headquarters of the Revolutionary Workers and other revolutionary groups. This commune assumed the powers previously vested in the Shanghai Party Committee and the municipal government, and rescinded all directives issued by these bodies after May 16, 1966. It then called upon the workers and peasants to return to work, and condemned the confiscation of state property, and above all, the slogan which the peasants had formulated in order to justify this practice: 'Eat everything share everything out'. The commune also instructed those Shanghai workers, who had been drafted to remote areas but had made their way back to Shanghai under cover of the cultural revolution, to return to their new homes.[5] Finally, it announced that individual persons, or groups of persons, who used firearms or explosives would be arrested, and that all covert anti-revolutionary organizations would be suppressed.

The Shanghai commune was acclaimed in the *Wen Hui Bao* as a new and splendid achievement, which had been inspired by the 'thoughts of Chairman Mao' and constituted a further important stage in both the Chinese and the world revolutions. Two members of the Committee for the Cultural Revolution were sent to Shanghai to help run the commune. (One of these was Yao Wen-yüan, whose attack on Wu Han had initiated the cultural revolution.) Meanwhile, the troops stationed in Shanghai affirmed their loyalty to the cultural revolution and promised to support the commune. All this would seem to indicate that the Shanghai commune had the approval of the Party leadership. On the other hand, the only newspapers to write about it at that time were those published in Shanghai. Later, a report appeared in the Peking *People's Daily* to the effect that a 'provisional organ of authority' had been established in Shanghai on February 5, 1967 in accordance with the principles of the triple alliance, which was to be known as the 'Revolutionary Committee for the City of Shanghai'. This report was published on February 28. But earlier (in a circular issued by the Party leadership on February 19, 1967), it was stated that the authorities in Shanghai had been instructed to call the new organ a 'commune'. Clearly, therefore, the leadership was divided over this issue, as we shall come to see in greater detail on a later page. As for the course of events in Shanghai, this was indicated by the first directive issued by the Revolutionary Committee which stressed the fact that it had the full support of the militia, the army and the 'people's militia'. It ordered all itinerant Shanghai workers to return to their factories, and all former Shanghai workers, who had made their way back to Shanghai from remote areas, to return to their new homes. It also expressly prohibited the confiscation of state property, acts of violence, the falsification of Party directives, and opposition to the armed forces. Finally, it stated that all anti-revolutionary and national organizations, including those founded by former soldiers, were to be dissolved. It is obvious from these provisions that during the period of the commune conditions in Shanghai must have been chaotic. There were two principal reasons for this.

Although in theory the revolutionary groups were answerable both to the Committee for the Cultural Revolution set up by the Central Committee and to the army, in actual fact they were largely autonomous, for their numerical superiority gave them great power in the commune, which was of course an essentially democratic institution. This naturally led to disputes between the rebels, the soldiers and Party cadres. Moreover, the revolutionary groups, who had also been exposed to bourgeois ideas, became divided into cliques, and after assuming the dominant role within the commune soon fell out amongst themselves. Some members of these groups, and even some groups themselves, secretly sympathized with the bourgeois camp, and sought consciously to create disturbances.[6] It was because of these disturbances that the leadership eventually prohibited the formation of professional groups (following the proscription of the national and composite groups).

The other reason why conditions in Shanghai were so chaotic was that the functionaries who were running the commune, were expected to implement directives issued by the leadership. However, the inhabitants of Shanghai were well aware of the functionaries' special role, and so took steps to eliminate them. But this posed an intractable problem, for the functionaries had been the only people with administrative experience. What was the leadership to do? If it had given the rebels a completely free rein, then by the time communes had been set up throughout China, it would have lost its *raison d'être*. This was clearly unacceptable, and consequently the Shanghai commune remained an isolated phenomenon.

Following the January revolution in Shanghai a new alternative model was required. The show place for this new apparatus was Taiyuen, the capital of Shansi province. Before the revolutionary groups seized power in Taiyuen conditions there had been as chaotic as in Shanghai or, for that matter, in any other of the major Chinese towns. Economism had been rife, and there had been frequent battles between the masses and the revolutionaries. On one occasion no less than ten thousand workers had joined forces to oppose the rebels.[7] But on January 12 the Party Committee and the government of both Taiyuen and the province of Shansi were deposed. The administration of the territory was then taken over by the headquarters company of 25 separate revolutionary groups. Two days later the rebels issued their first decree. They appear to have misunderstood the role which had been asisgned to them at that time, and the Party found it necessary to publish a leading article in the *People's Daily* on January 25, 1967, so as to clarify the situation. In this article major importance was attached to two new factors: (1) the army had helped the revolutionaries to seize power; (2) in Taiyuen the Party functionaries were not to be excluded from the new administration, as they had been in Shanghai. At the end of January 1967 the revolutionary workers in the city of Tsingtao and the provinces of Kweichow and Heilungkiang also seized power. The course of events, which was essentially the same as in Taiyuen and Shansi, is well illustrated by the developments in Heilungkiang, where local army units intervened in the struggle between revolutionary and anti-revolutionary rebel groups and successfully suppressed the anti-revolutionary groups. These groups were units of national organizations, which included the 'Army of Meritorious Veterans', the 'Army of the Red Flag', the 'Ever-ready Army', the 'Corps of August 8', and the 'Purple Guards'; similar units were to be found in all major towns including Peking and Shanghai. After the anti-revolutionary groups had been forced to yield, their leaders were condemned at specially convened mass meetings as a warning to their followers. A few days later the revolutionary rebels seized power in the province. The principal instigators of this 'rebellion' were the First Secretary of the Party Committee for the province and the chief army representative for the area. They selected suitable revolutionaries and persuaded them to participate in this 'revolution from the top' in order to crush the stubborn resistance of the local anti-revolutionaries. After the successful outcome of its venture in Heilungkiang province, the Maoist leadership recommended 'revolution from the top' as a particularly effective way of dealing with revisionist groups.

Even before the establishment of the Shanghai commune the Maoist leadership was at pains to point out that the 'revolutionary functionaries' would always be the mainstay of any attempt to seize power for the new revolutionary movement, and might eventually be placed in charge of such projects. Since they had greater political knowledge and greater organizational ability than the revolutionary workers, it was felt that they were better qualified – in purely technical terms – to conduct a successful revolution and set up an effective administration afterwards. And so the functionaries were called upon to co-operate with the rebels in order to ensure the successful implementation of such projects. At the same time, the rebels were reminded that they must always act in a disciplined manner. Above all, they were told that instead of resisting authority out of hand, they must learn to distinguish between just and unjust authorities. However, the leadership had not entirely abandoned the concept of the Paris Commune. Despite the problems of the Shanghai project, it was still contemplating the establishment of a commune in Peking.[8] But here too it was careful to point out that the rebel groups could not hope to seize power unaided and consequently could not afford to mistrust 'every person in a position of authority'. Incidentally, this guarded reference to the functionaries was made whilst the Shanghai commune was still in existence. Later, when the commune had been dissolved, Party functionaries were openly designated as the mainstay of the new revolutionary movement. The reason given by the leadership for upgrading the functionaries was that they were ideally placed to seize power, since they knew where it was concentrated and were able to identify the revisionist leaders who would have to be eliminated. The leadership also pointed out that the functionaries were well versed in administrative matters and had a better grasp of the general situation than the workers. Consequently, it recommended that, provided they had seen the error of their ways, even those functionaries who had made serious mistakes should be allowed to join the new administration, and should be given executive positions. It was calculated that by adopting such a course 95 per cent of all functionaries could be won over to the revolutionary cause.[9] And in point of fact, we find that in the province of Kweichow the plan to seize control of the local administration was first submitted for approval to the leading revolutionary functionaries in the Party Committee for that province. According to the *People's Daily* of February 23, 1967, this was the reason why the rebels in Kweichow achieved their objective so quickly.

Once the revolutionary groups in a number of different towns and provinces had seized power and established their new administrations it was possible to proceed with the next phase, namely the formation of revolutionary committees. Of course, the whole process was much more difficult in some localities than others. It was also rather more complex than I have indicated so far, for in many districts the rebels received crucial support, not only from the functionaries, but from the army as well. On January 23, 1967 the army was ordered to intervene in the cultural revolution – which until then had been essentially a civilian operation – so as to ensure that the left revolutionary groups succeeded in their bid for power and the rightist anti-revolutionary groups were suppressed. These objectives were to be achieved at all costs, even if it involved the use of arms. Two days later the leader writer of the army's newspaper exhorted the troops to afford the leftists every assistance, even if they were still in the minority. The most important regional departments of the State administration service were taken over and run by the army itself at the very outset of the 1967 revolutionary campaign. In addition, armed troops were sent to those districts in which the anti-revolutionary forces were particularly strong, in order to suppress them. The army also took charge of any administrative units or departments in which the revolutionary groups had failed to seize power. And after the seizure of power had been completed, it was the army that provided political education for the left-wing rebels in order to eradicate any remnants of bourgeois ideology. Political courses were held, at which the writings of Mao Tse-tung and army regulations could be studied. Soldiers' propaganda groups were formed in order to propagate and explain the Party's new directives. In suspect districts troops patrolled the streets day and night to preclude possible resistance on the part of anti-revolutionary elements.[10] Before long soldiers were also sent into the factories and mines to spread the new doctrine, for the political attitudes of the workers and functionaries had to be revolutionized so as to ensure that they fulfilled, and over-fulfilled, their production quotas.[11]

But despite these elaborate measures and the carefully framed directives, the carrying through of the cultural revolution remained an uphill task. The left wing rebels mistrusted the functionaries, whom they regarded as opportunists. Consequently, they continued to press for their removal,[12] and since the functionaries were supported by the army, we find frequent references in the Chinese press to clashes between rebels and soldiers at that time.[13] This was why the leadership decided to disband the rebel groups and reorganize the revolutionary masses. Everything had to make way for the revolutionary committees.

2. The Revolutionary Committees

Back in March 1966, i.e. several months before the cultural revolution had developed into a mass movement, the type of administrative system that had been developed in the Paris Commune was discussed in positive terms in an article published in *Hongqi*, the principal mouthpiece of the Communist Party leadership. The author of this article paid special attention to the fact that under this system all posts were to be elective and that all functionaries elected to them could be voted out of office at any time. This feature was also singled out in the resolution of August 1966, which called for the establishment of 'groups, committees and congresses of the cultural revolution' similar to those found in the Paris Commune. But at the beginning of 1967 the leadership's attitude to this type of administration became much more ambivalent; for on the one hand it called upon the rebels to take due note of the undesirable lack of discipline that had been such a marked feature of the Paris Commune whilst on the other hand it proceeded to establish an experimental commune in Shanghai, only to dissolve it a few weeks later when it proved unacceptable. From then on the terms 'commune', 'committee of the cultural revolution' and 'congress of the cultural revolution' were dropped in favour of 'revolutionary committee'.

But the revolutionary committees were preceded by two other kinds of organizations: the 'great alliance' and the 'triple alliance'. Great alliances were large-scale organizations composed of various revolutionary groups, which were frequently set up at the instigation of the army. Triple alliances, as the name implies, were tripartite organizations which were introduced after the rebels had succeeded in banishing the anarchy that had become so widespread towards the end of 1966. In these triple alliances the representatives of the revolutionary masses formed the 'foundation', the army representatives provided the 'main support', and the revolutionary cadres supplied the 'leadership'. The rebels' representatives continued in their normal employment, serving on the revolutionary committees on a part time basis. By and large, their committee duties consisted of giving interviews and answering letters.[14] As for the army representatives, they were responsible for keeping the politics and teachings of Mao Tse-tung in the forefront. The revolutionary functionaries carried out the administrative and political work of the committees. Clearly, the rebels' representatives were very much the junior partners. After playing a leading part in the revolution, they were reduced to the level of camp followers, whereas the cadres, who had been demoted at the outset of the revolution, fared much better. But the lion's share of the power went to the army, which provided the vast majority of the chairmen for the provincial committees. In the local committees the masses were usually well represented, especially in those formed at an early stage. But in the higher committees, and even in those local committees, formed later, they were less well represented. Many of the rebels were sorely tempted to stage a further rebellion. But rebellion was no longer 'justified', and would have been suppressed as an expression of bourgeois opposition.

3. The Opposition

Mao Tse-tung has said that people fall into one of three categories: the left, the right and the centre. He considers that these categories have always existed, and will go on existing 'for the next ten thousand years'. In China – according to Mao – the leftists and rightists, who between them form the minority group in the nation as a whole, are engaged in a constant struggle to win over those in the centre, who form the majority. It was because it was exposed to rightist attacks that the Maoist leadership took steps to protect the leftist minority during the cultural revolution. But all three of these categories are highly abstract, and defy precise definition. In practical terms it is by no means certain that the majority category, i.e. the centre, has ever really existed in China. In the cultural revolution, certainly, everybody was forced into a right or left wing position, even those who merely paid lip service to the revolution, or who stood silently in the wings. They were said to be in error, which was tantamount to being on the right. In actual fact, of course, such people occupied a central position. Meanwhile, the real rightists, i.e. the class enemies, continued to oppose the Maoist version of the dictatorship of the proletariat. Seen in this light, the composition of Chinese society can be redefined in terms of an absolute majority, consisting of supposed and real rightists, and a minority of leftists, whose task it was to convert the majority. But even the left revolutionaries were of suspect loyalty, for they had been exposed to bourgeois ideas, and unless they constantly scrutinized their own behaviour in the light of the Party's revolutionary criteria, there was always the danger that they might relapse into anti-revolutionary postures and become right wing deviationists.[15] In fact, the Maoist leadership openly conceded that, on occasions, counter-revolutionary ideology had been stronger than proletarian ideology.[16] And so, after directing the barb of the cultural revolution, first against the right and then against the centre, the leadership finally used this weapon in order to combat relapsed leftists.

Having first deposed a number of top-ranking Party leaders for their rightist activities at the very beginning of the cultural revolution the Maoist leadership went on to expose the 'capitalist bosses in the party' and their followers in the course of its anti-economism campaign in 1967. These despots, who had themselves started out in life as revolutionaries, kept black lists and used bugging devices in order to listen in on conversations between revolutionary workers;[17] they also bribed numerous workers to leave their jobs and tour the country in order to discuss their revolutionary experiences and, more significantly, rebel against the leadership; and in the rural areas they encouraged the egoism of the peasants by advising them to distribute communal property – tools, corn and money – amongst themselves and set up in farming on their own account.[18] The 'capitalist despots' sowed discord between different groups of workers, and between the workers and peasants. They also maintained contact with counter-revolutionary organizations, and even formed such organizations themselves. The members of these organizations had secret stores of small arms and ammunition, which they used against their opponents,[19] and it is known that one group at least, possessed a number of small artillery pieces.[20] I have already referred to some of the anti-revolutionary groups. Judging by their names, it would seem that the members of these groups were for the most part workers or former soldiers. The groups appear to have been organized on a national scale, for they had branches in various towns.

One of the most remarkable groups was the workers' militia, the so-called Purple Guards, which had branches in all the main industrial areas and appears to have had a very large membership. In one Shanghai factory with a staff of over 1,200 no less than 200 workers belonged to the counter-revolutionary Purple Guards whilst less than 170 were active cultural revolutionaries. And the worker's militia was only one of several counter-revolutionary organizations. The others included the 'Army of the Red Flag', the 'Army of Meritorious Veterans' and the 'Committee for Concerted Action'.[21] The protection provided by the Party for the leftist minority was obviously justified.

Not all these rightist organizations were in league with the capitalist despots in the Party. For example, the 'Battalion of May 16', a youth organization that was bent on deposing Premier Chou En-lai, had no such connexions;[22] nor had the 'Headquarters of the Red Working Rebels', which had convened a national conference of temporary workers to discuss their demands for better pay and conditions; nor had the Headquarters of the Battalion of Red Fighters', a Peking group which carried off eleven lorry loads of files from a government ministry and refused to return them despite repeated requests from the Committee for the Cultural Revolution.[23] And then there was a whole series of national organizations which were founded by the employees on state farms, workers, young people who had been directed into agriculture, and former soldiers. This must have been a particularly sore point with the Maoist Party leadership, for according to their theory only estate owners, kulaks, counter-revolutionaries and rightist elements, who were determined to sabotage the cultural revolution, would think of attacking Maoist organizations or high-ranking Maoist functionaries. In 1967 these, and other, composite and supraregional groups were exposed as counter-revolutionary organizations and proscribed by the leadership. But they were immediately replaced by new organizations which were equally 'reactionary', i.e. which also wanted to bring about a new form of socialism. The reactionaries – both groups and individuals – were extremely active at that time. They forced their way into military and civilian installations taken over by the army (such as airports, radio stations, prisons and secret archives) falsified or misconstrued Mao's directives and documents published by Party headquarters, sent anonymous reactionary letters, posted counter-revolutionary wall newspapers, distributed anti-Maoist leaflets, and spread rumours. They also encouraged the masses to withdraw large sums of money from their savings accounts, disrupted the economic and commercial life of the country, destroyed machinery, tools and cultural objects, and staged strikes and demonstrations.[24] In the end, the army was forced to intervene in order to restore proletarian discipline.

But the reactionaries were not the only ones who failed to carry through the cultural revolution in accordance with the intentions of the Maoist Party leadership. The revolutionaries were equally culpable in this respect. They committed numerous errors, and they staged street battles and attacked revolutionary functionaries. Their organizations were 'impure', with the result that they were all required to carry out a 'campaign for the rectification of their working methods', and some even had to be disbanded. The peasant revolutionaries tried to undermine the quadripartite campaign launched by Mao Tse-tung in person in order to purge the administration, the economy, the political life of the country and the mental attitudes of the people, whilst their urban counterparts collected incriminating material in order to depose Maoist leaders such as Chou En-lai and Chiang Ching.

The revolutionary rebels were in a particularly difficult position. Although they had been exposed to bourgeois influences in the past, it was imperative that they should not allow themselves to become isolated from the masses. On the contrary, they were expected to win their support. At the same time, counter-revolutionary elements were trying to infiltrate their organizations in order to destroy them. Not surprisingly, many of the less reliable members of these organizations had gravitated, either consciously or unconsciously, towards the revisionist camp. Some had even tried to secure the support of 'capitalist despots' in the Party in order to strengthen their own positions.[25] In some groups counter-revolutionary and non-revolutionary infiltration was so pronounced that the group leaders were voted out of office.[26] Sectarianism and the fragmentation of the revolutionary groups became such a serious problem that from mid 1967 onwards the Chinese press began to speak of a 'continuous civil war'.[27] The rebel groups had only one thing in mind: to acquire power within the Great Alliance[28] prescribed by the Maoist leadership, and to this end they were prepared to go to any lengths.[29] In order to equip themselves for their street battles they stole weapons, ammunition and lorries from the People's Liberation Army, and on occasions even went so far as to attack arms convoys.[30] As a result, the leadership was obliged to issue a directive at the beginning of September 1967 authorizing the troops to use their weapons in self-defence, and to disarm the masses. A number of factories had to stop production on account of the 'civil war', which also involved a large section of the rural population. Under their new slogan 'The Villages Encircle the Towns', the peasants marched into the urban areas and attacked government departments, industrial concerns and schools. We now see why the troops were sent into the factories, mines and villages in October 1967 to re-educate the workers and peasants along Maoist lines. In 1968 the composition of the anti-Maoist opposition was still essentially the same, and reactionary organizations – one of which had the temerity to call itself an 'Extraordinary Committee Attached to the Central Committee of the Communist Party' – were still active. As in the previous year, these organizations attacked the revolutionary Party leaders. In their pamphlets and wall newspapers they propagated the notion that the 'thoughts of Chairman Mao', and the Maoist system of government, were no longer relevant, and carried out a smear campaign against the three leading protagonists of the cultural revolution: Mao Tse-tung, Lin Piao and Chou En-lai. Amongst other things, they pointed out that Mao and Chou had served in the Kuomintang and that Lin had studied at the Whampoa Military Academy,[31] where Chiang Kai-shek, the arch enemy of the Chinese people, had been rector. Meanwhile, the counter-revolutionaries who had infiltrated the factories, people's communes, economic departments and revolutionary committees in the course of 1967 also continued with their subversive activities in 1968.[32] Thus, the threat to the army and the revolutionary committees was maintained, and street battles and sabotage remained a regular feature of Chinese life. When Mao Tse-tung warned the nation that the current phase of the cultural revolution constituted a continuation of the struggle between the Kuomintang and the Chinese Communist Party, the 'renegades, spies and other incorrigible counter-revolutionary elements' in the country agreed with his analysis but went on to cast the leadership in the role of the Kuomintang; and their interpretation was believed by the masses.[33] Maoist leaders were particularly wary of the 'old rebels' of the cultural revolution, and they warned that many of these had become conservatives and right wing opportunists. This was perfectly true. The rebels' representatives in the revolutionary committees had already shown themselves to be unreliable in 1967, when they had acquired the twin sobriquets of the 'Five-Many' and the 'Five-Few'. (Many were elected to the praesidium, many drove around in motor cars, many sat in their offices, many were cinemagoers, and many sported Mao Tse-tung insignia on their breasts; but few studied Mao's writings, few did any manual work, few practised self-criticism or self-perfection, few maintained contact with the masses, and few had a revolutionary outlook.) Although periodic purges were carried out in 1968 – about every two months – these representatives became even less revolutionary than they had been in the previous year.[34] They longed for peace, and turned their backs on the class war. They were concerned for their personal reputations, and were genuinely worried lest they should be regarded as the new bourgeois class. And when they were told to implement further revolutionary actions, they either argued that these were precipitate or unnecessary, or else they simply ignored the directives. In fact, self-interest, and the interests of their group, were the only criteria they recognized, a polycentric attitude which virtually denied the authority of the Maoist leadership. But then the attitudes and actions of the rebels' representatives in the revolutionary committees were characterized at all levels by polycentrism, fragmentation, capitulationism and conservatism.[35]

In 1969 the Party still had to contend with the sesame four evils. The Maoist leadership and the army were still primarily concerned with the implementation of the cultural revolution in the revolutionary committees, and with the exposure and elimination of actual and potential class enemies. We have already seen that class enemies are likely to survive in China for a long time to come, since their ranks are being constantly swollen by unreliable elements from the revolutionary camp. Consequently, it is impossible to foresee an end to the permanent revolution. All we can say with any certainty is that it will continue. According to Mao Tse-tung, it will continue for as long as there are people in China.

CHAPTER VII
THE PARTY AND THE ARMY

Our principle is that the Party commands the gun, and the gun must never be allowed to command the Party.

MAO TSE-TUNG

1. The Party Leadership

The onset of the cultural revolution has been given an earlier date by Peking than it actually had in order to stress the continuous nature of the class war. The reform of the Chinese opera, which was initiated in 1963 under the personal supervision of Mao Tse-tung and his wife Chiang Ching, is said to have constituted the first phase of this development. On that occasion the whole cultural and propaganda apparatus opposed Mao's attempted purge of the Chinese *litterateurs* and cultural functionaries, which was to have been the prelude to a large scale literary revolution. This was one of the reasons why Mao emphasized how important it was not to abandon the class war. Early in 1965 he stated that the principal object of the 'Socialist Educational Movement' was the elimination of capitalist despots, and in the autumn of the same year he issued a directive condemning Wu Han's drama 'Hai Jui is Relieved of his Post' as an attempt to rehabilitate the deposed Minister of Defence Peng Te-huai. But when the Communist Party headquarters set up the 'Five Man Group for the Implementation of the Cultural Revolution' under the chairmanship of Peng Chen in order to coordinate the campaign against the revisionist intellectuals in the Party, Mao was thwarted yet again. For Wu Han was Peng Chen's deputy in the Peking municipal government, and so instead of being attacked, Wu was protected by the five man group. This prompted Mao to issue a warning against the dangers of revisionism at Party headquarters. Shortly afterwards Mao left Peking to seek support for his policies in the provinces, and his followers in Shanghai mounted a press campaign, under the supervision of Chiang Ching, against the Peng Chen clique in the capital. In this campaign Mao received the backing of the army newspaper, which is published in Shanghai. Meanwhile, with the active approval of the senior functionaries in the propaganda departments, Peng

Chen sought to defend himself by reducing the 'highly political issue of anti-Party and anti-socialist behaviour to a "purely academic" question'. Then, acting in the name of the highest authority but without Mao's knowledge, Peng published his 'February Theses' in which he censured the cultural revolutionaries of Shanghai for 'treating a purely academic question in political terms' and trying to 'bludgeon' the people with dogmas. He suggested that it was preferable to persuade people by reasoned argument, and pointed out that if this was to be done, greater attention would have to be paid by all concerned to the real issues facing the Party. Peng insisted that the convinced leftists had also been infected by bourgeois ideas and were therefore liable to error. They would have to be purged politically and ideologically re-educated.

As yet no reliable information has come to hand concerning the part played by Liu Shao-chi – the Chinese Krushchev – and his group in the events leading up to the deposition of Peng Chen. Nor is there any means of establishing whether Liu proposed to hold an 'anti-Mao plenum without Mao' in July 1966 (similar to the Soviet plenum which deposed Krushchev). We can be sure, however, that when Mao moved against Peng Chen, the opposition to his policies within the Party had become quite powerful. Peng's 'February Theses' were published as an official document on February 12, 1966, and it took Mao until May 15 to have the 'Five Man Group' disbanded, and another month to have Peng removed from his numerous posts (he was a member of the Standing Committee, a First Secretary, and Mayor of Peking). Incidentally, because of the influence which Peng had exerted in Peking, Mao took the precaution of 're-organizing' the Peking Party Committee. And to complete the first of the five purges which he carried out at Party Headquarters Mao exposed as revisionists Lu Ting-i (the head of the propaganda department attached to the Central Committee), Lo Jui-ching (the Chief of the Army General Staff), and Yang Shang-kun (the head of the Central Committee's department for general affairs).

After this initial victory Mao Tse-tung let it be known that the purges were to continue. In July 1967 he was reported as saying that only a few of the 'reactionary capitalist revisionists' who had infiltrated the Party had been exposed and that 'others of Krushchev's sort are still snoring in our midst'.[1] It is, in fact, true that during Mao's absence from the capital Liu Shao-chi and Tang Hsiao-ping tried to bring the cultural revolution under central control and so render it impotent. Mao hit back by convening a plenary session of the Central Committee for August 1967 in the expectation that he would be able to force his policy through and have it endorsed by the plenum. But according to Soviet reports, only half of the members, and one third of the candidate members, of the Central Committee attended this assembly. Mao appears to have been undeterred, however, for we are told that he made up the necessary number by recruiting functionaries from various Party committees, members of the Group for the Implementation of the Cultural Revolution set up by the Central Committee[2] and 'representatives of the revolutionary lecturers and students at the Peking University colleges'. But for all Mao's astuteness, the plenary session ended in compromise. Lin Piao moved up to No 2 in the Standing Committee, which was a victory for Mao. But the Chinese Krushchev and his followers still remained members of the Standing Committee, albeit, demoted. Moreover, the new revolutionary masses were given only a subordinate part to play in the cultural revolution, the leadership of which was entrusted to the Party despite the presence of 'people of Krushchev's sort' at Party Headquarters and the unreliability of a majority of Party secretaries.[3] An even more pointed rebuff for Mao Tse-tung was the elimination of the army from active participation in the cultural revolution (which was later represented as an intrigue on the part of class enemies). After the compromises of the plenary session, which were regarded as a political defeat by Mao and his followers, the Red Guards and rebels were encouraged to purge the Party of its capitalist-revisionist officials.[4] By January 1, 1967 it was part of Mao's official policy that the mass of the workers and peasants, accounting for more than 90 per cent of the population, should be mobilized against the revisionist officials in the Party.

2. Local Party Committees

In view of the nature of the charges brought against Liu Shao-chi, Mao's decision to use outsiders in order to purge the Party must have seemed very strange to most Party members. For China's Krushchev was supposed to have done his utmost to introduce 'traitors, agents and counter-revolutionaries' into the Party and place them in positions of power. Certainly, Liu's theoretical writings were required reading for all candidate members, who were taught that it was permissible to 'join the Party in order to become an official', and that it was important for all Party members to obey their immediate superiors.[5] The situation was aggravated by the fact that the majority of Party secretaries at all levels had either failed to understand the cultural revolution or were not taking it seriously.[6] This was why the struggle between the Party functionaries on the one hand and the Red Guards and rebels on the other was so fierce. Again and again, the latter were branded as counter-revolutionaries, dismissed from their jobs, and even imprisoned. At the same time, the functionaries made full use of Party discipline to keep Party members under control and ensure that they did not join the revolutionaries. They also formed 'Armies for the Defence of Red Power' in order to protect themselves from attack,[7] and did their utmost to suppress the cultural revolution by insisting that priority be given to the needs of the production programme.[8] For a while this tactic succeeded, but eventually the workers defied the Party and walked out of the factories, whereupon the functionaries joined forces with the ideologically-backward workers and raised the 'ill wind of economism'. When this move also failed, they posed as leftist radicals and sought to sabotage the revolution by misinterpreting the directives issued by the Maoists at Party headquarters.

It was always claimed that there was only a handful of capitalist despots and revisionists in the Party. Their violent attacks on the revolutionaries were not a sign of strength but the hysterical acts of desperate men faced with certain defeat. On the other hand, the Maoists also maintained that even after they had been exposed, these despots were still a force to be reckoned with, and they pointed out that their lackeys had continued to wreak havoc in every Chinese town and every revolutionary organization, and had also acquired a considerable following amongst the population. In one factory in Shanghai, for example, it was discovered that every single department was under the control of these 'evil' Party functionaries (whom the Maoists divided into two categories: those who had acquired a 'capitalist soul' of their own accord and those who had been corrupted by revisionist colleagues).[9] Clearly, there must have been considerably more than a handful of revisionist functionaries. In fact, these people controlled virtually every Party committee in the provinces, the districts, the towns, the people's communes, and the industrial, cultural and educational units.[10] This was why, in spite of the assistance of the army, it took the cultural revolutionaries almost two years to seize power. And the Maoist leaders needed a full three years to undermine the prestige enjoyed by the 'Chinese Krushchev' amongst the Party membership. It was only after the cultural revolutionaries had seized power in every single province that the leadership was able to identify Liu Shao-chi as a reactionary, and expel him from the party.[11]

Against the entrenched power of the Party functionaries, the cultural revolution would probably never have succeeded had it not been for the intervention, at a very early stage, of the People's Liberation Army.

3. The Army

The Chinese People's Liberation Army forms an integral part of Chinese society. It has always recruited its soldiers from the peasantry, and its command structure has always been closely integrated with the power structure of the Communist Party. Before he became chairman of the Party in 1935, Mao Tse-tung served as political commissar in the army under Chu Te. Moreover, Mao has always held that armed conflict is the only way of conducting the class war in China. Consequently, the army has played a major part in the Chinese revolution. During the 'democratic revolution', for example, it was entrusted with a number of administrative and political tasks, in addition to its normal military role. Thus, troops were used 'to disseminate propaganda amongst the masses . . . to help them establish the new revolutionary authority, and to found Party organizations'.[12] Because it is so fully integrated into Chinese society, the army almost invariably reflects the conflicts which arise in that society. Thus, even before Peng Chen was deposed in the initial phase of the cultural revolution Lo Jui-ching, the Chief of the Chinese General Staff, was stripped of his powers. Lo was also a member of the Secretariat and of the Military Council of the Central Committee, acting Minister of Defence, and a

Deputy Premier. He was accused of trying to develop the army along purely military lines instead of introducing the troops to the thoughts of Mao Tse-tung and training them in accordance with the Maoist conception of the people's war. At the beginning of March 1966 a committee of army generals was set up to consider the case against Lo. One of the things to which this committee took exception was that instead of confessing his crimes against Mao Tse-tung and engaging in self-criticism Lo tried to commit suicide by jumping out of a window. After Lo had been removed from his command steps were taken to counter the influence he had exerted on both the Party and the army.

After this initial purge of the high comand, the army began to play an important part in the cultural revolution. Thus, in April 1966 troops were sent to occupy the offices of the Peking Party Committee, in which Peng Chen was first secretary.[13] Then, at the beginning of May, the army newspaper made a major contribution by demanding a purge of Party intellectuals. Incidentally, it was the army newspaper which coined the phrase 'cultural revolution'.[14] Later the same month the army's political department provided ideological courses for 'politically reliable' pupils and students, who subsequently formed the nucleus of the Red Guard units. And it was the army that organized transport for the Red Guards and other youth organizations when they visited Peking. In the capital these young people were looked after by soldiers and army functionaries, who 'lived, ate, and read and discussed the writings of Mao Tse-tung' with their charges. Thus, the army became involved in the cultural revolution from the outset. On the other hand, the famous 'sixteen points' specified by the Central Committee of the Party as the guidelines for the cultural revolution did not envisage an active role for the army. This would indicate a contradiction at Party headquarters, where there were a number of army leaders.

In January 1967 the army began to play a more important part in the cultural revolution. In Nanking, in the provinces of Hunan, Shansi and Heilungkiang, and even in a rural district near Peking, troops were deployed to protect the revolutionaries. At the same time, however, a number of army units were accused of having suppressed leftist groups. This deviation from the provisons of the 'sixteen point resolution' on the one hand and the anti-Maoist behaviour of individual military units on the other would suggest that the conflicts within the army had become acute. And, in fact, we find that a purge of the high command was carried out shortly afterwards. The most eminent of the victims of this campaign was Marshal Ho Lung,[15] who had been appointed 'Chief of the General Staff of the Red Guards' in the autumn of the previous year. According to the army newspaper, the class war within the army was both violent and complex, and was likely to decide the 'fate of the cultural revolution'. On January 23, 1967, following the eliminination of the opposition, the army was instructed officially to play an active part in the cultural revolution and, if necessary, to use arms in support of the leftist groups. Not long afterwards, the army was also instructed to set up revolutionary committees based on the principle of the 'triple alliance'. In some cases this was achieved speedily and efficiently, in others it proved a lengthy business, which can only mean that certain army units were less than enthusiastic about this project. In a number of places the army actually had to overcome open opposition from within its own ranks before it could proceed. The province of Heilungkiang is a case in point. On the very day they were ordered to take control of the local administration, loyal troops in the provincial capital of Harbin were still busily rounding up units of their own force which had defected to the counter-revolutionary camp. It took a full week for the army to seize power and set up a revolutionary committee in Harbin, and within a fortnight soldiers had to be redeployed to prevent this revolutionary committee from being overthrown. In fact, troops and gunboats were still being used against strongpoints occupied by 'anti-Maoist groups' at the end of February,[16] and it is inconceivable that these could have continued to hold out unless they had been stiffened by deserters. Nor was Harbin an isolated case. In Chekiang province the rightists in the Party and the army made common cause against their leftist opponents, staging street battles and posing such a serious threat to the local revolutionaries that the Maoist leadership was obliged to send representatives from both the 'superior military region' and Party headquarters to take control. A number of political commissars and army commanders were also exposed as capitalist despots in Szechuan, and Chinghai, and also in Inner Mongolia, where the army fired on the masses and made numerous arrests.[17] In some military regions the troops even staged 'revolutions from below', although this had been expressly forbidden.[18]

In the first half of 1967 the army was in a state of crisis. Of the 28 military regions, which correspond more or less to the administrative provinces, only 6 were reliable, a further 7 were unreliable, and the rest were keeping their options open whilst paying lip service to the revolutionary cause.[19] Peking sought to resolve this crisis by replacing the unreliable political commissars and military commanders, and by offering a sort of amnesty to local commanders, who were told that even if they had joined the ranks of the anti-Maoists, they could retrieve their position by self-criticism and correcting their errors.[20] But even after these measures had been put into effect, the army was still exposed to the threat of internal divisions, for class enemies constantly sought to undermine army unity and sow discord between the local military commands and the revolutionary committees. And there were still enough reactionary officers who were determined to wreck the new revolutionary movement. This became abundantly clear in March 1968 when Yang Cheng-wu, who had been appointed Chief of the General Staff in the course of the cultural revolution, was relieved of his post together with the political commissar for the Air Force, and the commander of the Peking garrison.

But despite the suspect loyalty of certain military regions the Maoist leadership was forced to rely on the army. For until the summer of 1967 only 28 per cent of the Politburo and Central Committee secretaries, 34 per cent of Central Committee members, 22 per cent of the candidate members of the Central Committee and 28 per cent of the first and second secretaries in the provinces remained politically active.[21] This naturally had a paralysing effect on the regular Party apparatus. By contrast, and despite repeated purges, the Party machine in the army (which was able to call on the services of about a million members) had remained pretty well intact. As soon as the army was authorized to intervene in the cultural revolution, the Military Commission attached to the Party Central Committee issued directives governing its implementation in different military establishments. They laid down that the revolution was to be implemented in full at all army headquarters (albeit by stages and under the supervision of the political commissar) but that at lower levels (i.e. corps or divisional level) only 'positive education' was to be provided. The commission also stipulated that 'revolutions from below', and the kind of discussions conducted by the Red Guards and the revolutionaries when they visited their colleagues in other towns to compare revolutionary experiences, were to be discouraged. The power structure of the army had to be preserved at all costs.[22] In order to ensure the politico-ideological reliability of the officer class, all officers were required to make class distinctions even in their own family circles, and to undertake class struggle and education with their own relatives. It was argued that 'peaceful coexistence' with reactionary wives or children was impossible and that consequently it was incumbent on all army officers to try to re-educate them along Maoist lines, since failure to do so must inevitably lead to their own corruption. 'Incurably reactionary' wives or children were to be reported to the competent authorities.[23]

Since it possessed the only effective administrative machine in the country, the army was obliged to undertake the duties normally performed by regional Party and government committees. Accordingly, it sent functionaries into the factories, mines, people's communes, financial and economic departments, and even the schools and provincial administrations, in order to help the revolutionary masses and local functionaries to set up revolutionary committees.[24] Officers, soldiers and political commissars were also sent to factories and communes, where together with the workers and peasants they lived, ate and worked, studied Mao's writings and directives, undertook political education, and maintained 'work discipline'. They arranged meetings at which the revolutionary workers and peasants remembered the injustices and cruelties of the bourgeois regime and expressed their gratitude for the achievements of the cultural revolution and their resolve to obey its directives to the letter.[25] Meanwhile, the army cadres kept a close watch on the workers' and peasants' representatives in the revolutionary committees, investigated their families, and organized everything with such exemplary zeal that before long they came to be regarded as the mainstay of the Maoist administration.

Needless to say, this extension of the army's activities into the administrative sphere increased and intensified the conflicts between the army and the people. Peking was quick to notice this undesirable trend, and from the beginning of April 1967 the army was told not to take military action against any revolutionary groups, but to confine itself to political work. They also had to apply for permission to Party headquarters before branding any such groups as reactionary or counter-revolutionary, and they were not allowed to retaliate when attacked by crowds. At the same time, the masses were told that their rating as proletarian revolutionaries depended on the attitude they adopted to the army.[26] However, relations between the army and the people remained as bad as ever with the result that in August 1968 the leadership was obliged to repeat its warning in stronger terms. If was suggested that if anyone had a grievance against an army comrade, it should be reported to his immediate superior. On no account were public accusations to be made either against individuals or against the army. The revolutionaries were told that they could rely on the army authorities to take speedy action to rectify any lapses or errors on the part of individual soldiers or military functionaries. But as late as 1969 the Chinese press was still reporting cases of personal inadequacy amongst army personnel. Some were accused of adopting a scornful attitude towards erring revolutionaries, others of being over-cautious in their approach to members of the revolutionary groups. There were also those who failed to implement the leadership's directives because they found them too complex, and those who distorted them to suit their own leftist leanings. And there were others who were afraid of rehabilitating, and restoring to office, local functionaries whom they had previously opposed, or who refused to expose known reactionaries for fear of the consequences.[27] Finally, there were some army personnel whose heads had been turned by the public acclaim they had received after the initial phase of the cultural revolution and who had subsequently acquired a distinctly bourgeois outlook.[28] But quite apart from the conflicts between the army and the masses, there were further conflicts both between the regional army staffs and the troops under their command, and between the different army groups.

It was clear from the outset that the army personnel should not be allowed to use their own judgement in such complex civilian operations, which called for the constant supervision of political commissars. Consequently, some 80 per cent of the army's political functionaries accompanied the officers and soldiers when they were sent to the factories and people's communes. But there were still not enough functionaries to go round, which meant that the smaller detachments had to operate without supervision. This was a potentially dangerous situation, and in order to exercise some measure of control a number of the functionaries responsible for the activities of these detachments gave strict instructions that they were always to work as groups, so as to enable individual soldiers to supervise one another. But although it helped security, this arrangement proved extremely cumbersome. Difficulties also arose when companies which had been seconded from their army groups to perform civilian duties in other military districts, ignored the local garrisons, thus causing unnecessary friction and jeopardizing their mission. A similar threat was posed in other districts, where military units or companies seconded from different branches of the army wasted a great deal of time bickering with one another instead of making common cause against the class enemy. But the greatest threat of some leading political cadres in the army to isolate themselves from the ordinary soldiers and live their lives in the 'rarefied atmosphere of privilege'. Because of this tendency, the leadership was for ever reminding these cadres of the qualities that they were supposed to bring to their work. Basically, the ideal political commissar was a man who never lost his temper, even when wrongly accused, and who was able to collaborate with colleagues who held different views from his own without betraying his Maoist principles; he was also politically conscious and knew precisely which persons he had to win over and which to combat; he engaged in constant self-criticism, thus purging himself of all egoistic notions and desires, and read the works of Mao Tse-tung at all times, drawing on them for guidance whenever he was faced with an intractable problem.[29] The army certainly needed such men, for it was confronted with the difficult task of reconstructing and reactivating the Party.

4. The Reconstruction of the Party

Points 5 and 8 of the '16 point resolution', which was ratified by the Party Central Committee on August 8, 1966, stated that the capitalist despots constituted only a small minority of Party functionaries, 95 per cent of whom were either 'good' or 'fairly good' and were therefore to be regarded as allies. However, the Red Guards and revolutionaries tended to look upon all functionaries as revisionists and did their best to expose them as such. From the end of August 1966 onwards the Maoist propagandists insisted again and again that the overwhelming majority of functionaries were really on Mao's side, but they failed to make any lasting impression on the Guards and revolutionaries, who were clearly intent on deposing all figures of authority. In the end the Maoist leadership was obliged to condemn this attitude as egoistic and anarchistic. But the leadership still had to provide some explanation for the fact that Party functionaries, who should really have set an example to the masses, had themselves fallen into error. It did so partly by invoking the old theory of the 'poisonous plant', partly by blaming the period of misrule under the 'Chinese Krushchev', but partly also by accusing those who wanted to see *all* Party functionaries removed from office of trying to exploit this difficulty in order to save the capitalist despots in the Party. The leadership knew well enough that there were large numbers of functionaries who held bourgeois views and were guilty of every kind of ideological error. But they insisted that the revolutionary masses, whom it credited with very considerable analytical powers, knew that not every functionary was a capitalist despot. It called upon the masses to adopt a benevolent attitude to those functionaries who had erred, thus enabling them to return to the socialist fold and once again become leaders of the revolution. This exhortation to the masses was combined with a warning to the erring functionaries, who were told that if they failed to make common cause with the revolutionary workers and peasants, they would indubitably become anti-revolutionaries and anti-Maoists.

After revolutionary committees had been set up on a nation-wide basis, and the Party functionaries had been rehabilitated by the army in the autumn of 1968, special training centres were opened in practically every district in which revisionist cadres could purge themselves of their bourgeois ideas and learn to adopt a proletarian *weltanschauung* through physical work. They could then be appointed to positions of authority in the Maoist administration. There was some resemblance between Maoist and Liuist practice in this respect, for it will be remembered that under the 'capitalist' system evolved by Liu, Party functionaries had to work long and hard during the early stages of their careers in order to qualify for senior positions later on. But this resemblance reflects the way in which the Maoist leadership kept moving to the right in the course of the cultural revolution. The first clear indication of this rightist tendency was given when the revolutionary committees were set up. According to paragraph 9 of the '16 point resolution' of August 8, 1966 these should have been called 'cultural revolutionary groups, committees and congresses'. In the event, however, the crucial word 'cultural' was dropped, and no attempt was made to establish congresses. Moreover, according to the original resolution, the membership of these committees was to have been decided by the method used at the time of the Paris Commune. In other words, the revolutionary masses were to compile a list of candidates and, after holding preliminary discussions, to elect the members from that list; and as an additional safeguard against the emergence of authoritarian or bureaucratic practices the masses were also to be empowered to vote out of office any member whom they found unsatisfactory. But this blueprint was unrecognizable in the actual committees. The resolution of August 8 made no reference whatsoever to the participation of revolutionary functionaries or army personnel, yet in the event the army representatives and, to a lesser extent, the representatives of the revolutionary functionaries – neither of whom were chosen by the masses – assumed the dominant role. This volte-face was preceded by a series of conflicts between different sections of the Maoist leadership, which set in following the abortive attempt to establish a commune in Shanghai. We have already seen that two members of the Committee for the Implementation of the Cultural Revolution set up by the Central Committee to co-ordinate different facets of the cultural revolution were sent to Shanghai to help with the establishment of the commune; and we have also seen that whereas the local Shanghai newspapers hailed the commune as a victory for the 'thoughts of Chairman Mao', the national press did not refer to it at all until it had come to an end. The reason it was dissolved was that the masses had more power than the Party and the army, and this did not correspond to the power structure of the Chinese People's Republic. But the advocates of the Shanghai commune laid the blame for its demise at the door of the 'arch bureaucrat' – the name given to Chou En-lai by the Red Guards during the late phase of the cultural revolution. The conflict between Chou En-lai and his 'bureaucratic clique' on the one hand and the Committee for the Cultural Revolution on the other came to a head when the Committee members persuaded a number of Red Guard units in Peking to join forces in the 'Corps of May 16' in order to expose Chou as a second 'Chinese Krushchev' and so bring about his downfall.[30] Subsequently, the Committee members tried to implement the cultural revolution within the army, which also had its fair share of capitalist despots. But in doing so it overreached itself, for the army was then the only body capable of maintaining public order, and the leadership could not condone any attempt to undermine its authority. As a result, many of the Committee members were exposed as class enemies and severely disciplined. The *Red Flag*, the official mouthpiece of the Central Committee, was a further casualty of this purge; it was proscribed from the end of 1967 to July 1968 because both its chief editor, and its assistant editor, had been members of the Committee for the Implementation of the Cultural Revolution.[31] Moreover, the fact that Mao's wife made far fewer public appearances and was seldom mentioned in the Chinese press from 1968 onwards must also have been linked with this anti-leftist campaign, for she was the deputy head of the Committee for the Implementation of the Cultural Revolution and one of the most ardent champions of the cultural revolution in its original form. Just how much power she lost at that time became apparent when she spoke at the mass meeting held on September 7, 1968 to celebrate the setting up of the new revolutionary committees on a nationwide basis. In her speech she said that she had not even known that there was to be a mass meeting until she had been asked – just a few hours before – to address the delegates. After making this revealing remark, she went on to urge her audience not to forget the splendid achievements of the Red Guards during the early and transitional phases of the cultural revolution, with which she herself had been intimately connected.

Following the elimination of those Maoists who had stubbornly adhered to the original version of the cultural revolution the leadership was able to turn its attention to the reconstruction of the Party apparatus. On January 1, 1968 this was officially stated to be one of the principal tasks facing the Party. Accordingly, the cultural revolution was represented from then onwards as an 'open-ended reorganization of the Party'. But before it could implement this new policy the leadership felt compelled to carry out a large scale purge in order to 'root out' the counter-revolutionaries amongst the general population. For it was argued that if the Party was to regain its vitality, it must first rid itself of all such undesirable elements and replace them by 'new blood' from among those factory workers who had shown themselves to be 'activists in the study of the thoughts of Mao Tse-tung'. But if it was to reconstruct the Party, the leadership also had to elect a new Central Committee, and it proposed to do this at the 9th Party Congress which it hoped to convene in the autumn of 1968. However, this project met with considerable opposition. Since the Party apparatus had broken down there was no established procedure for deciding the composition of such a congress. The Party headquarters wanted to appoint the majority of the delegates (i.e. all except the delegates from the army, which had its own Party apparatus), and it was actively supported in this respect by the Party's propaganda organs which criticized 'superstitious adherence to formalism', arguing that 'our power' was vested in 'us' – i.e. in the surviving members at Party headquarters – by more than 90 per cent of the population. But despite such propaganda, the Party headquarters was unable to get its own way and instead of a Party congress had to content itself with a 12th plenary session of the old Central Committee. Over half the members of this plenum, which sat from October 13 to 31, 1968, had been specially co-opted to replace those members who had been deposed, and according to Party statutes these co-opted members were not entitled to vote. But this did not prevent the plenum from expelling Liu Shao-chi from the Party, even though a two-thirds majority was required, which in the circumstances was clearly unobtainable. In addition, the plenum relieved Liu of all his official posts, both inside and outside the Party, although this also constituted a clear breach of the Party statutes. Strictly, such action could only have been taken by a National People's Congress, which the Maoist leadership had in fact planned to convene in the late autumn of 1968, immediately after the 9th Party Congress. But when the Party congress proved impossible, the plan for a National People's Congress was dropped. It has yet to be revived.

After the 12th plenum the Party members in the army, and

in the revolutionary committees, met to *elect* delegates to the 9th Party Congress. The procedure adopted in these elections varied in different provinces. Some convened general assemblies attended by Party members from all types of revolutionary committee whilst others convened separate assemblies for each different type of committee (i.e. from district level upwards). Eventually, the 9th Party Congress was convened on April 1, 1969, and it elected 170 members and 109 candidate members to the new Central Committee. The full members consisted of 77 professional soldiers (45·3 per cent), 52 functionaries (30·59 per cent), 25 workers (14·67 per cent), 11 peasants (6·49 per cent), 3 scientists (1·77 per cent) and 2 persons whose occupations are unknown (1·18 per cent). The candidate members consisted of 50 professional soldiers (45·87 per cent), 17 functionaries (15·59 per cent), 14 workers (12·85 per cent), 13 peasants (11·93 per cent), 2 scientists (1·84 per cent) 2 Red Guards (1·84 per cent) and 10 persons whose occupations are unknown (10·08 per cent). In both categories the professional soldiers were the largest single group. But although this un-doubtedly reflected the importance of the army in China, it does not mean that Chinese politics were controlled by the military. For political decisions were still taken either by the Politburo or by its Standing Committee, and were merely presented to the Central Committee for ratification. The mem-bers of the Standing Committee were Mao Tse-tung, Lin Piao, Chou En-lai and two other 'bureaucrats', a combination which struck a reasonable balance of power between the professional soldier Lin Piao, who was Mao's 'closest comrade in arms', and the bureaucrats, whose numerical superiority offset any ad-vantages Lin might otherwise have possessed. The only person in the Standing Committee whose authority was unquestioned was Mao himself, for the other four members had all demon-strated their unswerving allegiance to him. The composition of the Politburo also appeared to have been arranged so as to ensure that all interests were represented, for the membership included ultra-leftists from the Committee for the Implementa-tion of the Cultural Revolution, followers of Lin Piao, regional army commanders who were not followers of Lin's, and the surviving members of the old Politburo, who showed little enthusiasm for the cultural revolution and were even subjected to fierce attacks by its protagonists. It has also been established that no more than a third of the professional soldiers in the Central Committee were members of Lin Piao's group,[32] and although Lin was officially designated as Mao's successor in the new Party statutes, it was far from certain that he would inherit the absolute power and the great prestige enjoyed by the present chairman.[33] At the 9th Party Congress Mao alluded to this problem: 'We hope that this Party congress will be a victory for Party solidarity, and that even greater victories will be achieved after the congress.'

But although a Party congress was held, the Party had yet to be reconstructed. In the two year period from the beginning of 1968 to the beginning of 1970 only one district Party Committee in the whole of China was completely reorganized; and although Party cells were formed in a number of factories or factory departments, and the army (which played an active part in the whole of this reconstruction programme) opened offices and 'experimental centres for the reorganization of the Party', no real headway was made. According to the leader writer of the *Red Flag*, this was largely due to the fact that many rank and file Party members simply were not able to understand Mao's directives.[34] Inevitably, such people neglected the requirements of Party policy. Many considered that provided they followed the Party's general line, they could afford to interpret its directives as they pleased; others felt that it was up to their superiors to decide how specific directives were to be interpreted; whilst yet others were firmly convinced that Party directives undermined popular initiative,[35] and so instead of carrying out those directives, they did what the masses wanted them to do, even when it was demonstrably wrong, in the belief that they were implementing the 'mass line'. They had overlooked the all-important fact that Mao Tse-tung represented 95 per cent of the people, and were unaware that the implementation of the mass line really meant educating the masses so that they would be able to understand and appreciate the policies pursued by the leadership on their behalf.[36] The ideological attitudes of the masses at that time can be seen from the example of the peasants. The leadership had been forced to allow them to rear pigs for their own use, keep their personal property, cultivate their vegetable patches, and work on their own account even during the peak agricultural periods. Once again egoism had gained the ascendancy. The peasants preferred to work on their own land rather than in the communes, and the local functionaries either could not, or would not, do anything about it. In the circumstances, it is hardly surprising that the leadership's protracted endeavours to reconstruct the Party should have met with such little success.

Because it was so unsuccessful, this campaign was seldom reported in the Chinese press. But we are able to form a general idea of the way in which this campaign was planned from the information provided about a number of prestige projects that were carried out in different parts of China.[37] In these projects the first step was the formation of a hard core of Party members (revolutionary functionaries, 'outstanding workers' and relatives of the soldiers attached to the factories) who were placed under the supervision of the local army unit and made to study those writings of Mao Tse-tung which dealt with the reconstruction of the Party. Subsequently, special study courses were devised to interest the 'broad mass' of Party members and non-members in the task of Party-building. Discussions were then held to decide whether anybody should be expelled from the Party, given further study courses, or punished for misdemeanours. Any class enemies also had to be identified and exposed at this stage. And if Party members found it impossible to reach agreement with non-members, the army provided further courses on the teachings of Mao Tse-tung until there was unanimity on all sides. If non-members who had applied for Party membership were present, their individual motives would be examined and at the same time there would be mass criticism of Liu Shao-chi's thesis that entry into the Party was simple a necessary first step in building a career. Finally, when the Maoists and the masses had reached total agreement on all issues, the Party members elected leadership groups for the individual Party branches, and then went on to elect Party committees. Above all, these committees had to combat actual and potential cases of fractionalism, anarchism, economism and egoism. They were advised to pay close attention to the younger workers, who were considered to be particularly unreliable 'because they had had no experience of the suffering in the old society' and consequently were unable to make a 'proper comparison between the old and the new China'. But the Party committees were not only required to conduct the class struggle, they also had to intensify it, especially if they found that Party members and the masses had conceived the 'false notion' that the country was at peace. In order to counter this notion the committees were instructed to 'root out' class enemies from the ranks of the workers and to encourage the masses to furnish information about them so that they could be exposed. Courses in Maoist doctrine, for Party members and non-members alike, were held at frequent intervals to ensure that people's attitudes remained ideologically sound, and special courses were also held for those whose work was below standard.

One question of crucial importance was the relationship between the new Party committees and the old revolutionary committees. This question was answered quite unequivocally by the Maoist leaders, who insisted that 'the relationship between the Party and the revolutionary committees must be a relationship between those who lead and those who are led'. Thus, the revolutionary committees had to implement the resolutions passed by the Party committees. However, in practical terms this situation hardly ever arose, for in the majority of cases the members of the revolutionary committees were also members of the Party committees. Moreover, the administrative work of these committees was executed by the same departments. So what really happened was that the revolutionary committees were more or less incorporated into the new Party committees. The Party functionaries have therefore regained the positions which they held prior to the cultural revolution, and the advantages which the revolutionary workers obtained in the course of the cultural revolution have largely been taken away from them. The only way in which they can now acquire positions of authority and power is by joining the Party, and those who do are now suspected of career-opportunism.

It was in 1956 that Mao Tse-tung first acknowledged the existence of conflicts in Chinese society. Today, those conflicts are as prevalent as ever. If anything, the principal conflict – between those who lead and those who are led – has become even more pronounced over the years. For Party members 'those who are led' are the non-members, for the members of Party committees they are the rank and file Party members plus the non-members. This relationship between superior and inferior sections of the community extends right up the scale to the Party leadership itself, and is found in every sphere of Chinese life. And no matter who leads, those who are led are the masses.

CHAPTER VIII
MAOISM

Comrade Mao Tse-tung is the greatest Marxist-Leninist of our times. With his all-embracing creative genius comrade Mao Tse-tung has taken over, defended and elaborated the Marxist-Leninist heritage; he has raised Marxism-Leninism to a completely new level.

LIN PIAO

The phenomenal success of Maoism throughout the whole of China would not have been possible without the support given by Lin Piao, 'Mao Tse-tung's closest comrade in arms'. After taking command of the army following the overthrow of the Minister of Defence, Peng Te-huai, in 1959 Lin applied the thoughts of Mao Tse-tung in the military sphere, and eventually succeeded in replacing the code under which the army had operated during Peng's ministry with a new code based on political criteria. The training methods used to re-educate the pupils, students, workers, employees and peasants during the cultural revolution – i.e. the 'Four Primaries', the 'Three-and-Eight Working Method', the 'Four-Good-Companies' and the 'Tripartite Democratic Method'[1] – were originally devised by Lin Piao prior to the revolution for use in the army. And the famous 'Little Red Book' of quotations from Mao, which became required reading for the entire population, was also compiled by Lin Piao for this purpose. Moreover, it was Lin who insisted that 'everybody must study the works of Chairman Mao, heed his words, act in accordance with his directives, and become a champion of Chairman Mao'; and he described the thoughts of Mao Tse-tung as a 'source of infinite power and a spiritual atom bomb of incalculable strength'. As for Lin himself, he was acclaimed from the beginning of the cultural revolution onwards, as Mao's greatest comrade in arms and his best disciple, and was held up as a 'perfect example' of how to study and apply the thoughts of Mao Tse-tung. At the 11th plenary session of the 8th Central Committee, which was held in August 1966, Lin emerged as Mao's right hand man, and from then onwards there were even occasional references to 'the thoughts of Lin Piao'. Finally, in the new Party statutes, which were adopted at the 9th Party congress in April 1969, Lin was officially designated as Mao's heir.

1. The Democratic Revolution

Maoism as propagated and defended by Lin Piao consisted of two principal parts, both of which were based on the experiences of the Chinese Communist Party. Both constituted a departure from traditional Marxism-Leninism. The first, which is particularly relevant to the oppressed peoples of Asia, Africa and Latin America, concerns the democratic revolution, i.e. the initial phase of the revolution, and the seizure of power by force of arms. Peking argued that since the reactionary ruling classes now have such a powerful grip on the cities, the Communist Parties in developing countries should emulate the Chinese Communist Party by concentrating on their rural areas, since these are the weakest link in the capitalist system. The first step in a modern democratic revolution is a peasant movement based on a programme of agrarian reform. When the estate owners and kulaks have been dispossessed by armed peasants and their lands redistributed, guerilla warfare can be developed by a partisan force drawn from the ranks of the peasants which will be able to establish military strong points in all liberated villages, and gradually encircle and capture the towns.[2] Lin Piao has gone further than this, carrying Mao's doctrine of the armed democratic revolution over into the international sphere. In a pamphlet, *Long Live the People's War*, he suggested that the relationship between developing and industrial nations was basically the same as the relationship between villages and towns. The struggles of the oppressed peoples of the world against imperialism would eventually liberate their oppressed fellow workers at the heart of the imperialist metropolis. In other words, the 'international villages' would encircle, and finally liberate, the 'international towns'.

2. Contradictions in Socialist Society

The second major component of Maoism concerns the furtherance of the revolution under a dictatorship of the proletariat, and is designed to prevent the emergence of revisionism. It is considered valid for all socialist countries. The original Marxist conception from which it was developed was based on three assumptions: (1) that different social classes are the product of different historical phases in the development of production;

(2) that the class struggle will lead to the establishment of a dictatorship of the proletariat; and (3) that this dictatorship is a transitional phase leading to the dissolution of all social classes and the creation of a classless society.[3] Lenin took Marxist theory further on the question of seizing State power in a revolutionary situation and setting up a dictatorship of the proletariat. However, he warned that the transition from capitalism to Communism would embrace a whole historical epoch, and that until such time as the transition had been completed, the exploiting classes would continue to hope for the restoration of capitalism, and that these *hopes* would inevitably lead to *attempts* at such a restoration. Lenin argued that opposition by the bourgeoisie would be *ten times as strong* after they had been overthrown, and reminded his followers that the power of the bourgeoisie came, not only from the strength of international capital and international bourgeois associations, but also from *force of habit* and the strength and tenacity of *small scale production*. He was particularly perturbed by the existence of small businesses which, he said, contributed to the growth of capitalism and the bourgeoisie 'daily, hourly ... and on a massive scale. In this connexion Lenin also claimed that a 'new bourgeoisie' was emerging from the ranks of 'our Soviet employees'.[4] But although Lenin had seen the problem, he was unable to furnish theoretical or practical solutions. It had not really occurred to him that in a socialist society the ultimate victory of the proletariat could be in doubt. He therefore left open the question as to how the proletariat was to maintain and consolidate its power. It was Mao Tse-tung, the 'modern Lenin', who found in the cultural revolution a solution to this central question, and so inaugurated a new era of international communism. It is unlikely that Lenin would have reached this solution, for despite his voluntarist leanings, he firmly believed that social consciousness is determined by social activity, and not *vice versa*. And although Mao Tse-tung has never actually denied this Marxist position in so many words,[5] he has none the less made it perfectly clear that he gives priority to consciousness. Accordingly, Maoist writers have tended to attach great importance to mental attitudes. They are particularly apprehensive about economism, which both gratifies and promotes the natural egoism found in all human beings. A further source of apprehension is the constant emergence of revisionists and

reactionaries in both the Party and the army, who try to u
power from within. It was because of this threat that the lea
ship formed a special group within the proletariat, the '
letarian revolutionaries', to safeguard proletarian power.

By Maoist definition, a proletarian cultural revolution
political revolution of the proletariat against the exploit
classes within the framework of a socialist State. In China
constituted a continuation of the protracted war waged
tween the Communist Party and its followers on the one ha
and the Kuomintang on the other, i.e. between the proletari
and the capitalists. There were three distinct phases in th
revolutionary process. In the first, secret opponents of the regim
were exposed; in the second, power was seized by the revolu
tionary forces; and in the third, that power was consolidated
The Party, the army and the revolutionary masses were to rall
behind the 'proletarian headquarters', which was under th
personal command of Mao Tse-tung and his deputy Lin Piao
After the seizure of power, revolutionary committees were set
up as provisional administrative organs. At provincial level the
revolutionary committees had jurisdiction over Party, political
and financial matters. But they did not have jurisdiction over
the local army units. These revolutionary committees – which
were formed in accordance with the 'triple alliance' by the
revolutionary masses, the revolutionary functionaries and the
representatives of the army (the only group not to be desginated
as a revolutionary force) – were supposed to constitute a
'proletarian government'. In fact, this did not happen. Although
the revolutionary committees have not actually been abolished,
they now have only a nominal existence. Since most of the
members of these committees are also Party members, it is
clearly impossible for the revolutionary committees to control or
supervise Party functionaries.

The most important aspect of Maoism in terms of the cultural revolution was the decision to use the army for civilian
duties. All revolutionary committees were placed under the
ultimate control of soldiers, and soldiers were stationed in
the factories, mines, financial and commercial departments,
schools, and cultural centres. The local party committees were
also organized, and subsequently controlled, by soldiers. But,
above all, the soldiers propagated the Maoist doctrine cham-
pioned by their Commander in Chief, Lin Piao, and in doing

so established Lin's reputation as Mao's foremost disciple. And so they launched, and supervised, a truly remarkable popular movement. From the beginning of the cultural revolution to the middle of 1968 the masses were themselves in control and the working class as a whole was officially designated the leader of the cultural revolution. With the passage of time, however, their role was progressively undermined until by mid 1968 they were effectively eliminated from all positions of authority. The leadership also shifted its ground by representing the cultural revolution as a personal revolution that takes place in the soul of each individual. In this connexion great significance was attached to Lin Piao's statement that everybody should regard himself, not only as the driving force behind the revolution, but also as the 'end object of the revolution'. In the second half of 1968 the cultural revolution came to be interpreted in these terms. And at the beginning of 1969 a new slogan was formulated: 'Unity based on centralism'. From then on, all aspects of the revolutionary process – politics, leadership, theoretical insights, planning – had to be unified. But if this was to be done, the Chinese people had to acquire a common sense of purpose, a common will. Accordingly, they were told that since Mao Tse-tung represented 95 per cent of the Chinese population and had the support of over 90 per cent of the world population, it was incumbent on them to 'pay reverence, unreservedly and eternally', to the proletarian headquarters commanded by Mao and his deputy and successor Lin Piao.

However, all such attempts to unite the country were vitiated by one major contradiction, brought about as a result of the tactics pursued by the Maoists themselves. For in order to continue the proletarian revolution the leadership had been obliged to adhere to the national front policy which it had pursued in the democratic revolution. In the cultural revolution it had to rely on the leftists and win over the centre before it could hope to implement its anti-rightist campaign with the backing of 95 per cent of the population. Lin Piao commented on this aspect of Party policy in his report to the 9th Party congress: 'It helps to consolidate the dictatorship of the proletariat, and to divide and undermine our enemies, if we handle the contradictions between ourselves and the enemy as if they were contradictions among the people.' This highly subjective approach to the problem merely confused the issue by introducing

heterogeneous elements into the Party's own ranks. Consequently, the leadership found itself constantly obliged to examine the class affiliations of its functionaries, combat reactionary and revisionist ideologies and their advocates, criticize the bourgeois outlook of Party members, and take steps to re-educate all those who became contaminated.

The Maoist leadership is not unaware of the contradiction between objective reality and its own subjective approach. It knows perfectly well what is happening, and accepts it as a reality in its own right. That is why Peking has given its assent to the conception of the permanent revolution. It considers that it will take several hundred years, and several cultural revolutions, before a Communist society can be achieved in China, and it insists that during this transitional period all necessary measures must be taken to ensure that the proletarian dictatorship, under the control of the Party, is constantly strengthened. It is in this sense that Mao's decision to use the army as a means of supervising and controlling every sphere of activity in the People's Republic – industry, agriculture, finance, commerce, culture, propaganda and the administration – constitutes the most important aspect of his creative development of Marxism-Leninism. By now it is perfectly clear that the continuing revolution is destined to go on for ever. Admittedly, we are told that when the proletariat has succeeded in liberating the whole of humanity, it will then have achieved its own emancipation. But we are also told that, in politico-ideological terms, the class war will *never* come to an end and that the mental revolution, i.e. the battle for men's minds, has no fixed time limit. The reason why Liu Shao-chi was condemned by the Maoist leadership was that he regarded the Communist society as a perfected – i.e. a static – society and equated it with the 'harmonious society' described by Confucius. However, Mao Tse-tung has also stated that one of the ultimate objectives of the Chinese Communist Party is to establish just such a 'harmonious society', both in China and in the world at large. This particular aspect of Mao's teachings is not mentioned in China today. But it is entirely feasible that it will be propagated at some future date as an essential component of Maoism, for the day will surely come when the continuous and growing tensions of the class war prove intolerable. And when that happens, the Chinese must either submit to a further cultural revolution, or else the process of peaceful evolution, which the Maoist leadership has always feared, must set in.

3. Maoist Culture and Maoist Man

In 1963 Mao Tse-tung said that drama and the cinema, the fine arts, ballet, the opera, poetry and prose writings were all dominated by the 'dead', i.e. by traditional ideas and traditional artists. In 1964 he said that, far from reflecting the socialist revolution and the construction of socialism, these art forms had become even more revisionist. Speaking in the same year, Mao's wife – who had become a cultural functionary at the beginning of 1963 – complained that the characters portrayed by the three thousand or so theatrical and opera companies in China were all either emperors or ministers or feudal or bourgeois lovers. It is, in fact, perfectly true that in the early 1960's socialist art and letters were at a low ebb in China. In 1962, for example, Mao's *Selected Works* appeared in an edition of 50,000 copies whilst the 1962 edition of the 'feudalistic' novel *The Dream of the Red Chamber* ran to 140,000 copies. It has also been estimated by the Maoist leadership that prior to the cultural revolution 7,500 tons of paper were used for printing feudalistic and bourgeois 'poison' whilst only 72 tons were used for the works of Mao Tse-tung. Even the army's cultural departments produced ideologically suspect works at that time. In 1967 the leadership reminded the Chinese people of the fearful consequences of the cultural policy pursued by Stalin, who had incorporated the whole of Russian classical literature into Soviet culture without criticizing it in any way, and it insisted that they must hold fast to Mao's ideas, for his 'Jenan Speech on Literature' had provided the 'first real summary of literature in the history of mankind'.[6] The principle underlying Mao's cultural and literary philosophy is very simple: culture and literature must serve the interests of the workers, peasants and soldiers. Accordingly, the first task which the Chinese artists and writers were asked to undertake was the creation of a new proletarian hero. In the twenty odd years since the proclamation of the People's Republic, this task has been fulfilled by 5 modern Peking operas, 2 revolutionary ballets and 1 orchestral symphony. The best known of these works is the opera *Conquering Tiger Mountain with Tactical Skill*, the final version of which was approved by the Party and prescribed for all performances.[7]

This opera, which was written and first performed in 1958, was redrafted from the beginning of 1963 under the supervision of Mao's wife. Thus, the final version bears the imprint of Chiang Ching, and has remained the model for all subsequent revolutionary operas. The action of *Conquering Tiger Mountain with Tactical Skill* takes place in Manchuria during the revolutionary war against the Kuomintang. The leading role is played by the People's Liberation Army, which is now the most important group in Chinese society and which at that time was commanded in Manchuria by Lin Piao, who carried out Mao's instructions to 'consolidate communist power in Manchuria'. The most important role is played by the revolutionary masses – peasants and two railwaymen – whilst the villains are represented by the 'bandits', i.e. the Kuomintang troops. The opera is full of class warfare. The bandits plunder and murder, and earn the inveterate hatred of the masses. Then, the People's Liberation Army appears on the scene, defeats the Kuomintang and saves the local populace. In the course of the campaign the army mobilizes the peasants to build a railway line, and encourages them to organize themselves, and train as a militia force. But although the army is the real hero of this opera, there is of course a personal hero as well. He is a soldier who comes from a poor peasant family, is a Party member, and has been brought up on the thoughts of Mao Tse-tung. He is also wise and courageous, and imbued with a hatred of the class enemy. Whilst carrying out his dangerous mission the soldier thinks constantly, not only of the Chinese revolution, but also of the world revolution that is to follow it. He does not shrink from adversity, or even from death itself. As an individual hero he is as fearless as a tiger, and as a class hero he dances rings around the Kuomintang. Even when he consciously puts his life at risk by disguising himself as a Kuomintang leader in order to penetrate the enemy ranks, he knows no fear, for he carries the 'morning sun in his breast', which is the source of all wisdom and strength (and is also one of the signs representing Mao Tse-tung). In ideological terms, it is impossible to fault this opera. Between them, the Liberation Army and the soldier hero represent all the qualities of Maoist man. However, in 1965 the cultural revolution was implemented, and from then onwards

Maoist man acquired a further dimension. Prior to the revolution he had been expected to spurn fame and affluence, to fear neither adversity nor death, and to dedicate himself to the revolutionary cause and the service of the people. Now he also has to undergo a 'total rebirth'. Apart from equipping himself for his daily occupation, the post-revolutionary Chinese has to acquire a thorough knowledge of politics, military strategy and culture, and be able to work in industry and agriculture, as a forester and a fisherman. He also has to combat his own egoistic and revisionist tendencies, constantly read the thoughts of Mao Tse-tung, and seek to change his own soul in the light of Mao's teachings. Finally, he has to 'root out' and expose class enemies, albeit with a measure of restraint since otherwise the opposition might become too numerous. If the young soldier who helped conquer Tiger Mountain were to be transported to present day China, one cannot be sure that he would still be hailed as a class hero.

4. Religious Elements of Maoism

Paul Tillich has tried to show an affinity between Communism and religion.[8] Similarly, C. Y. Yang, the regligious sociologist, has attempted to demonstrate that Chinese Communism is a kind of faith,[9] and Robert Lifton that quasi-religious considerations – such as the quest for revolutionary immortality and the insistence on revolutionary purity – were important motivating factors in the cultural revolution.[10] In this connexion it is often said that the God-substitute in present day China is provided by the people. But in the last two sections of this book, in which I hope to demonstrate the indebtedness of Chinese Communism to popular belief, I shall try to show that in China the godhead has been reincarnated, not in the people, but in their leader.

In Chinese mythology the heavens are represented as a pantheistic deity, and it was because of this supernatural association that the Chinese emperor was traditionally called the 'son of heaven'. Heaven is now the symbol of Mao Tse-tung, and reactionaries who try to usurp his power have been accused of behaving 'as if the gifts of heaven really came from them'. But Mao is represented not only by heaven, but by mother earth as well, and the sun symbol is now also reserved exclusively for Mao. Thus, the revolutionaries were said to have seized power so as to enable the 'infinitely radiant sun of the "thoughts of Mao Tse-tung" to shine forth and the heaven to become a "Mao-heaven" and the earth a "Mao-earth"'. Similarly, when the revisionists sought to divert the cultural revolution on to a non-Maoist path they were accused of trying to steal the heaven and to substitute a false sun. Fortunately, these dark clouds had been unable to blot out the radiant sunshine of the 'thoughts of Chairman Mao'. But quite apart from shining in the heavens, where its rays bring benefit to all mankind, the 'Mao-sun', which is the 'reddest of all red suns', also dwells in the hearts of men and enables them to overcome all their difficulties and achieve all their objectives. Yet another celestial body is used as a symbol for Mao: the polestar. In Taoist mythology the polestar is a pantheistic deity exercising a function similar to that of the Three Fates in Greek and Roman mythology; and although it might be held that the 'Mao-sun, -earth and -heaven' are simply imaginative terms which were coined in order to express a 'poetic truth', this can hardly be argued in respect of the 'Mao-polestar', whose mystical associations are quite explicit. This preoccupation with mysticism is reinforced by other expressions. Thus, the 'thoughts of Mao Tse-tung' are said to be a 'magic treasure house' and a 'magic weapon', and his 'three early publications' are a Marxist-Leninist 'book of magic[11] that gleams like gold', that transforms the 'soul' and provides a 'magic charm' that will protect the country from revisionism and peaceful evolution. The 'Little Red Book' of Mao quotations is also a 'book of magic that gleams like gold' and strengthens belief. In the Taoist myths and legends mortals mysteriously acquire books of magic charms, which they learnt by heart, thus gaining mastery over the elements and eventually becoming immortal. And in Taoist mythology such books invariably emit either golden or bright, multicoloured rays, as do all benevolent and beneficial treasures of magical origin. The similarities between the Taoist myths and the Mao symbols are, of course, self-evident. But Mao's writings are imbued with further magical properties. His 'Jenan Speech on Literature', for example, is said to be a 'magic mirror', which exposes all demons in human shape and forces them to revert to their original form. In fact, Mao's whole doctrine is considered to be an all-conquering weapon, just like the Buddhist or Taoist doctrines, which vanquished all evil and demonic forces. Religious elements are also found in the language used to describe Mao's opponents.[12] Thus, the Chinese reactionaries are described as 'cow-ghosts and snake-gods', as 'demons, ghosts and evil animals in human form', as 'man-eating ghosts which have slipped into a painted human skin', and as fiends which inflict the most awful torments on human beings in hell. As for the departments controlled by these adversaries, they are known as the 'palaces of the demon princes'. Here, of course, the terminology is predominantly of Buddhist provenance. In the ancient myths and legends the appearance of fiends is invariably accompanied by a threatening storm, whilst the deeds of contemporary Chinese demons are compared with dark, wet, frightening or black winds, with wild driving rain, ghostly flames, and such like phenomena. And we are told that these demons are quite incapable of 'laying aside their butchers' knives to become Buddhas'. But there are even more significant similarities between Buddhism and Maoism. For example, when a Party member commits ideological errors, he is often subjected to a crude form of shock therapy which is remarkably similar to the therapeutic method used by the Buddhists for people who were possessed by demons or had fallen into a stupor. In both cases the therapist suddenly shouts at the afflicted person at the top of his voice in the hope that this will arouse him to a new awareness of his situation. Moreover, when functionaries or workers failed to implement the cultural revolution with the necessary sense of urgency, Peking warned them that unless they mended their ways, they were likely to fall back into the 'sea of bitterness', a specifically Buddhist expression traditionally used as a synonym for human existence. Those who had erred in this way were exhorted to abandon the 'primrose path' and revert to the path of Maoism, since this represented the *Tao*, which should be *revered* by one and all with a deep sense of class solidarity.

5. The Mao-Cult

Religious Maoism possesses its own formal cult: the Mao-cult. And Mao's position as an international figure has been established in accordance with ideological cum theosophical criteria. He is the contemporary Lenin, the greatest leader and the

greatest genius in the world. His infinitely radiant ideas shine
forth on the whole world. In all five continents there is nothing
that is beyond the grasp of his infinite wisdom. The love felt
for Chairman Mao by the peoples of the world is 'deeper than
the four great oceans'. The people of China and the people of
the world hope that he will 'live for ever'. The Mao-cult has
already established certain set rituals. We have seen on an
earlier page that instead of saying 'good morning' to one another
and to their teachers, Chinese schoolchildren now start the
day by chanting in unison 'May Chairman Mao live ten thousand
times ten thousand years'. We are also told that many Chinese
villages have dedicated 'rooms of loyalty' to the thoughts of
Chairman Mao and that many peasant households have their
own 'tablets of loyalty'. These are clearly derived from the
ancestral temples and tablets of the old China; mornings and
evenings the villagers gather, either in their communal room,
or in front of their family tablets, to pay reverence to Mao Tse-
tung. Apparently, they also make this act of reverence before
every meal, and before retiring to bed. In addition to 'rooms of
loyalty', Mao-statues have been erected in all towns and
villages visited by Mao; and people also gather in front of these
statues, which are upwards of 10 metres in height, to sing songs
in honour of their great leader and to wish him eternal life.
Special 'exhibition halls' have been built to commemorate the
life of Mao Tse-tung, and these too contain Mao-statues, which
are offset by mosaic floors decorated with sunflowers. The halls
face east because that is the source of light and hence symbolic
of Maoism, just as the old imperial palaces faced south because
that was the source of warmth. The roads leading up to these
halls are made of red concrete and flanked by columns sur-
mounted by torches. The halls are built as an act of reverence
by the local inhabitants, who receive no payment for their
labours, a custom which also harks back to Buddhist times when
the people built temples as an act of reverence, and without
payment, in order to atone for their sins or gain indulgences in
the afterlife. To enable pilgrims to visit these 'sacred shrines' –
this is the term used by the Chinese press – special railway lines
have been laid to link them with the national grid. In 1949 Mao
Tse-tung recommended to the 8th National Congress that a
resolution should be passed making it illegal to celebrate the
birthdays of Party members in public or to name towns, streets

or buildings after Party members. Today, this recommendation has been discreetly forgotten.

There is just one last point to be mentioned in connexion with the Mao-cult. Between 1966 and 1968 740 million 'Mao quotations' and 150 million copies of Mao's *Selected Works* were printed. Prior to the cultural revolution it took 13 presses, working full time, to print Mao's publications; in 1967 it took 171, and in 1968 300. In 1969 a *single* press in Peking produced no less than 1,612 thousand million pictures of Mao. This massive glorification of Mao Tse-tung calls to mind an old Chinese proverb: In the whole of history there was no one like *Him*, and after *Him* there will be no one who can vie with *Him*.

Notes

Introduction

1 See 'Long Live the Great Proletarian Cultural Revolution', *Hongqi*, No 8, 1966.
2 See 'The New Phase of the Socialist Revolution in China', *Renmin Ribao*, July 17, 1966.
3 *Fundamentals of Marxism-Leninism* (Berlin, 1960), p 522.
4 See V. I. Lenin 'The Attitude of Social-Democracy towards the Peasant Movement'.
5 See Karl Marx, 'The Class Struggles in France: 1840–1850'.
6 See the 'Resolution on Different Aspects of the People's Communes', of December 10, 1958.
7 See Leo Trotsky, *The Permanent Revolution*.
8 'A Great Revolution which Moves Men's Souls,' *Renmin Ribao*, June 2, 1966.
9 See *Mao Tse-tung Hsuan-chi*, Vol IV, p 1347.
10 See *ibid*, Vol IV, pp 1346 and 1350.

Chapter I

The Youth of China

1 See *Tongji Gongzuo Tongxun* (Statistical Report), No 20, 1956.
2 See Tseng Chao-lun, 'Higher Education in New China' in *People's China*, No 12, June 16, 1953, pp 6–10.
3 See Chien Chun-jui, 'The Key to the Reform of Higher Education' in Stuart Fraser (Ed) *Chinese Communist Education: Records of the First Decade* (Nashville, 1965), pp 122–125.
4 See Tseng Chao-lun, 'Higher Education in China' in *People's China*, No 12, June 16, 1953, pp 6–10.
5 See Ma Hsu-lun, 'Success of People's Education' in Stuart Fraser (Ed), *op cit*, p 132. The total given in the *People's Manual* (Chinese edition; 1957, p 583) is 194,000.
6 See *Tongji Gongzuo Tongxun*, No 20, 1956.
7 See *ibid*.
8 See Chang Chung-lin, 'We Must Do All in Our Power to Improve the Poor Quality of University Education', *Renmin Ribao*, June 30, 1955.
9 See Yang Hsui-feng, 'University Education (speech delivered to the delegates to the plenary session of the First National People's Congress in July, 1955) in *Current Background*, No 351, August 24, 1955, pp 215–221.
10 See *Tongji Gongzuo Tongxun*, No 20, 1956.
11 The statistics published by the Chinese People's Republic are often contradictory. The drop-out figure of 7,000 was given by Yang Hsiu-feng in his speech to the National People's Congress (see Note 10). Yang also claimed that these 7,000 represented 3·5 per cent of the new student intake. But according to *Tongji Gongzuo Tongxun*, No 20, 1956, the intake

for the year 1953–1954 was 81,000, which would give a percentage of over 11·5.

12 Chu Wen-pin, 'Why are the Students so Nervous?', *Renmin Jiaoyue* (National Education), No 11, 1956.

13 See *Renmin Ribao*, October 10, 26 and 29, 1956 and January 23, 1957.

14 This point was made in *Zhongguo Quingnian* (Chinese Youth), No 5, 1957.

15 See the Reuter report from David Chipp in Peking of April 13, 1957.

16 The version put out by the *Renmin Ribao* on August 8, 1957 was quite different: the incident was engineered by an organized clique operating on a nationwide basis. But no firm evidence has been produced to show that such a clique ever existed, and its alleged leaders, Chang Po-chun and Lo Lung-chi, were never brought to trial, whereas the local 'counter-revolutionaries' were tried and executed. This would suggest that the Hanyang revolt was a spontaneous local action, similar to the countless revolts launched by the Red Guards and other pupil and student organizations during the cultural revolution.

17 See the Reuter report from David Chipp in Peking of April 13, 1957.

18 See the report distributed by the *New China News Agency* on May 27, 1957.

19 Chou En-lai, 'Our Work on the Cultural and Educational Front' in Stuart Fraser (Ed), *op cit*, pp 308–315.

20 See *Renmin Ribao*, November 21 and 22, 1964 and February 3, 1965, and *Zongguo Qingnian Bao*, January 19, 1965.

21 See Yang Hsiu-feng, 'China's Educational System Passes through the Great Revolution and the Great Evolution', *Renmin Ribao*, October 8, 1959.

22 See *Renmin Ribao*, March 10, 1961.

23 See *Guangmin Ribao*, December 2, 1961.

24 This problem was first broached in 1963. See the editorial in *Renmin Ribao*, May 4, 1963.

25 See *Renmin Ribao*, February 2, 1963.

26 See *Guangmin Ribao*, June 27, 1963.

27 See *Guangmin Ribao*, February 27, 1963.

28 See *Zhongguo Qingnian Bao*, December 27, 1962.

29 See *Zhongguo Qingnian Bao*, September 16, 1963.

30 See *ibid*.

31 See *Guangmin Ribao*, July 4, 1962.

32 See *Renmin Ribao*, May 30, 1959.

33 See *Guangmin Ribao*, July 31, 1965.

34 See *Zhongguo Qingnian Bao*, September 7, 1965.

Chapter II

The Intelligentsia

1 In 1957 there were 56,000, and in 1958 72,000 graduates (see National Bureau of Statistics (Eds), *The Great Decade* [Chinese edition], Peking, 1959); in 1959–1960 there were 135,000, and in 1961 162,000 graduates

(see *Renmin Ribao*, August 4, 1961); in 1962 there were 172,000 graduates (see *Renmin Ribao*, August 29, 1962).

2 See *New China News Agency*, January 1, 1956.

3 See *Xuexi*, March 16, 1950, pp 17 ff.

4 See *Xinhua Ribao*, October 6, 1950.

5 See *People's China*, I and VIII, April 16, 1950, p 24.

6 See Chien Chun-jui, 'The Key to University Reform' in *Guangmin Ribao*, November 2, 1951.

7 See *Current Background*, 182, May 15, 1925, p 15.

8 See Wu Ta-kun, 'Let Professors Teach Independently', *Renmin Ribao*, August 19, 1956.

9 See *Wenyi Boa*, No 23, 1954, p 46.

10 See *Renmin Ribao*, January 1, 1955.

11 See *Wenyi Bao Supplement*, January 1955, p 11.

12 See *Renmin Ribao*, June 10, 1955 and July 27, 1955, and *Zhongguo Qingnian*, No 14, July 16, 1955.

13 Robert Guillain, *Six Hundred Million Chinese* (New York, 1957), p 176.

14 See *Guangmin Ribao*, May 11, June 12 and July 3, 1957.

15 See *Renmin Wenxue*, No 9, 1956, p 58.

16 Wang Meng. The story was published in *Renmin Wenxue*, September, 1956, pp 29–44.

17 See *Renmin Ribao*, September 24, 1957.

18 See *Renmin Ribao*, July 17, 1964.

19 See *Guangmin Ribao*, December 22, 1961.

20 See *Zhexue Yanjiu* (Philosophical Studies), No 1, 1963.

21 It is interesting to note that the author of one of these biographies reproduced the duel scenes from Sir Walter Scott's *Ivanhoe* almost verbatim. See Shih Ko, *Lo Chen* (Peking, 1962), pp 16 ff and 91 ff.

22 See *Renmin Ribao*, May 31, 1957.

23 Excerpts from Kang Cho's speech were eventually reproduced in *Yangcheng Wanhao* (Canton Evening News), July 7, 1966.

Chapter III

Workers and Peasants

1 See, *inter alia*, *Zhongguo Gongren* (China's Workers), No 15, April 1951.

2 See *Guangmin Ribao*, May 22, 1953.

3 See *Renmin Ribao*, December 3, 1957.

4 See *Lao Dung*, November 24, 1959.

5 See *Renmin Ribao*, March 5, 1960.

6 See *Renmin Ribao*, October 17, 1960.

7 See *Yangcheng-Wanhao*, February 9, 1963.

8 See *Xuexi*, June 16, 1950.

9 See *Shansi Ribao*, November 30, 1952.

10 See *Shansi Ribao*, June 26, 1952.

11 See *Renmin Ribao*, April 2, 1953 and *New China News Agency*, February 9, 1953.

12 See *Chekiang Ribao*, January 27, 1952.

13 See *Shansi Ribao*, August 22, 1951.

14 See *Renmin Ribao*, February 3, 1953.

15 See Chinese Academy of Sciences (Eds) *Collected Material on the Agricultural Cooperatives During the Reconstruction of the National Economy* (Chinese edition; Peking, 1957), pp 1057, 1088 and 1167.

16 See *Renmin Ribao*, February 11, 1953.

17 See *Shansi Ribao*, June 30, 1952.

18 An's speech was reproduced in *Renmin Ribao*, February 12, 1953.

19 See Kenneth R. Walker, 'Collectivisation in Retrospect: The "Socialist High Tide" of Autumn 1955–Spring 1956' in *The China Quarterly*, No 26, 1966, pp 1–43.

20 See Tung Ta-lin, *Agricultural Co-operation in China* (Peking, 1959), p 28.

21 These figures were given in National Bureau of Statistics (Eds), *Statistical Records and Distribution of the Products of the Agricultural Collectives in 1955* (Chinese edition: Peking, 1957).

22 See *Xinhua Banyuekan*, No 1, 1957, pp 88–90.

23 See *ibid*.

24 See 'Materials Relating to an Enquiry into the Distribution of the Products of 228 Collectives in 1957 based on Spot Checks' in *Xinxua Banyuekan*, No 18, 1958, pp 21–30.

25 National Bureau of Statistics (Eds) *The Great Decade* (Peking, 1959), p 105.

26 See *Tongji Gongzuo*, No 20, 1958, p 23.

27 See the 'Resolution on Different Aspects of the People's Communes' ratified by the Central Committee on December 10, 1958 and published in *Xinxua Banyuekan*, No 24, 1958, pp 3–11.

28 The movement towards 'de-communization' first set in 1959. See *Renmin Ribao*, November 2, 1959 and *Xinhunan Bao*, November 19, 1959. See also Chapter IV of this study.

29 See *Renmin Ribao*, December 30, 1959.

30 See *Hongqi*, August 1, 1962. For further accounts of these irrigation projects and the alkaline effects of the well water see *Renmin Ribao*, April 10, 1960 (p 14), May 5, 1961 and November 8, 1961.

31 See *Renmin Ribao*, January 29, 1965 (p 2).

32 See *Nanfang Ribao*, October 11, 1964.

33 See *Renmin Ribao*, October 11, 1964.

34 This radio programme, which was transmitted on June 20, 1964, has been reproduced in *Current Scene*, No 22, 1965, p 6.

35 See *Hubei Ribao*, December 20, 1964.

36 See *Nanfang Ribao*, May 3, 1963.

37 See *Nanfang Ribao*, September 1, 1964.

38 See *Renmin Ribao*, April 10, 1964 (p 2).

Chapter IV

The Party

1 See Mao's speech to the 8th Plenary Session of the 8th Central Committee in Lu Shan in July 1959 in Union Research Institute (Eds), *The Case of Peng Te-huai* (Hongkong, 1968), pp 15–26.

2 See Mao's Tse-tung's observations on culture, which were published during the cultural revolution in *Hongqi*, No 9, 1967.

3 Chou Yang's 'crimes' were enumerated by Yao Wen-yuen in an article entitled 'On the Anti-revolutionary Renegade Chou Yang' in *Hongqi*, No 1, 1967. Prior to the cultural revolution Yao had been an insignificant cultural functionary, but after publishing this article he was promoted to the upper echelons of the party. Most of Yao's material was drawn from private conversations and unpublished speeches and so cannot be verified. I have accepted only those statements about Chou Yang which seem to me to be credible.

4 This may well have been intended as a pun, for in spoken Chinese 'chumao' means 'a pig's bristle'.

5 See Liu Pei-yu, *Biography of General Chu Te* (Chinese edition; 1941). Quotation taken from 'The Confessions of Chu Te' in *Xinheita*, No 39, February 24, 1967. This passage also appears in Ming Pao (Eds), *Material Relating to the Great Sino-Communist Proletarian Cultural Revolution*, Vol I (Chinese edition; Hongkong, 1967), pp 594–610.

6 See *ibid*, p 601. Other sources also name Chu Te as the author of these tactics. See Hsiao Jen-ho, 'Chu Te: From Hsiu Tsai to Soldier' (Chinese version) in *Ming Pao Monthly*, No 39, 1967, pp 29–34.

7 I have based my account of this incident on the article 'The Reactionary Film "Liao Yuen" and the Chinese Chrushchev' in *Hongqi*, No 7, May 20, 1967, pp 33–44.

8 'To reach one's hundredth year' means 'to die'. This euphemism, which is of feudal origin, is still employed by the Chinese communists, who seem loth to speak of Mao's 'death' lest they should invoke it.

9 See *Hongqi*, No 15/16, August 1, 1962, p 36.

10 Excerpts from these speeches, and statements by other anti-Maoists, were reproduced in the article written by the editors of *Renmin Ribao*, *Hongqi* and *Jiefangjun Bao* on September 1, 1968.

11 The four categories were: (1) functionaries who took part in the Long March; (2) functionaries who served in the Sino-Japanese war; (3) functionaries who served in the War of Liberation; and (4) functionaries who changed sides in the closing stages of the War of Liberation. In this connexion see Ezra F. Vogel, 'From the Revolutionary to the Semi-Bureaucrat: The Regularization of Cadres' in *The China Quarterly*, No 29, pp 36–60, and A. Doak Barnett, 'Social Stratification and Aspects of Personnel Management in the Chinese Communist Bureaucracy' in *The China Quarterly*, No 28, pp 8–39.

Chapter V

The Young Rebels

1 According to a Japanese source, this school formed the first Red Guard cell on May 21, 1966. Others claim that the organization was founded in March 1966 by the secondary school attached to Peking University. In this connexion see John Israel, 'The Red Guards in Historical Perspective' in *The China Quarterly*, No 30, p 7.

2 This charge was brought against Peng in a Central Committee statement on May 16, 1966, which was published in *Renmin Ribao*, May 17, 1967.

3 See *ibid*.

4 On May 25, 1966 seven students in the Philosophy Department at Peking University published an article in a wall newspaper in which they accused the university rector, the First Secretary of the Party Committee attached to the university and members of the Party Committee for the city of Peking of anti-party activities. For a verbatim account of this article see *Renmin Ribao*, June 2, 1966.

5 See letter of June 6, 1966 from Class 4 of the final year pupils at the 1st Peking Secondary School for Girls to the Central Committee and Chairman Mao in *Renmin Ribao*, June 18, 1966.

6 This apparently spontaneous action may, of course, have been carefully planned.

7 See *New China News Agency*, August 22, 1966.

8 For a detailed account of these four categories see 'Resolution of the Central Committee on the Great Proletarian Cultural Revolution' of August 8, 1966 in *Renmin Ribao*, August 9, 1966.

9 In this connexion see the pamphlet published by the Red Guard organization at the secondary school attached to the Chinghua University on July 20, 1966 in which the 'capitalists' were accused of vilifying and trying to destroy the children of the revolutionary functionaries. An English translation of this pamphlet appeared in *China News Analysis*, No 636, November 11, 1966.

10 See the editorial in *Wen Hui Bao*, March 6, 1967.

11 See *ibid*, and also the article published on behalf of the 3rd Headquarters of the Peking Red Guards in *Renmin Ribao*, January 31, 1967.

12 See the speeches given by Chou En-lai and Chiang Ching at the Red Guards Congress staged by the Peking secondary schools on March 23, 1967.

13 See the speech given by Chou En-lai at the mass meeting of August 31, 1966 (German version) in *Peking Rundschau*, No 36, September 6, 1966. Chou appears to have been the first to question the wisdom of allowing the Red Guards to roam the country. At the first mass meeting – held on August 18, 1966 – he was the only speaker to insist that each institution must be allowed to conduct its own cultural revolution. In other words, the Red Guards were not to think they could claim a monopoly.

14 See the reports in *Neue Zürcher Zeitung*, September 7, 1966.

15 The text of the directive issued by the Party Headquarters, the Council of State, the Military Committee and the Committee for the Cultural

Revolution Attached to the Central Committee has been published in Union Research Institute (Eds), *CCP Documents* (Hongkong, 1968), pp 461–462.

16 See the article published by the Shanghai Red Guards 'Where is the Lu Hsün Corps Going?' which was reported by the *New China News Agency* on February 25, 1965.

17 See *Asahi* (Tokyo), January 28, 1967 and *Wen Hui Bao*, January 18, 1967.

18 See *Renmin Ribao*, May 22, 1967.

19 See *Ming Pao*, July 31, 1967.

20 For an account of these events see *Jiefangjun Bao*, July 27, 28 and 30, 1967. The incident was also reported by the *New China News Agency* on July 30, 1967.

21 See the editorial in *Wen Hui Bao*, February 15, 1967.

22 See *Wen Hui Bao*, February 18, 1967.

23 See *Wen Hui Bao*, March 12, 1962.

24 The triple alliance in the Chinese schools was based on the revolutionary teachers, pupils and workers.

25 Amongst others, Peng Chen and his followers, and the members of the Party Committee at Peking University, were overthrown on this account. See the documents published in *Renmin Ribao*, May 17, 1967.

26 See the report from the marines unit attached to the 89th Secondary School in Peking, which was published in *Hongqi*, No 11, July 9, 1967, pp 43 ff.

27 It seems surprising that the soldiers should have had to explain the bourgeois educational system to the pupils. This would indicate that the non-revolutionary pupils had taken no interest in the cultural revolution and that their revolutionary colleagues were interested only in private vendettas and the overthrow of anti-revolutionary despots.

28 See the report from the army unit attached to the Jenan Secondary School in *Renmin Ribao*, March 8, 1968.

29 See *Renmin Ribao*, April 28 and June 14, 1968.

30 See *Renmin Ribao*, February 21 and March 5, 1968.

31 One third were representatives of the revolutionary masses, one third revolutionary functionaries, and one third soldiers.

32 This was stated in a programme on the Chekiang radio network on July 15, 1968. Excerpts from the script were reproduced in *China News Analysis*, No 719, August 2, 1968.

33 See *ibid*.

34 See *Peking Rundschau*, No 43, October 29, 1968, pp 10–11.

35 See 'Neuartige Schule, wo Theorie und Praxis miteinander übereinstimmen' in *Peking Rundschau*, No 44, November 5, 1968.

36 In the old China it was customary to wish the emperor 'ten thousand years of life'. In fact, this expression was reserved exclusively for him, with the result that he came to be known as 'the one who lives for ten thousand years'.

37 See 'Von armen Bauern und unteren Mittelbauern geleitete Schulen' in *Peking Rundschau*, No 46, November 19, 1968, pp 12 ff.

38 (1) Faced with a choice between people and weapons, people take

precedence. (2) Faced with a choice between political and non-political work, political work takes precedence. (3) Faced with a choice between ideological work and routine political work, ideological work takes precedence; and faced with a choice between the practical and theoretical aspects of ideological work, the practical aspects take precedence.

39 The 'Three-and-Eight Working Method' involves: (1) A firm and ideologically correct political attitude; (2) a straightforward and careful approach to work; (3) strategical and tactical agility. It further involves: (a) a sense of solidarity; (b) enthusiasm; (c) gravity; (d) vitality. The name 'Three-and-Eight Working Method' comes from the Chinese formulation of these requirements, which consists of three sentences and eight symbols.

40 A 'Four-Good-Company' must have: (1) a good political and ideological record; (2) a good 'Three-and-Eight Working Method'; (3) a good military training; and (4) a good basic organization.

41 'Five-Good-Fighters' must have: (1) exemplary political attitudes; (2) a good 'Three-and-Eight Working Method'; (3) a good military training; (4) a good fighting record; and (5) a good physique.

42 Previously, there had been only one hundred such groups at the Chinghua University.

43 This would seem to indicate a certain lack of solidarity between the workers seconded to the universities and those in the factories.

44 In 1968–1969 the leadership again stressed the importance of class affiliations, although at that time not only the workers, but also the peasants and smallholders, were considered ideologically acceptable. During this period a premium was placed on Party and Youth League membership.

45 See 'Ausbildung von roten Ärzten aus den Arbeitern' in *Peking Rundschau*, No 6, February 11, 1969, pp 7 ff.

Chapter VI

Worker and Peasant Rebels

1 See the (joint) editorial in *Renmin Ribao* and *Hongqi*, January 1, 1967.

2 See the editorial in *Renmin Ribao*, December 26, 1966.

3 The information on the January revolution has been taken from the following sources: *Wen Hui Bao*, January 5, 1967; *New China News Agency*, January 11 and 12, 1967; *Renmin Ribao*, January 10, 1967; and the editorials in *Renmin Ribao* and *Hongqi*, January 12, 1967.

4 Later, this view of the cultural revolution was repudiated by the leadership.

5 Two corps of 'Workers who Have Returned to Shanghai from the North signed the 'urgent command of January 9, 1967'. See *Renmin Ribao*, January 12, 1967.

6 It was no accident that the *Renmin Ribao* chose to attack these groups on February 22, 1967.

7 See the first statement issued by the 'Headquarters of the Revolutionary

Rebels of Shansi' on January 14, 1967, which was reproduced in *Renmin Ribao*, January 25, 1967.

8 See the editorial and commentary in *Hongqi*, No 3, February 3, 1967. At about this time the wall newspapers were saying that a commune was to be set up in Peking. In this connexion see *Asahi*, February 11, 1967, p 3 and *Yomiuri*, March 4, 1967, p 3.

9 See editorial in *Hongqi*, No 4, March 1, 1967.

10 See *Renmin Ribao*, February 28, 1967.

11 See the editorial in *Jiefangjun Bao*, March 22, 1967.

12 See the editorials in *Hongqi*, No 4, March 1, 1967 and *Wen Hui Bao*, February 28, 1967.

13 See the editorials in *Hongqi*, No 5, March 30, 1967 (first published in *Renmin Ribao*, March 10, 1967), *Renmin Ribao*, February 28 and March 2, 1967, and *Wen Hui Bao*, February 18, 1967.

14 See *Renmin Ribao*, April 6, 1968.

15 See *Renmin Ribao*, January 22 (editorial), January 31 and February 12, 1967.

16 See the editorial in *Hongqi*, No 15, 1967.

17 See *Renmin Ribao*, January 21 and 25, 1967.

18 See *Renmin Ribao*, February 1, 1967.

19 See *Renmin Ribao*, February 1, 1967.

20 See *Ming Pao*, May 14, 1967.

21 See *Renmin Ribao*, January 31, 1967.

22 See *Hongqi*, No 14, 1967 and Chiang Ching's speech of September 5, 1967, which was reproduced in Union Research Institute (Eds), *CCP Documents* (Hongkong, 1968), pp 512 ff.

23 See *ibid*, pp 501–502.

24 See *New China News Agency*, January 21, 1967, *Renmin Ribao*, February 28, 1967 and, Union Research Institute (Eds), *CCP Documents* (Hongkong, 1968), pp 512 ff.

25 See *Hongqi*, No 5, 1967.

26 See *Jiefangjun Bao*, June 8, 1967.

27 See, *inter alia*, the editorial in *Jiefangjun Bao*, September 16, 1967.

28 See the editorial in *Renmin Ribao*, October 19, 1967.

29 See the editorial in *Wen Hui Bao*, September 14, 1967.

30 See Union Research Institute (Eds), *CCP Documents* (Hongkong, 1968), pp 505–506.

31 Many of the anti-Maoist party leaders were overthrown because of their former connexions with the Kuomintang. That was why these organizations concentrated on the 'murky' past of the three top men.

32 See *Wen Hui Bao*, June 12, 1968 and the communiqué issued after the 12th Plenary Session of the Eighth Central Committee which was published in *Renmin Ribao*, November 2, 1968.

33 See the editorials in *Xin Anhui Bao*, June 30, 1968.

34 See *Hongqi*, No 10, 1967.

35 See the (joint) editorial in *Renmin Ribao* and *Jiefangjun Bao*, April 20, 1968.

Chapter VII

The Party and the Army

1 See *New China News Agency* (Peking), August 14, 1967.
2 Only 3 of the 18 members of this group belonged to the Central Committee.
3 See the statement issued by the Central Committee on May 16, 1966 and the editorials in *Renmin Ribao*, *Hongqi* and *Jiefangjun Bao*, May 17, 1968.
4 Liu Shao-chi was condemned in person by the Red Guards in their wall newspapers back in 1966. It was not until March 30, 1967 that the official anti-Liu campaign was launched in *Hongqi*, and even then Liu was referred to as 'the Chinese Krushchev' and not by his own name.
5 See the editorial in *Hongqi*, No 4, 1967.
6 See the statement issued by the Central Committee on May 16, 1966.
7 See *Hongqi*, No 12, 1967.
8 See *New China News Agency*, January 21, 1967.
9 See *Renmin Ribao*, January 23, 1967 and the editorial in *ibid*, December 26, 1967.
10 See, *inter alia*, *Renmin Ribao*, January 12, 23, 25, 26 and 30.
11 In the provinces of Yunnan and Fukien revolutionary committees were not set up until August 1968.
12 *The Words of Chairman Mao Tse-tung* (Peking, 1967), p 118.
13 See Jürgen Domes, *Kulturrevolution und Armee* (Bonn, 1967), p 85.
14 See the editorial in *Jiefangjun Bao*, May 4, 1966.
15 Marshal Ho Lung was also a member of the Politburo, Deputy Prime Minister and Deputy Chairman of both the National Defence Council and the Military Commission of the Central Committee. The other victims of this purge included: General Hsü Kuang-ta (Deputy Minister of Defence and Commander in Chief of the Chinese Armoured Divisions); General Hsiao Hsiang-jung (Director of the Department for General Affairs in the Ministry of Defence; General Liu Chih-chien (Deputy Director of the General Political Department in the People's Liberation Army and Head of the 'Group for the Cultural Revolution in the Army', which was set up in October 1966); and General Wang Shang-jung (Director of the Operations Department at the Headquarters of the People's Liberation Army). For further information on this purge see Jürgen Domes, *Kulterrevolution und Armee* (Bonn, 1967), pp 92 ff.
16 See *New China News Agency*, March 1, 1967.
17 See Union Research Institute, *CCP Documents* (Hongkong, 1968), pp 383–384, 415–416, 431 ff and 441–442.
18 See the directive issued by the Military Commission of the Central Committee on January 28, 1967 in *ibid*, p 209.
19 The reliable military regions were the cities of Peking and Shanghai and the provinces of Shansi, Shantung, Kiangsu, Kweichow and Heilungkiang. The unreliable military regions included the city of Tientsin and the provinces of Chekiang, Hopei, Szechuan, Chinghai, Inner Mongolia and Sinkiang.
20 See the editorial in *Hongqi*, No 12, 1967.

21 See C. Neuhauser, 'The Impact of the Cultural Revolution on the Chinese Communist Party Machine' in *Asian Survey*, June 1968, p 466.

22 See the directives issued by the Military Commission of the Central Committee on January 1, February 11 and February 16, 1967 in Union Research Institute (Eds), *CCP Documents* (Hongkong, 1968), pp 209, 263 ff, and 287.

23 See *ibid*, p 209 and *Jiefangjun Bao*, June 8, 1967.

24 See the editorial in *Hongqi*, No 5, 1967.

25 See *Renmin Ribao*, May 28, 1969.

26 See the editorial in *Hongqi*, No 5, 1967.

27 See *ibid*. Such behaviour was also reported on the Kweichow radio network on February 22, 1969.

28 See *Guangmin Ribao*, December 24, 1969.

29 See *Renmin Ribao*, May 29 and June 3, 1969.

30 See Ting Wuan, 'Studies on the Composition of the Committee for the Cultural Revolution set up by the Central Committee' in *Ming Pao Monthly*, No 49, p 67 (text and footnote).

31 Only the assistant editor was purged. Although the chief editor was the chairman of the committee, he had been a loyal disciple of Mao's for many years and took no part in the anti-Chou campaign.

32 See *Ming Pao Monthly*, No 44, 1967.

33 Lin Piao's report to the 9th Party Congress was enlarged and revised by the delegates and subsequently re-edited by the secretariat of the Party praesidium. The re-editing took 13 days to complete.

34 Reported by the *New China News Agency* on March 14, 1969.

35 See *Renmin Ribao*, December 11, 1968.

36 See the editorial in *Renmin Ribao*, February 17, 1969.

37 My principal sources were the two reports on the new Party branch at the Hsinhua printing works in Peking and the report on the new Party branch at the machine tool workshop at the Chuchuo Rolling Stock Factory in the province of Hunan. These reports were reproduced in the *Peking Rundschau*, Nos 1, 2 and 3, 1970. See also the analysis in *Jenwu yü Ssuhsiang*, No 33, 1969, pp 31 ff.

Chapter VIII

Maoism

1 The 'Tripartite Democratic Method' presupposes political, economic and social democracy. For definitions of the other concepts see Chapter V, Section IV of this book.

2 See Lin Piao's speech at the mass meeting held to commemorate the fiftieth anniversary of the October Revolution. See also the editorial in *Hongqi*, No 12, 1967.

3 See Karl Marx and Friedrich Engels, *Selected Letters* (Chinese edition), p 63.

4 See Lenin, *Collected Works*, Vol 28 (Chinese edition), p 235; Vol 31, p 6; and Vol 29, p 162.

5 See *Renmin Ribao*, August 28, 1967 and the editorial in *Hongqi*, No 15, 1967. If Mao were to repudiate this fundamental tenet of Marxism in so many words he could not call himself a Marxist.

6 See Chen Po-tas' article in *Renmin Ribao*, May 24, 1967.

7 This version was reproduced in *Hongqi*, No 11, 1969, together with two commentaries. I have drawn on the material supplied in these commentaries for my analysis of this opera.

8 Especially in *Dynamics of Faith*, New York, 1957.

9 See C. K. Yang, *Religion in Chinese Society* (Berkeley and Los Angeles, 1967), Chapter XIV.

10 See Robert Jay Lifton, *Revolutionary Immortality: Mao Tse-tung and the Chinese Cultural Revolution* (New York, 1968).

11 I have translated Chinese 'pao' as 'magic'. Basically, this word means 'valuable'. But a 'Pao-Shu' is much more than a 'valuable book' because 'pao' has a supernatural connotation which 'valuable' does not possess.

12 There are many Chinese expressions which denote the forces of evil. Unfortunately, many of them are untranslatable.

Bibliography

The works listed in this bibliography are works dealing specifically with China. The various editions of Marx, Engels and Lenin have not been included, nor have publications concerned with general aspects of Marxist theory. I have listed all relevant newspapers and periodicals, but not individual articles.

Newspapers

A. Chinese Newspapers

1. National Dailies

Dagong Bao
– Daily newspaper catering primarily for technicians who are not members of the Communist Party.
Gongren Ribao
– Trade union newspaper catering for the workers.
Guangmin Ribao
– Daily newspaper catering for intellectuals who are not members of the Communist Party.
Jiefangjun Bao
– Daily newspaper published by the People's Liberation Army.
Renmin Ribao
– People's Daily, the official government newspaper.
Zhongguo Qingnian Bao
– Daily newspaper catering for Chinese youth, the official organ of the Communist Youth League.

2. Regional Newspapers

Beijing Ribao
– Peking Daily.
Chekiang Ribao
– Daily newspaper for the province of Chekiang.
Chengdu Ribao
– Daily newspaper for the town of Chengdu (in the province of Sizhuan).
Fukien Ribao
– Daily newspaper for the province of Fukien.

Gansu Ribao
– Daily newspaper for the province of Gansu.
Gianxi Ribao
– Daily newspaper for the province of Gianxi.
Guanxi Ribao
– Daily newspaper for the province of Guanxi.
Heilungkiang Bao
– Daily newspaper for the province of Heilungkiang.
Honan Ribao
– Daily newspaper for the province of Honan.
Hubei Ribao
– Daily newspaper for the province of Hubei.
Hunan Ribao
– Daily newspaper for the province of Hunan.
Nanfang Ribao
– Daily newspaper for the South of China.
Qingdao Ribao
– Daily newspaper for the town of Qingdao.
Shansi Ribao
– Daily newspaper for the province of Shansi.
Sizhuan Ribao
– Daily newspaper for the province of Sizhuan.
Wen Hui Bao
– A Shanghai newspaper.
Xin Anhui Bao
– Newspaper for the province of Anhui.
Xinhua Ribao
– New China Daily, published in Nanking.
Xinhunan Bao
– Newspaper for the province of Hunan.
Yancheng Wanbao
– Canton Evening Newspaper.

B. Hongkong Newspapers

Because of its geographical position, Hongkong has always been an excellent source of information about events in China. But since it is seldom possible to check such information, it should always be evaluated in the light of information obtained from sources in the People's Republic.

Ming Pao
– a non-Party newspaper.
Sing Tao Jih Pao
– a non-Party newspaper.

C. Japanese Newspapers

The only foreign correspondents allowed to remain in China when the cultural revolution was launched were the Japanese. During the late phase of the revolution they too were asked to leave the country.
Asahi
Mainichi
Yomiuri

Periodicals

A. Chinese Periodicals
1. National Periodicals

Hongqi
– The 'Red Flag', the official organ of the Central Committee of the Chinese Communist Party.
Lao Dung
– 'Work,' one of the trades union organs.
Xinxua Banyuekan
– 'New China,' an advanced theoretical magazine published fortnightly by the Chinese Communist Party.
Xuexi
– 'Studies,' an older theoretical magazine published by the Chinese Communist Party.
Xinxua Yuebao
– 'New China,' a monthly theoretical magazine which succeeded *Xuexi* as the official organ of the Chinese Communist Party.
Zhongguo Gongren
– 'China's Workers,' another trades union organ.
Zhongguo Qingnian
– 'China's Youth,' the organ of the Chinese Communist Youth League.

2. Regional Periodicals

Qanxian
— 'The Front,' the organ of the Party Committee for the city of Peking.
Xinbeita
– Peking University students' magazine.

3. Technical Periodicals

Bejing Wenvi
– Peking literature.
Jinji Yanjiu
– Economic studies.
Renmin Jiaoyue
– National education.
Renmin Wenxue
– Popular literature.
Tongji Gongzuo
– Statistics.
Tongji Gongzuo Tongxun
– Statistical work.
Wenxue Pinglun
– Literary criticism.
Wenyi Bao
Literary Gazette.
Xuexu Luntan
– Scientific discussions.
Zhexue Yanjiu
Philosophic studies.
Zhüben
– Theatre magazine.

4. Foreign Language Periodicals Published in the Chinese People's Republic.

Chinese Literature
– A monthly magazine printed in English and containing translations and criticisms of Chinese literature.
Pekinger Rundschau
– A weekly magazine printed in German and containing all important news items and commentary on events in China.

People's China
– A monthly magazine published in English by the Chinese government.

5. Hongkong Periodicals

Hsüehsi Chungshu
'Study manuals.' These manuals contain Party directives and major items of Chinese news. They are published by a Communist press in Hongkong for local Chinese Communist Party members.
Jenwu yü Ssuhsiang
'People and Ideas.' This magazine publishes Chinese communist documents which are otherwise difficult to obtain.
Ming Pao Monthly
– A non-partisan magazine which publishes regular articles on China.

6. Western Magazines

Asian Survey (Berkeley, Cal.)
– An American university magazine devoted to Asian studies which contains articles on China.
Aus Politik und Zeitgeschichte (Supplement of the Hamburg weekly *Das Parlament*)
– This magazine publishes occasional articles on China.
Aussenpolitik (Freiburg im Breisgau)
– This magazine publishes occasional articles on China.
China News Analysis (Hongkong)
– An English language magazine which provides a weekly analysis of Chinese news. This is an extremely well documented publication and is quite indispensable for any student of Chinese affairs.
The China Quarterly (London)
– The foremost periodical dealing with modern China.
Current Scene (Hongkong)
– An English language magazine published three times a month by the United States Information Service.
Europa Archiv (Bonn)
– A general magazine dealing with all aspects of international politics.

Ost-Probleme (Cologne)
– This magazine publishes German translations of articles and reports on the socialist countries of the world.
Survey of China Mainland Press (Hongkong)
– This magazine is published by the American Consulate in Hongkong and contains English translations of articles appearing in the Chinese press.

Books

A. Official Chinese Communist Publications

Department for Agricultural Work (Eds), *Questions Relating to Agricultural Work* in 1955 (Chinese edition). Peking, 1955.

Eighth National Congress of the Chinese Communist Party: Documents. Peking, 1956.

Lan Kuang, *et al*, *Sixan Wenti*. Peking, 1950.

Mao Tse-tung, *Four Philosophical Publications of Chairman Mao* (Chinese edition). Peking, 1961.

Mao Tse-tung Hsüan-chi, 4 Vols. Peking, 1965.

Ma Yin-chu, *My Economic Theory, Philosophy and Political Views* (Chinese edition). Peking, 1958.

National Bureau of Statistics, *Statistical Records and Distribution of the Products of the Agricultural Collectives in 1955* (Chinese edition). Peking, 1957.

National Bureau of Statistics (Eds) *The Great Decade* (Chinese edition). Peking, 1959.

People's Manual (Chinese edition). Peking, 1957.

The Chinese Academy of Sciences (Eds), *Collected Material on the Agricultural Cooperatives During the Reconstruction of the National Economy* (Chinese edition). Peking, 1957.

The Words of Chairman Mao Tse-tung. Peking, 1967.

Ti-Tan, *Wu Hsün Chuan*. Peking, 1951.

Tung Ta-lin, *Agricultural Co-operation in China*. Peking, 1959.

Zhonghua Hoye Wenxuan. Shanghai, 1965.

B. Documents

Anonym. *Communist China 1055–1959: Policy Documents with Analysis*. Cambridge (Mass), 1962.

Compton, Boyd. *Mao's China: Party Reform Documents, 1942–1944*. Seattle, 1952.

Doolin, Denis J. *Communist China: The Politics of Student Opposition*. Stanford, 1964.

Fraser, Stuart. *Chinese Communist Education: Records of the First Decade*. Nashville, 1965.

Kao Yin-tsu. *Chung-hua mon-huo ta-shih-chi* (Chronological Development of the Chinese People's Republic). Tapei, 1957.

MacFarquhar, *The Hundred Flowers Campaign and the Chinese Intellectuals*. New York, 1960.

Ming Pao Monthly. *Material on the Great Sino-Communist Proletarian Cultural Revolution*. 8 Vols. Hongkong, 1967 *et seq*.

Schram, Stuart. *Die permanente Revolution in China: Dokumente und Kommentar*. Frankfort, 1966.

Szu-mien Lü, *Chung-kuo Tung-shin* (General History of China). 2 Vols. Hongkong, 1952.

Union Research Institute (Eds). *The Case of Peng Te-huai*. Hongkong, 1968.

Union Research Institute (Eds). CCP: *Documents of the Great Proletarian Cultural Revolution*. Hongkong, 1968.

Wang Chao-tien. *Wo shih i-ko hung-wei-ping* (I was a Red Guard). Taipei, 1967.

C. Studies on China

Barcate, Louis. *China in der Kulterrevolution: Ein Augenzeugenbericht*. Vienna, 1967.

Bertram, J. M. *Crisis in China: The Story of the Sian Mutiny*. London, 1937.

Chen, Jerome. *Mao and the Chinese Revolution*. London, 1965.

Chow, Tse-tung. *The May Fourth Movement: Intellectual Revolution in Modern China*, 2 Vols. Cambridge (Mass), 1959.

Domes, Jürgen. *Kulturrevolution und Armee*. Bonn, 1967.

Goldman, Merle. *Literary Dissent in Communist China*. Cambridge (Mass), 1967.

Guillain, Robert. *Six Hundred Million Chinese*. New York, 1957.

Heinzig, Dieter. *Die Krise der Kommunistischen Partei Chinas in der Kulturrevolution*. Hamburg, 1969.

Lifton, Jan. *Revolutionary Immortality: Mao Tse-tung and the Chinese Cultural Revolution*. New York, 1968.

Tillich, Paul. *Dynamics of Faith*. New York, 1957.

Weggel, Oskar. *Die Chinesischen Revolutionskomitees*. Hamburg, 1968.

Wetzel, Heinrich. *Liu Shao-chi; le Moine rouge*. Paris, 1961.
Yang, C. K. *Religion in Chinese Society*. Berkeley and Los Angeles, 1967.
Yu. T. C. *Mass Persuasion in Communist China*. New York, 1964.